Lucky☆Star

5

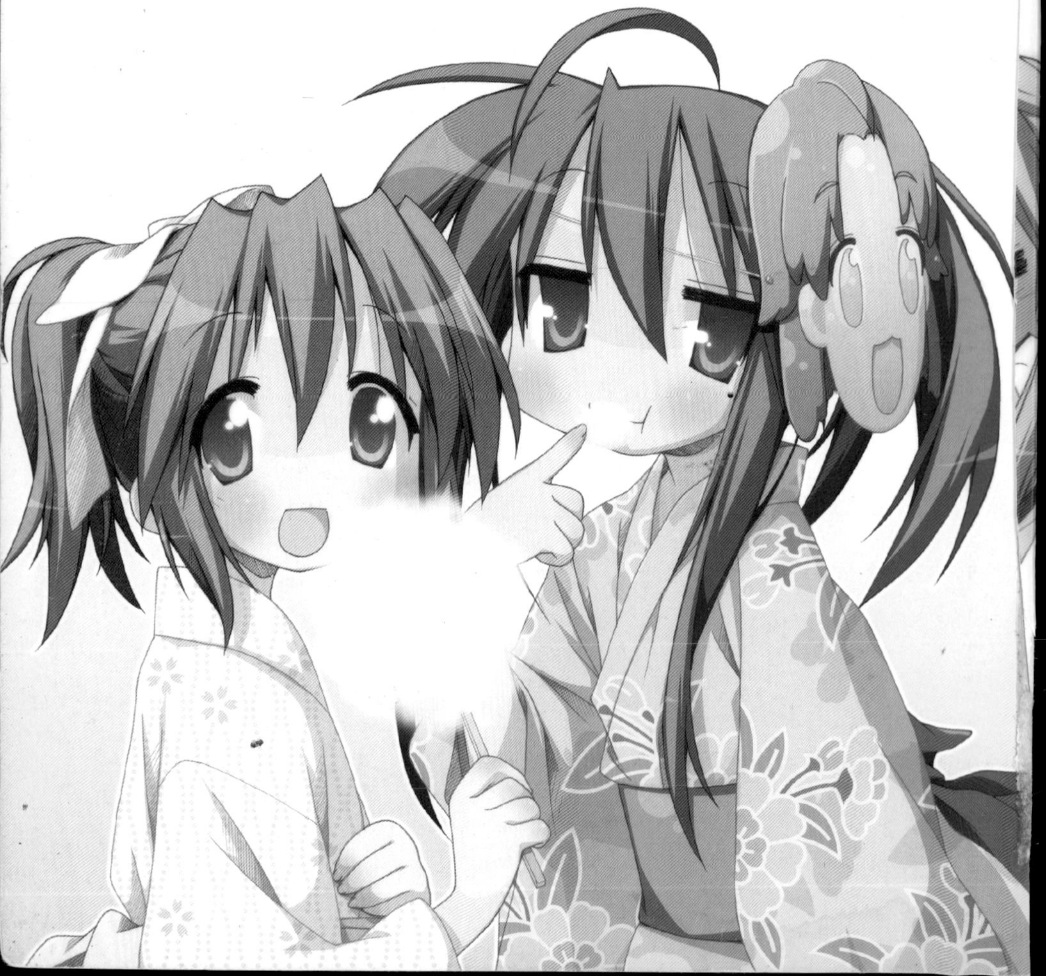

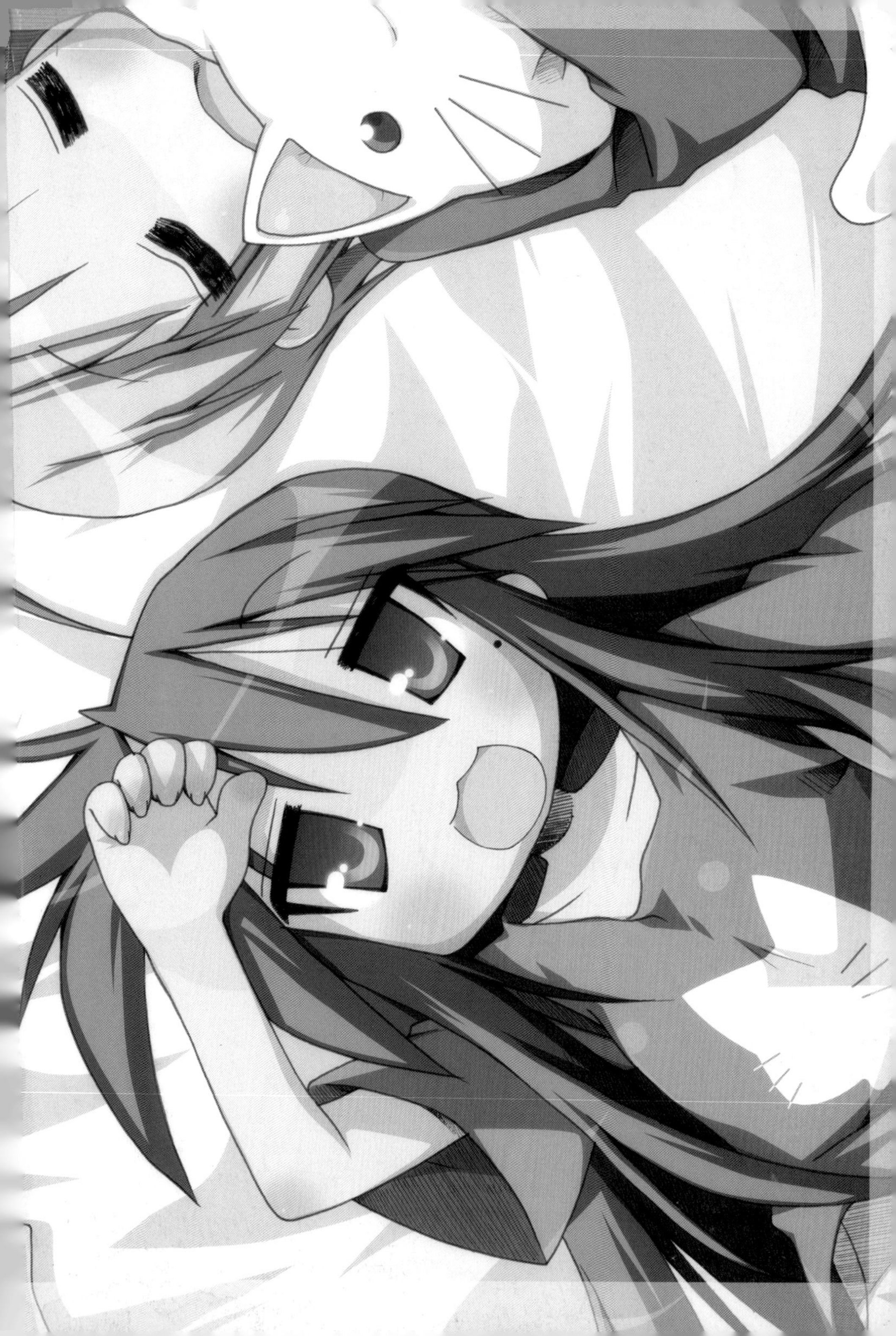

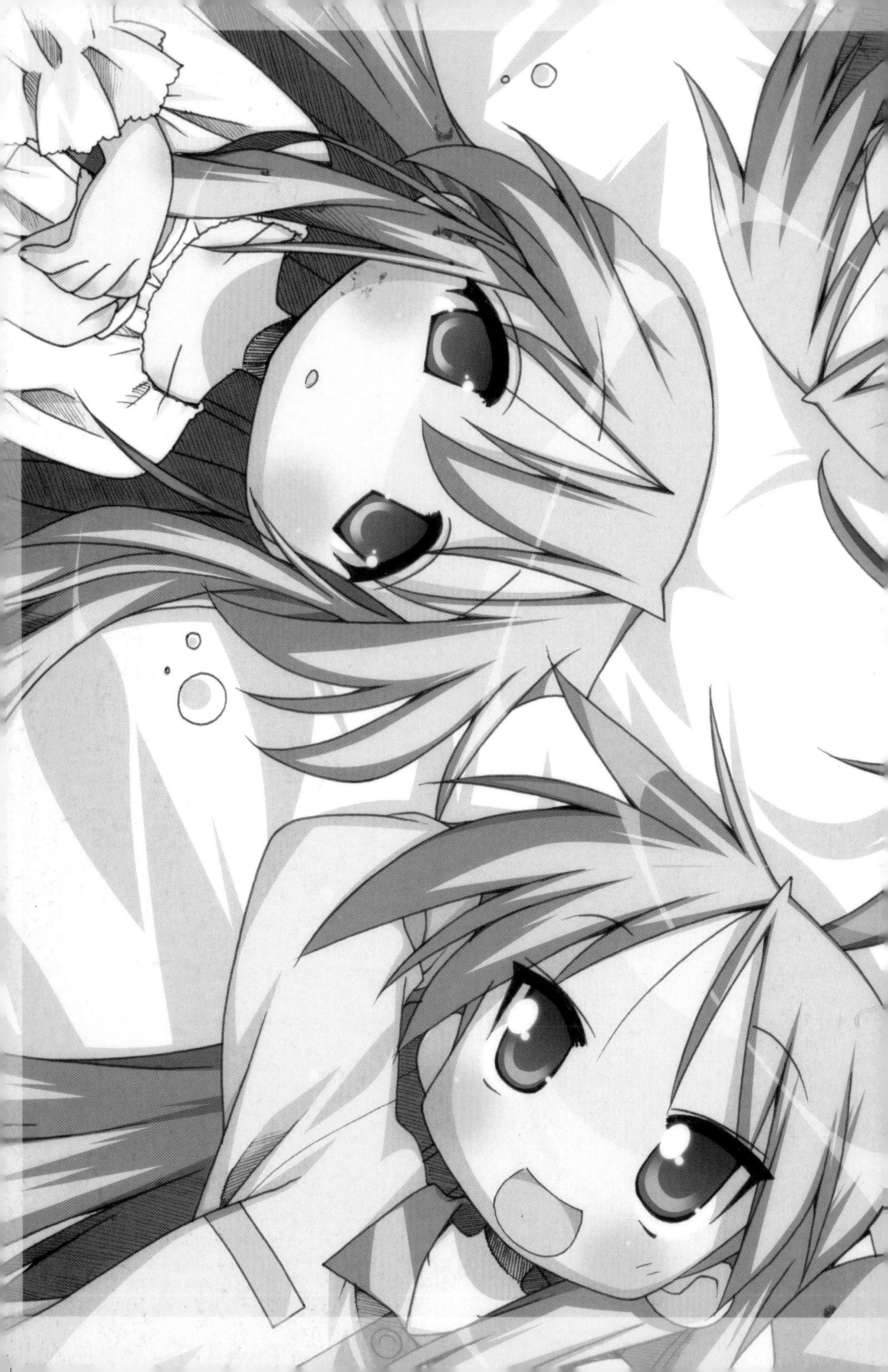

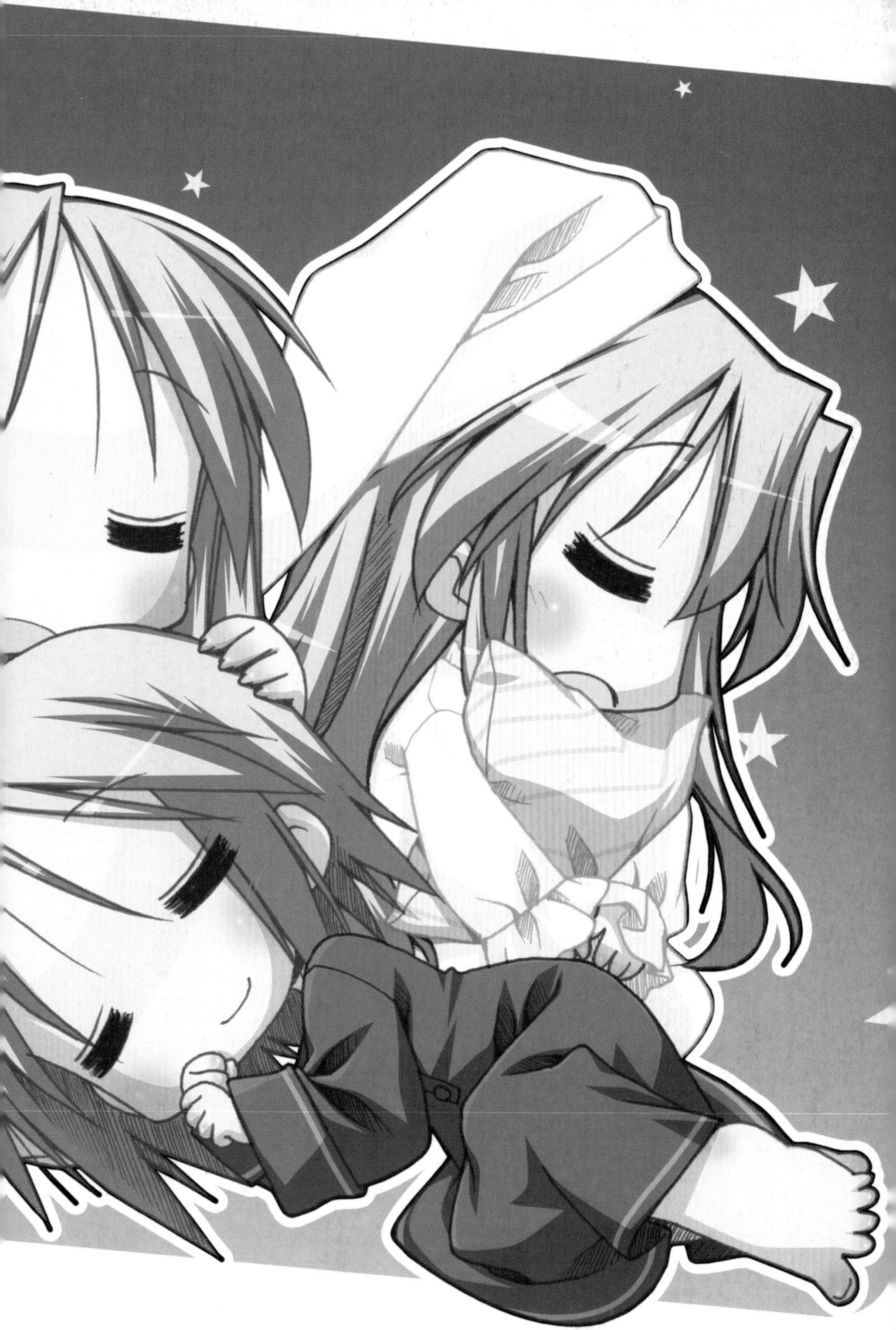

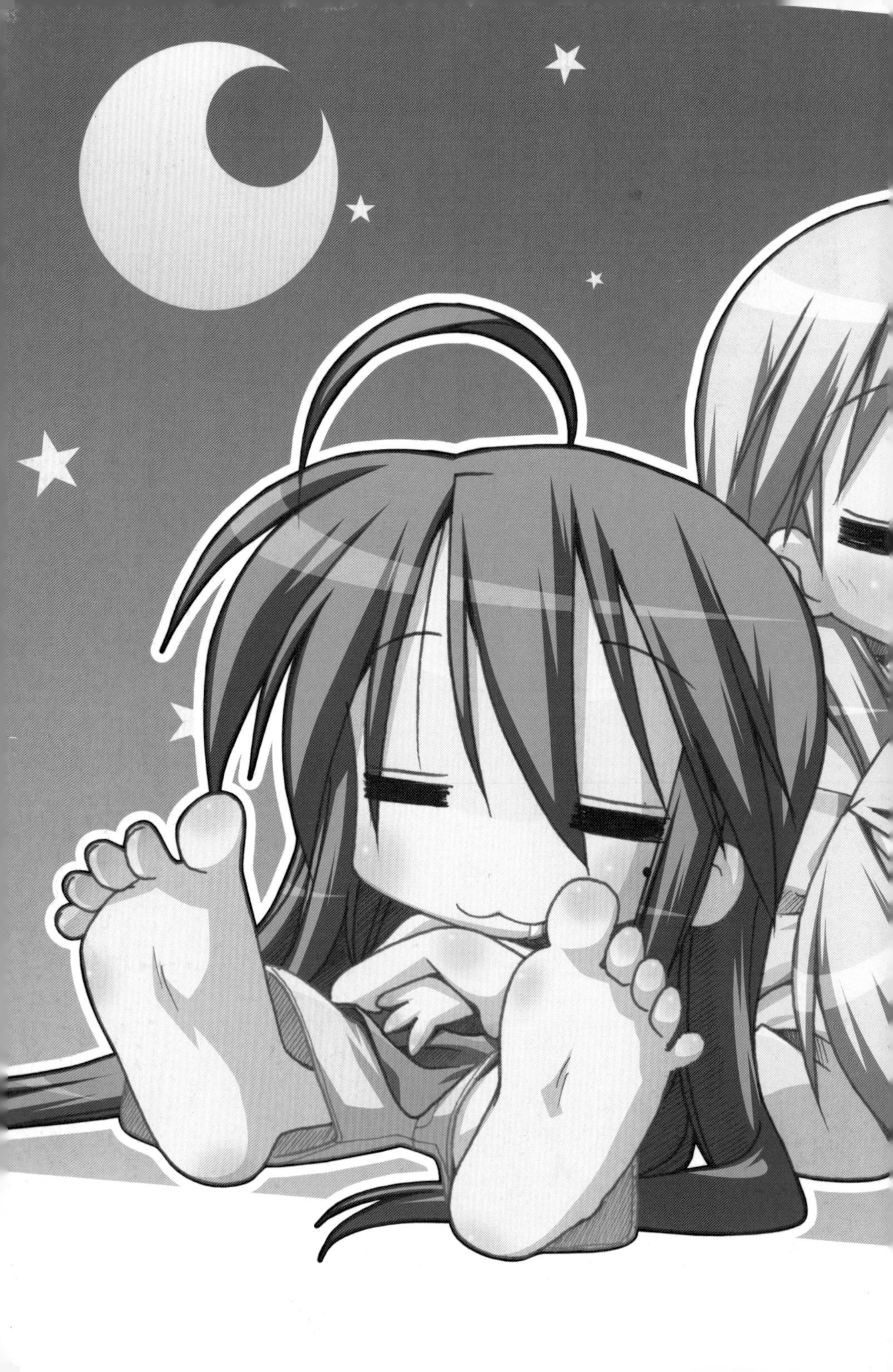

special

bonus 1

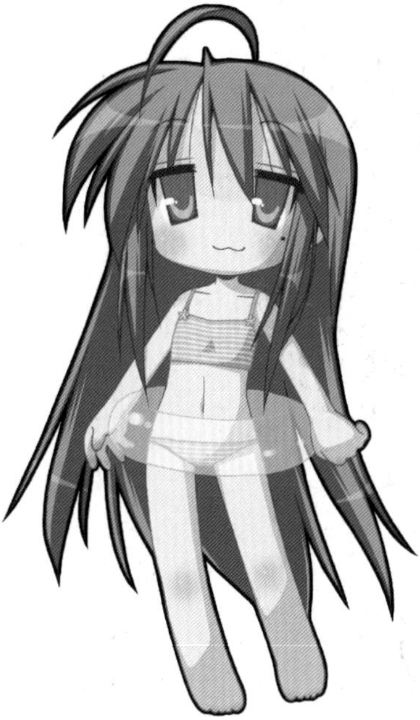

ah-ya story

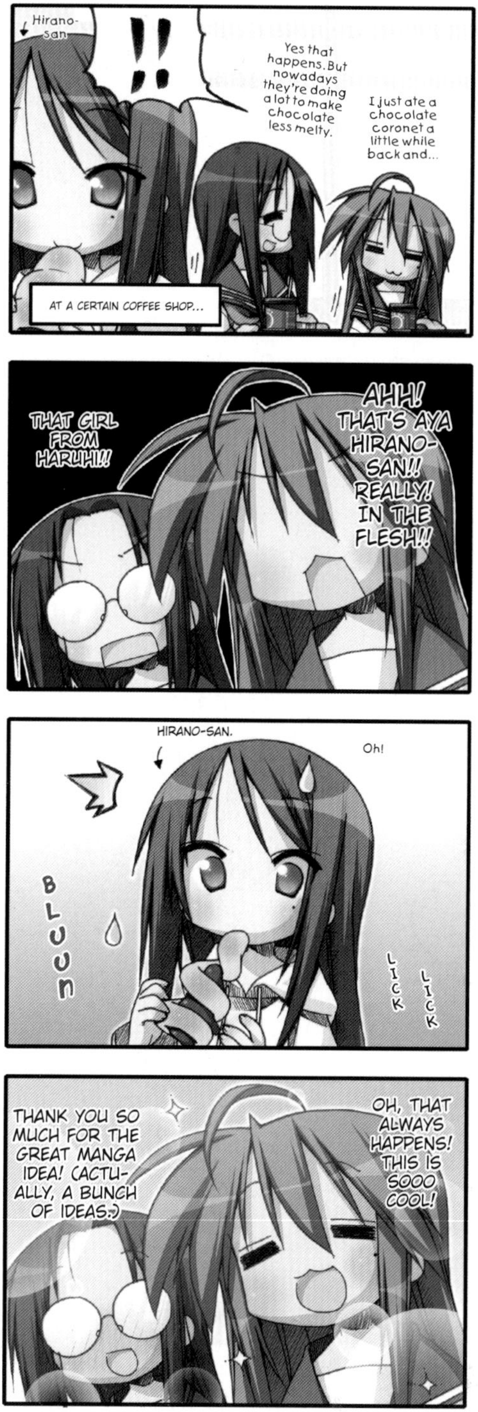
I just ate a chocolate coronet a little while back and...
Yes that happens. But nowadays they're doing a lot to make chocolate less melty.
!!
Hirano-san
AT A CERTAIN COFFEE SHOP...
AHH! THAT'S AYA HIRANO-SAN!! REALLY! IN THE FLESH!!
THAT GIRL FROM HARUHI!!
Oh!
LICK LICK
HIRANO-SAN.
BLUUN
OH, THAT ALWAYS HAPPENS! THIS IS SOOO COOL!
THANK YOU SO MUCH FOR THE GREAT MANGA IDEA! (ACTUALLY, A BUNCH OF IDEAS.)

special bonus 2

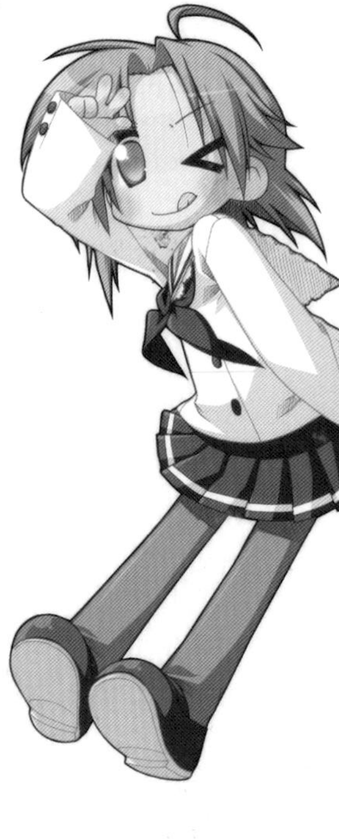

a momentary lapse

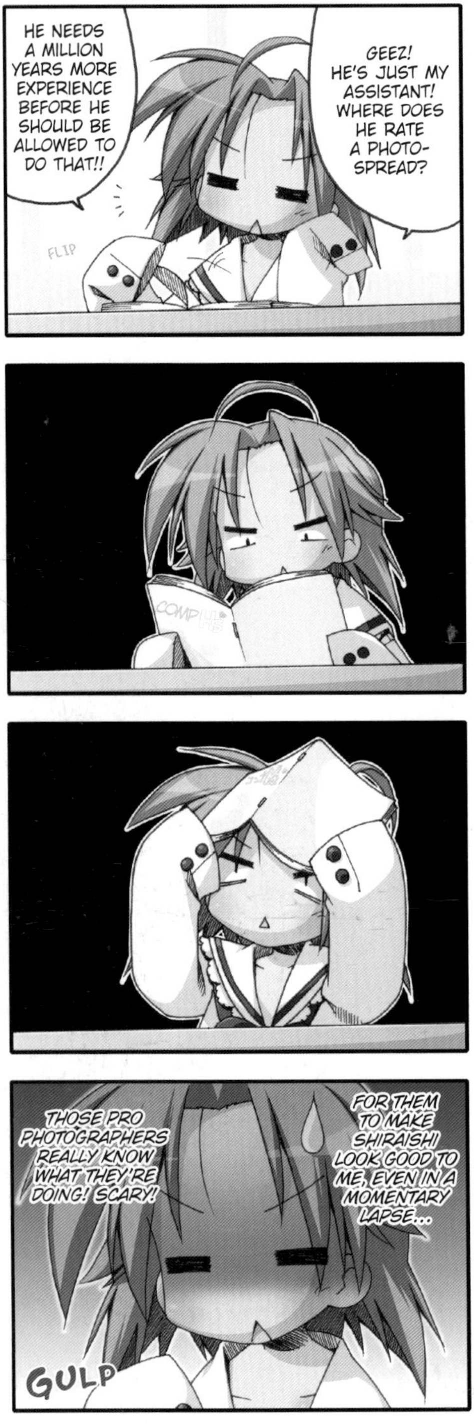
GEEZ! HE'S JUST MY ASSISTANT! WHERE DOES HE RATE A PHOTO-SPREAD?
HE NEEDS A MILLION YEARS MORE EXPERIENCE BEFORE HE SHOULD BE ALLOWED TO DO THAT!!
FLIP
COMP
FOR THEM TO MAKE SHIRAISHI LOOK GOOD TO ME, EVEN IN A MOMENTARY LAPSE...
THOSE PRO PHOTOGRAPHERS REALLY KNOW WHAT THEY'RE DOING! SCARY!
GULP

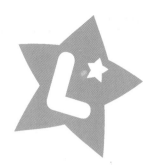

contents

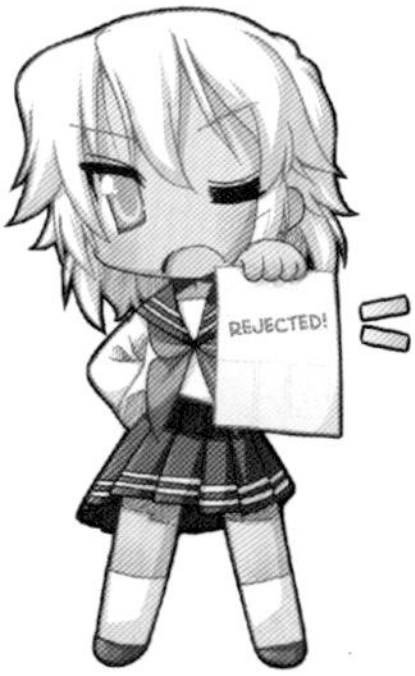
REJECTED!

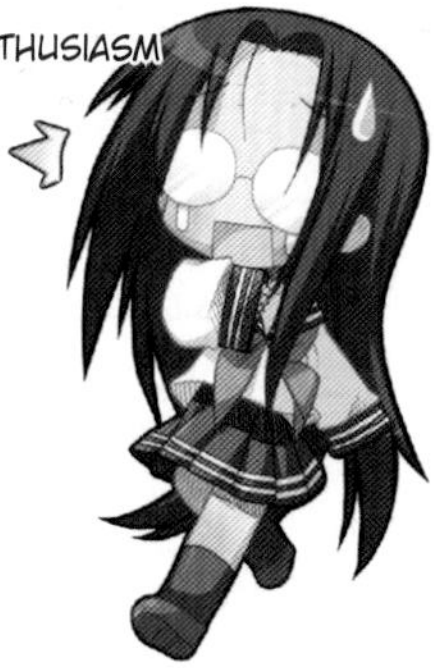

Lucky☆Star

episode 125
imagination

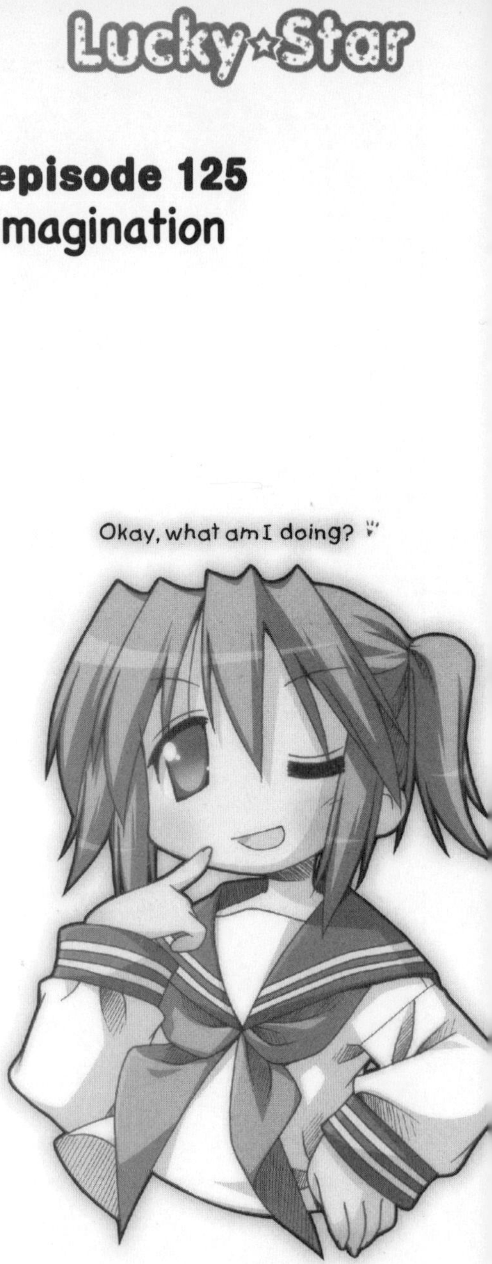
Okay, what am I doing?

● Comptiq, May 2007 issue

our strength

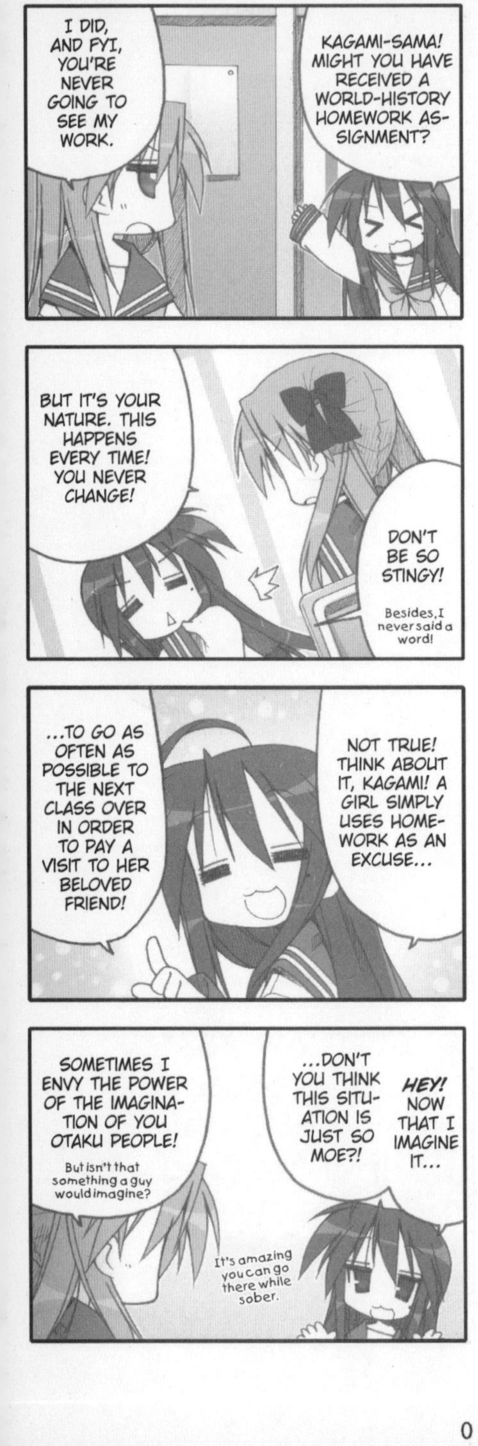
KAGAMI-SAMA! MIGHT YOU HAVE RECEIVED A WORLD-HISTORY HOMEWORK AS-SIGNMENT?
I DID, AND FYI, YOU'RE NEVER GOING TO SEE MY WORK.
DON'T BE SO STINGY!
Besides, I never said a word!
BUT IT'S YOUR NATURE. THIS HAPPENS EVERY TIME! YOU NEVER CHANGE!
NOT TRUE! THINK ABOUT IT, KAGAMI! A GIRL SIMPLY USES HOME-WORK AS AN EXCUSE...
...TO GO AS OFTEN AS POSSIBLE TO THE NEXT CLASS OVER IN ORDER TO PAY A VISIT TO HER BELOVED FRIEND!
HEY! NOW THAT I IMAGINE IT...
...DON'T YOU THINK THIS SITU-ATION IS JUST SO MOE?!
SOMETIMES I ENVY THE POWER OF THE IMAGINA-TION OF YOU OTAKU PEOPLE!
But isn't that something a guy would imagine?
It's amazing you can go there while sober.

one's ideal reality

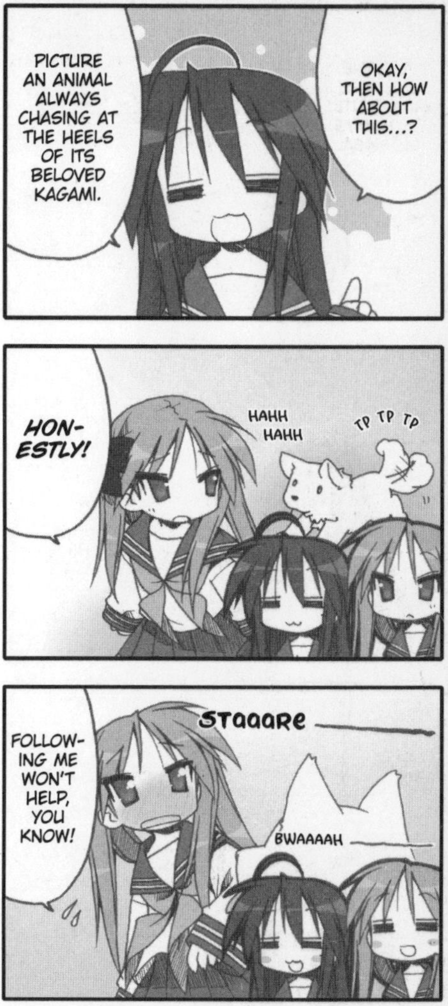
OKAY, THEN HOW ABOUT THIS...?
PICTURE AN ANIMAL ALWAYS CHASING AT THE HEELS OF ITS BELOVED KAGAMI.
TP TP TP
HAHH HAHH
HON-ESTLY!
STaaaRE
BWAAAAH
FOLLOW-ING ME WON'T HELP, YOU KNOW!
DOOM
Yeah, I see the point...
YOUR COMPARISON IS REALLY RUDE! APOLOGIZE TO THE ANIMAL WORLD!
WHAT DID YOU SAY?!
That I'm lower than a dog?

boundary line

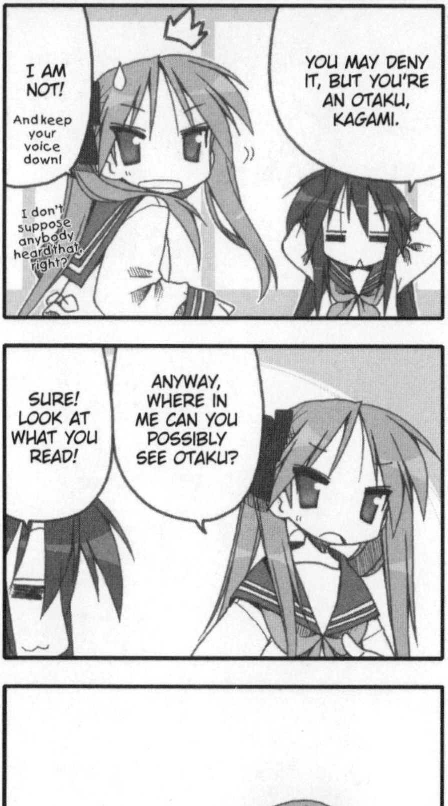
YOU MAY DENY IT, BUT YOU'RE AN OTAKU, KAGAMI.
I AM NOT!
And keep your voice down!
I don't suppose anybody heard that, right?
ANYWAY, WHERE IN ME CAN YOU POSSIBLY SEE OTAKU?
SURE! LOOK AT WHAT YOU READ!
HUH? YOU MEAN READING LIGHT NOVELS MAKES YOU AN OTAKU?
EH? YEAH, SURE. PROBABLY.

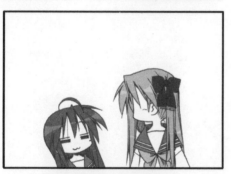

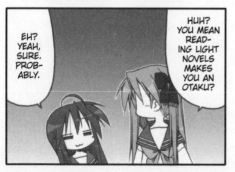

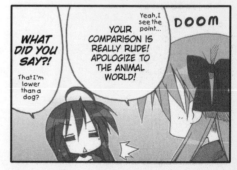

suspicion

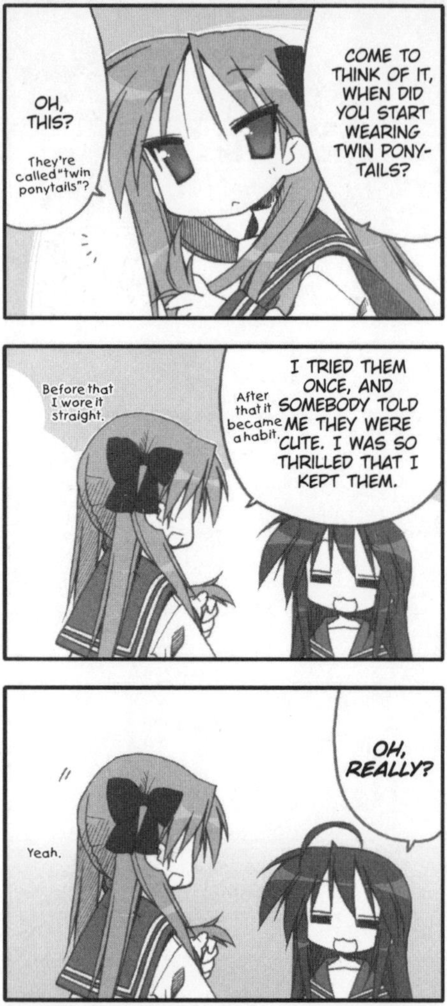
COME TO THINK OF IT, WHEN DID YOU START WEARING TWIN PONYTAILS?
OH, THIS?
They're called "twin ponytails"?
I TRIED THEM ONCE, AND SOMEBODY TOLD ME THEY WERE CUTE. I WAS SO THRILLED THAT I KEPT THEM.
After that it became a habit.
Before that I wore it straight.
OH, REALLY?
Yeah.
WHO SAID THAT?
IT'S THAT FACE YOU'RE MAKING THAT ANNOYS ME!
Like you've got some awful image in you're mind!
GRIN
GRIN

cute girl

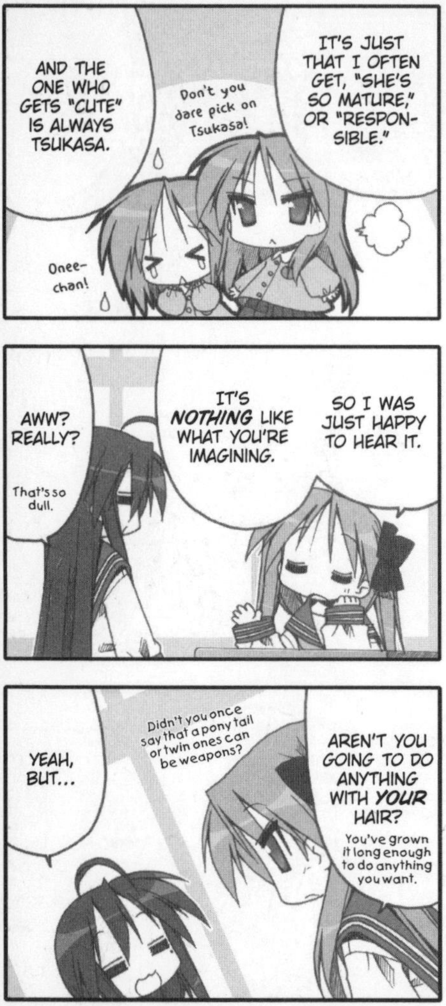
IT'S JUST THAT I OFTEN GET, "SHE'S SO MATURE," OR "RESPONSIBLE."
Don't you dare pick on Tsukasa!
AND THE ONE WHO GETS "CUTE" IS ALWAYS TSUKASA.
Onee-chan!
SO I WAS JUST HAPPY TO HEAR IT.
IT'S NOTHING LIKE WHAT YOU'RE IMAGINING.
AWW? REALLY?
That's so dull.
AREN'T YOU GOING TO DO ANYTHING WITH YOUR HAIR?
You've grown it long enough to do anything you want.
Didn't you once say that a pony tail or twin ones can be weapons?
YEAH, BUT...
IT'S NO FUN JUST PLAYING AROUND WITH IT ON MY OWN.
It would be more moe doing it when others could see.
I-IS THAT RIGHT...?

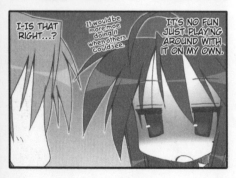

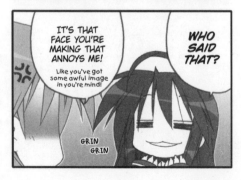

THE OTAKU WORLD'S MOE FIGHTING SPIRIT!

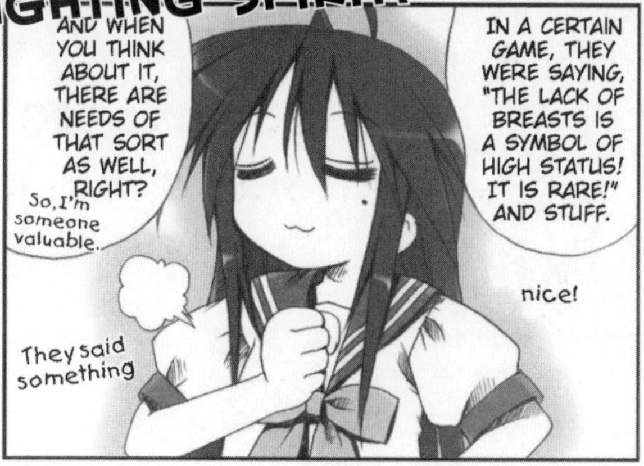
IN A CERTAIN GAME, THEY WERE SAYING, "THE LACK OF BREASTS IS A SYMBOL OF HIGH STATUS! IT IS RARE!" AND STUFF.
AND WHEN YOU THINK ABOUT IT, THERE ARE NEEDS OF THAT SORT AS WELL, RIGHT?
So, I'm someone valuable.
nice!
They said something

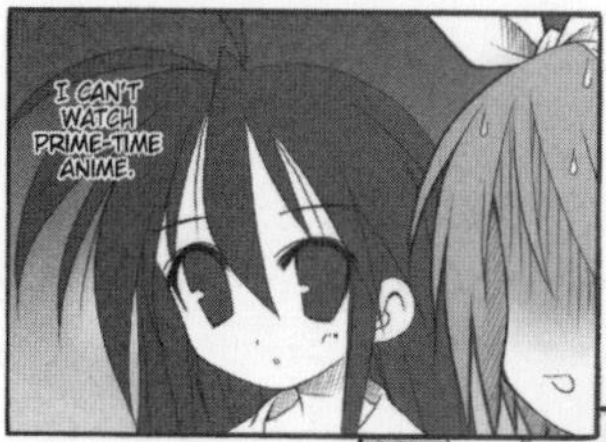
I CAN'T WATCH PRIME-TIME ANIME.

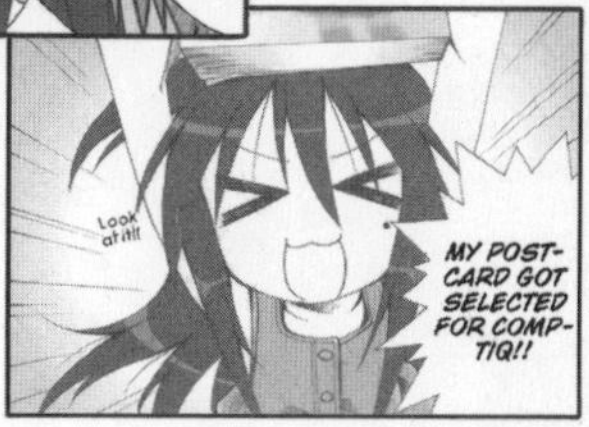
MY POST-CARD GOT SELECTED FOR COMP-TIQ!!
Look at it!!

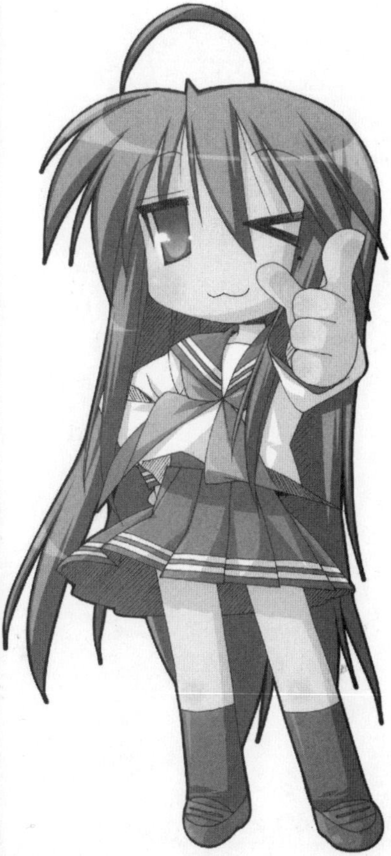

- A mole under her eye
- Excellent athletic skills
- Otaku

KONATA IZUMI

Lucky☆Star

episode 126
always doing things like that.

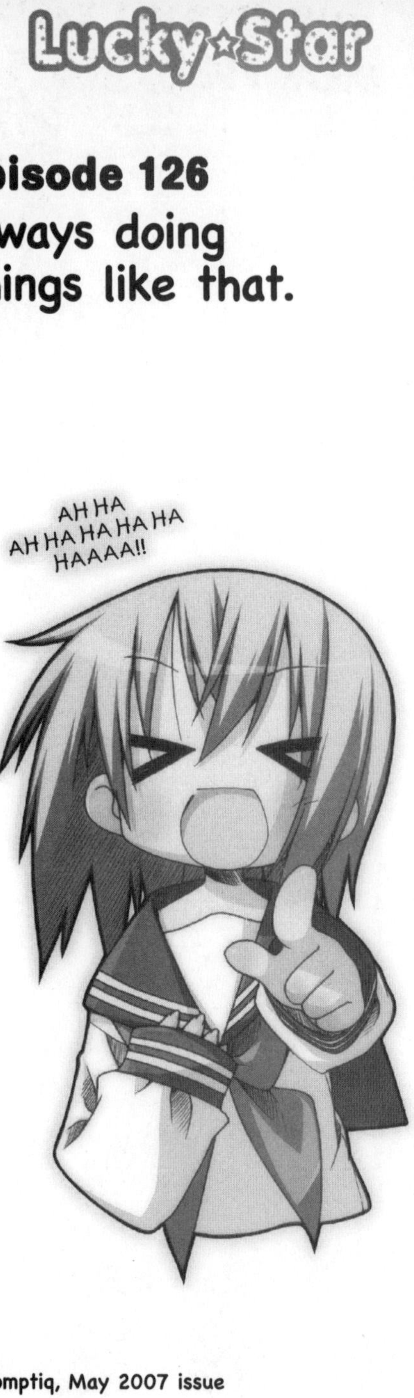
AH HA
AH HA HA HA HA HA
HAAAA!!

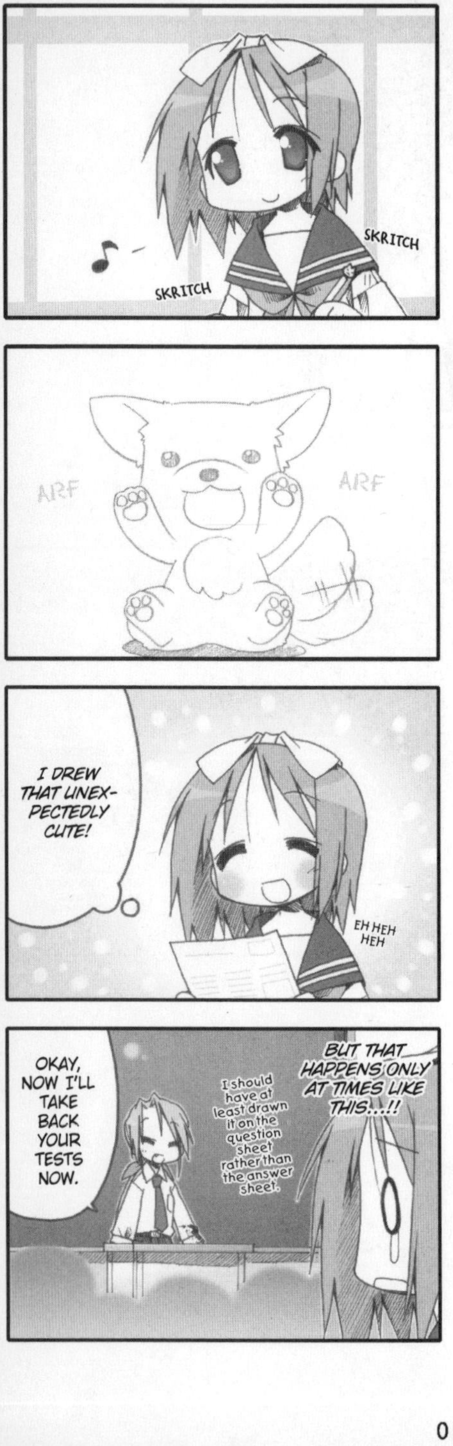
SKRITCH
SKRITCH
ARF
ARF
I DREW THAT UNEXPECTEDLY CUTE!
EH HEH HEH
BUT THAT HAPPENS ONLY AT TIMES LIKE THIS...!!
I should have at least drawn it on the question sheet rather than the answer sheet.
OKAY, NOW I'LL TAKE BACK YOUR TESTS NOW.

● Comptiq, May 2007 issue

ball dropped between players

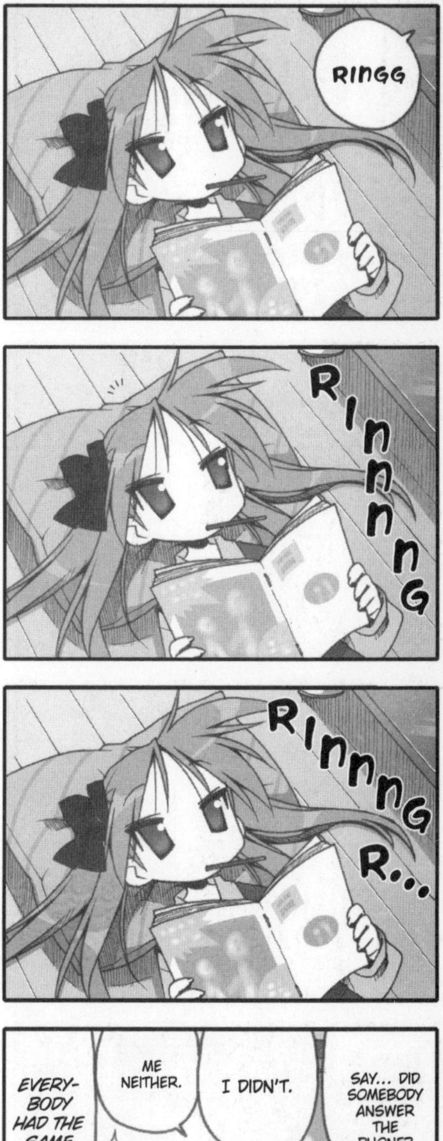
RINGG
RINNNNG
RINNNNG
R...
SAY... DID SOMEBODY ANSWER THE PHONE?
I DIDN'T.
ME NEITHER.
EVERYBODY WAS HOME, SO I FIGURED THAT SOMEBODY ELSE WOULD ANSWER IT.
EVERY-BODY HAD THE SAME IDEA.

the conclusion

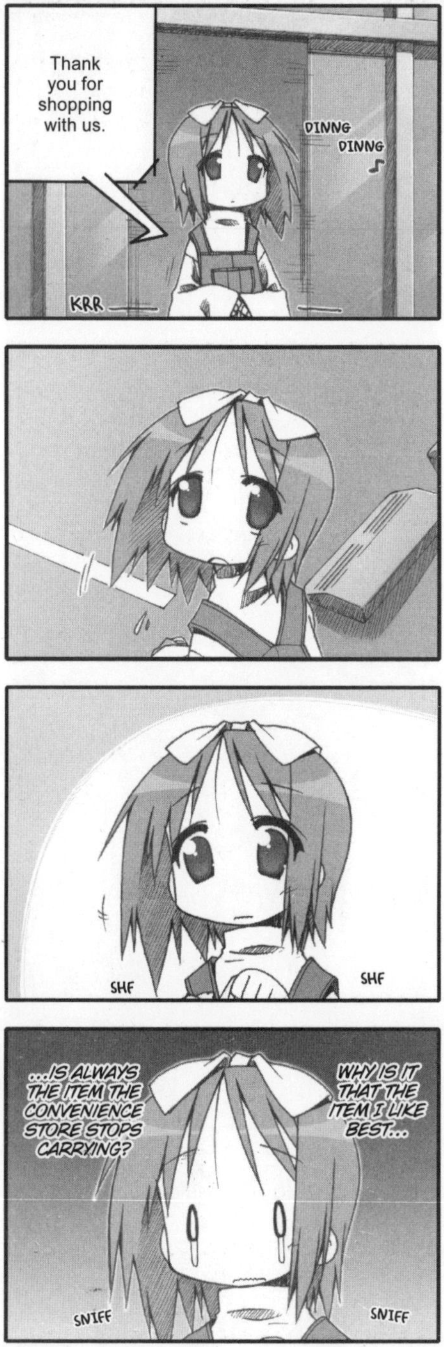
DINNG
DINNG
Thank you for shopping with us.
KRR
SHF
SHF
WHY IS IT THAT THE ITEM I LIKE BEST...
...IS ALWAYS THE ITEM THE CONVENIENCE STORE STOPS CARRYING?
SNIFF
SNIFF

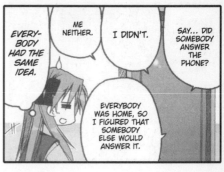

ms. right and correct

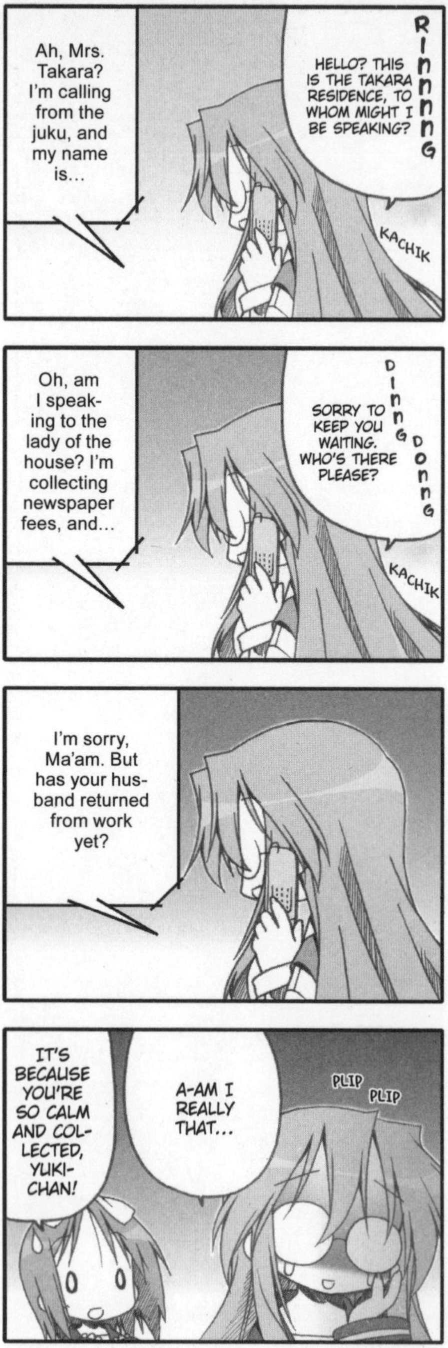
Rinnng
HELLO? THIS IS THE TAKARA RESIDENCE, TO WHOM MIGHT I BE SPEAKING?
KACHIK
Ah, Mrs. Takara? I'm calling from the juku, and my name is...
Dinng Donng
SORRY TO KEEP YOU WAITING. WHO'S THERE PLEASE?
KACHIK
Oh, am I speak-ing to the lady of the house? I'm collecting newspaper fees, and...
I'm sorry, Ma'am. But has your hus-band returned from work yet?
PLIP PLIP
A-AM I REALLY THAT...
IT'S BECAUSE YOU'RE SO CALM AND COL-LECTED, YUKI-CHAN!

ms. mischievous

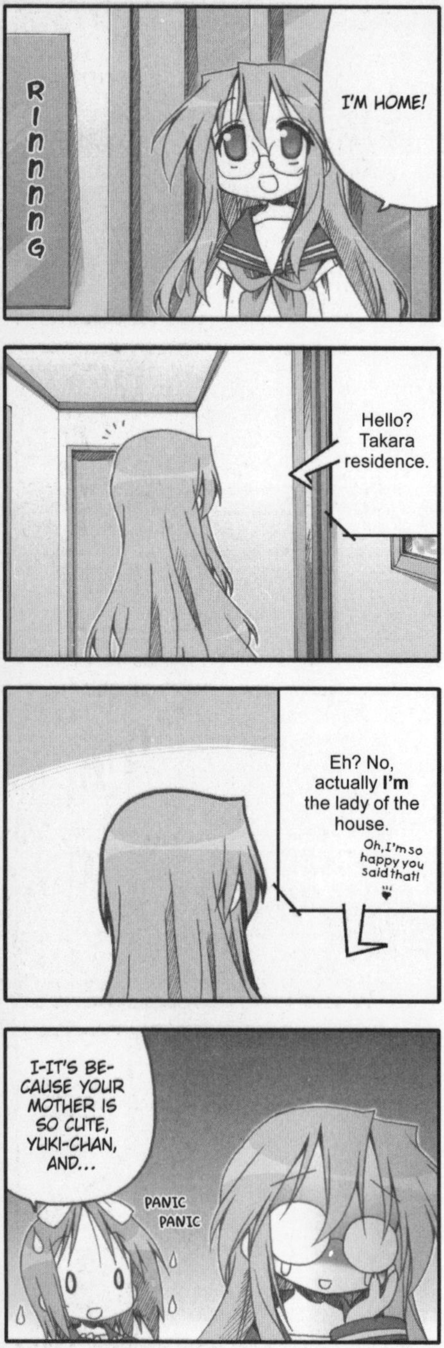
I'M HOME!
Rinnnng
Hello? Takara residence.
Eh? No, actually **I'm** the lady of the house.
Oh, I'm so happy you said that!
I-IT'S BE-CAUSE YOUR MOTHER IS SO CUTE, YUKI-CHAN, AND...
PANIC PANIC

AN AIRHEAD WHO ALWAYS GOES AT HER OWN PACE

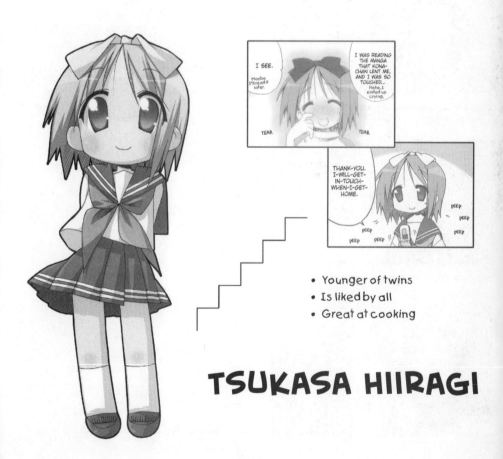

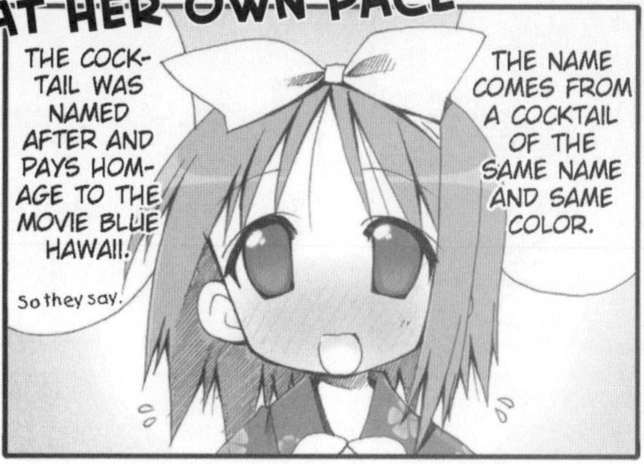
THE NAME COMES FROM A COCKTAIL OF THE SAME NAME AND SAME COLOR.
THE COCK-TAIL WAS NAMED AFTER AND PAYS HOM-AGE TO THE MOVIE BLUE HAWAII.
So they say.

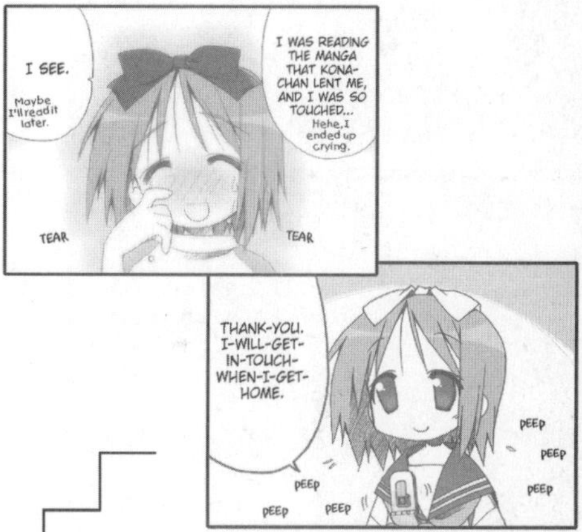
I WAS READING THE MANGA THAT KONA-CHAN LENT ME, AND I WAS SO TOUCHED...
Hehe, I ended up crying.
I SEE.
Maybe I'll read it later.
TEAR
TEAR
THANK-YOU. I-WILL-GET-IN-TOUCH-WHEN-I-GET-HOME.
PEEP
PEEP
PEEP
PEEP
PEEP
PEEP

- Younger of twins
- Is liked by all
- Great at cooking

TSUKASA HIIRAGI

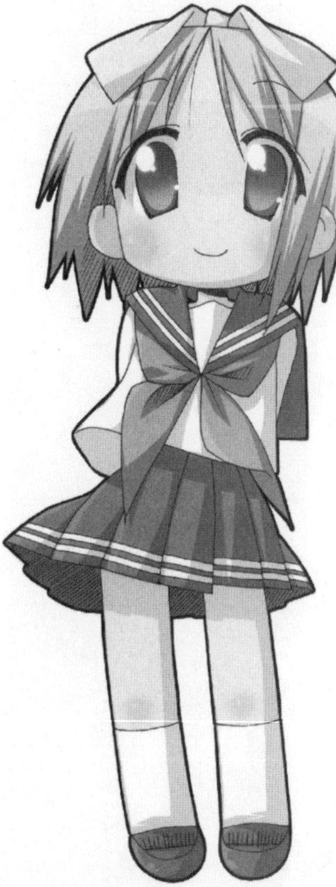

Lucky☆Star

episode 127
similar oddities

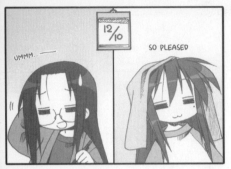

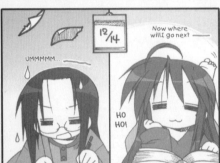

That's right.
It's so embarrassing...

● Comptiq, May 2007 issue

active and passive

12/10
SO PLEASED
UMMM...
12/14
Now where will I go next
HO HO!
UMMMMM...
12/18
I'm going to be going there!
EXCITEMENT
Arrg! I'm so sleepy!!
I can't wait for the New Year!
AND ON THE FATEFUL NEW YEAR'S EVE...!!
Oh, time! Please stop!!
I'll never make it!!
I'm going to miss the deadline!!

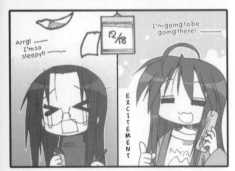

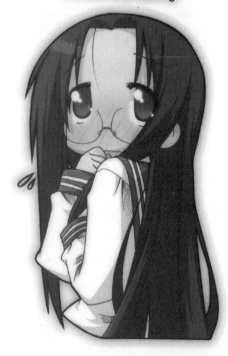

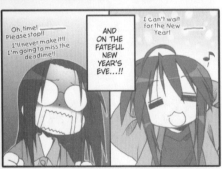

i beg your pardon

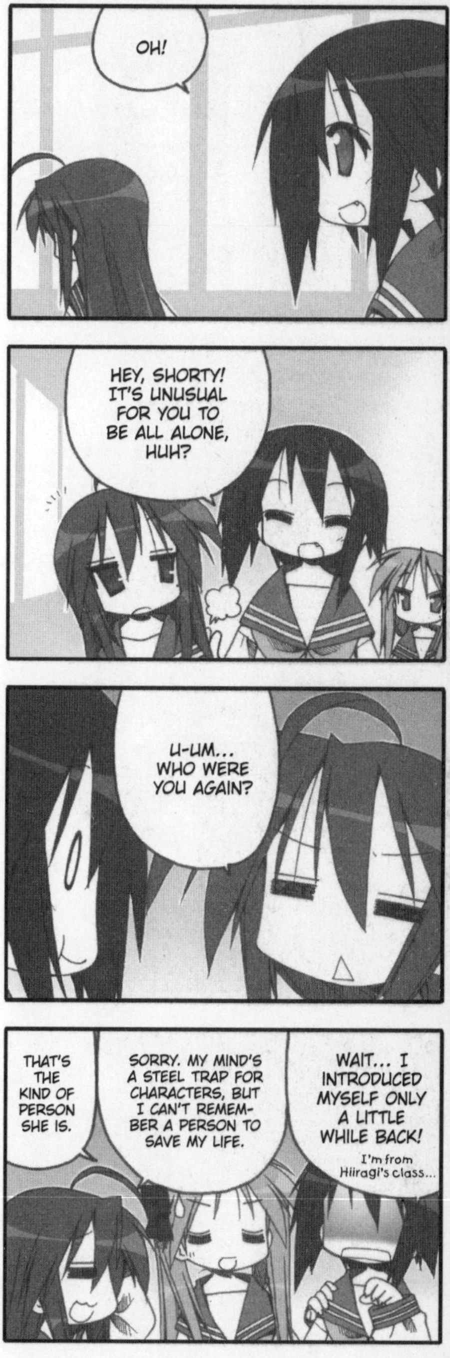
OH!
HEY, SHORTY! IT'S UNUSUAL FOR YOU TO BE ALL ALONE, HUH?
U-UM... WHO WERE YOU AGAIN?
WAIT... I INTRODUCED MYSELF ONLY A LITTLE WHILE BACK!
I'm from Hiiragi's class...
SORRY. MY MIND'S A STEEL TRAP FOR CHARACTERS, BUT I CAN'T REMEMBER A PERSON TO SAVE MY LIFE.
THAT'S THE KIND OF PERSON SHE IS.

smell

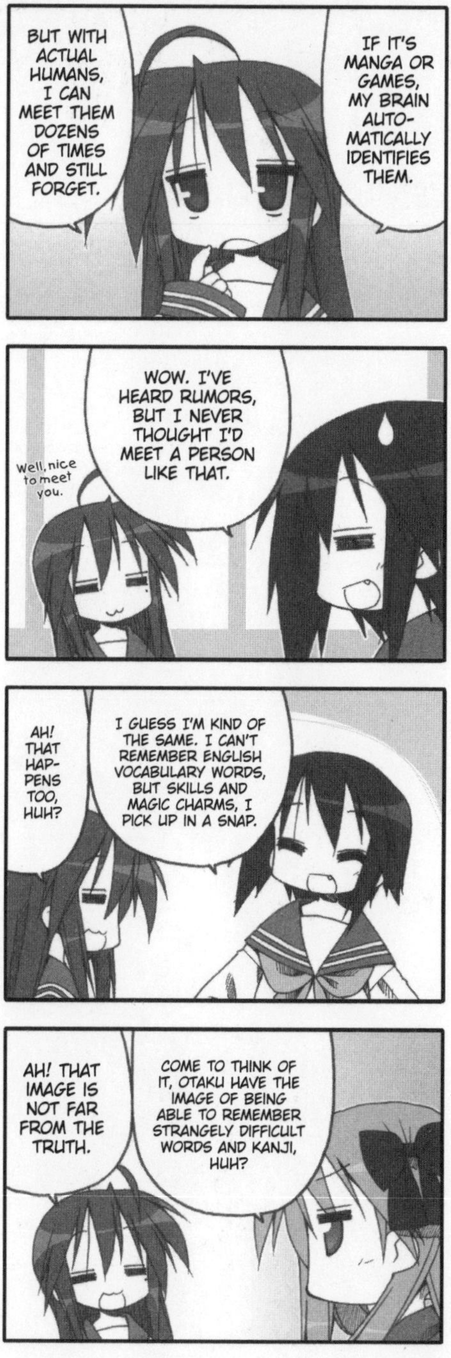
IF IT'S MANGA OR GAMES, MY BRAIN AUTOMATICALLY IDENTIFIES THEM.
BUT WITH ACTUAL HUMANS, I CAN MEET THEM DOZENS OF TIMES AND STILL FORGET.
WOW. I'VE HEARD RUMORS, BUT I NEVER THOUGHT I'D MEET A PERSON LIKE THAT.
Well, nice to meet you.
I GUESS I'M KIND OF THE SAME. I CAN'T REMEMBER ENGLISH VOCABULARY WORDS, BUT SKILLS AND MAGIC CHARMS, I PICK UP IN A SNAP.
AH! THAT HAPPENS TOO, HUH?
COME TO THINK OF IT, OTAKU HAVE THE IMAGE OF BEING ABLE TO REMEMBER STRANGELY DIFFICULT WORDS AND KANJI, HUH?
AH! THAT IMAGE IS NOT FAR FROM THE TRUTH.

the mist descends

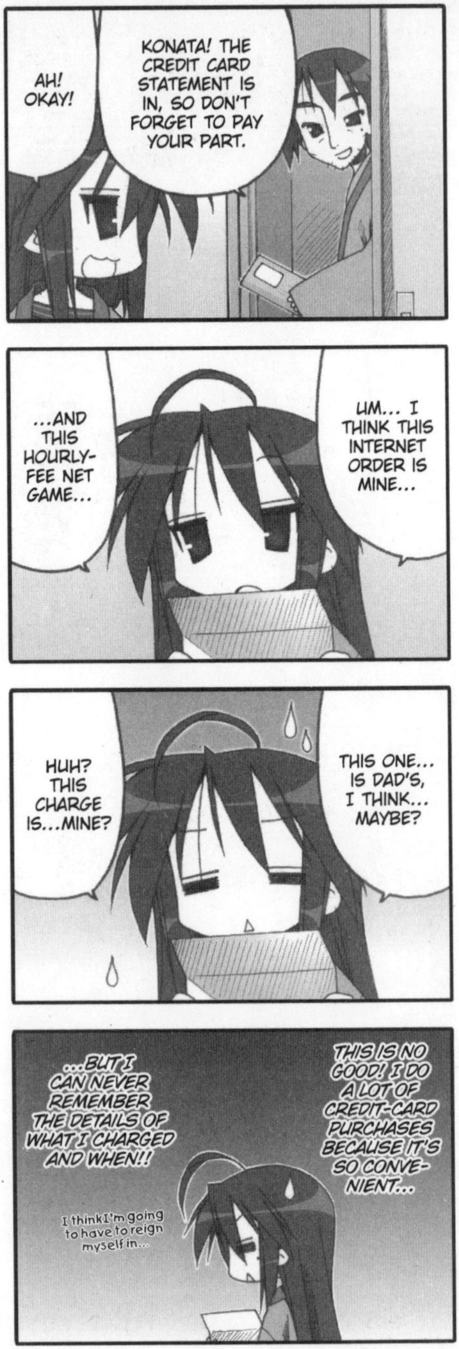
KONATA! THE CREDIT CARD STATEMENT IS IN, SO DON'T FORGET TO PAY YOUR PART.
AH! OKAY!
UM... I THINK THIS INTERNET ORDER IS MINE...
...AND THIS HOURLY-FEE NET GAME...
THIS ONE... IS DAD'S, I THINK... MAYBE?
HUH? THIS CHARGE IS...MINE?
THIS IS NO GOOD! I DO A LOT OF CREDIT-CARD PURCHASES BECAUSE IT'S SO CONVE-NIENT...
...BUT I CAN NEVER REMEMBER THE DETAILS OF WHAT I CHARGED AND WHEN!!
I think I'm going to have to reign myself in...

transparency

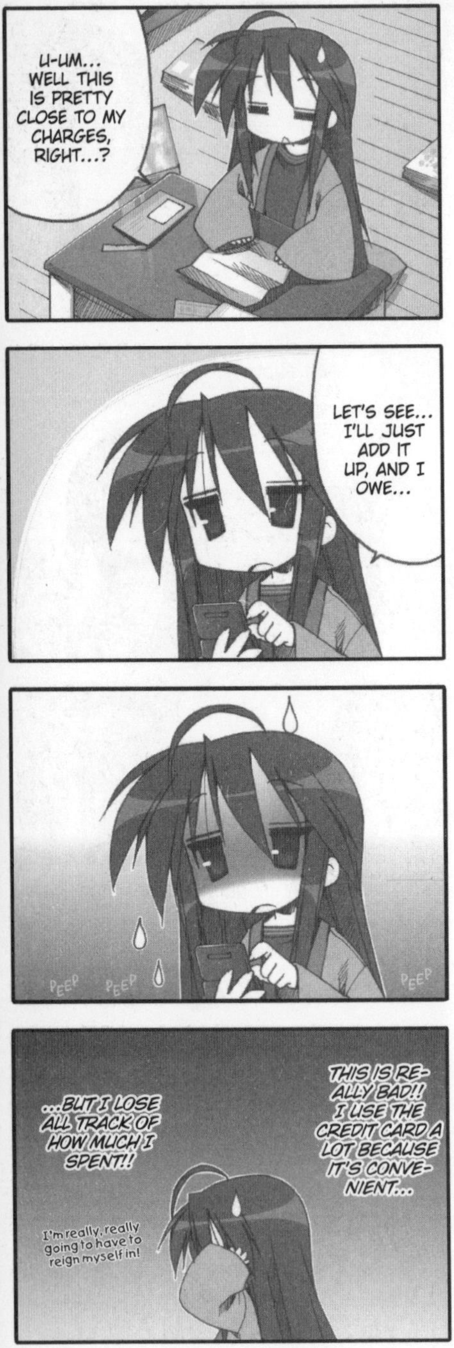
U-UM... WELL THIS IS PRETTY CLOSE TO MY CHARGES, RIGHT...?
LET'S SEE... I'LL JUST ADD IT UP, AND I OWE...
PEEP
PEEP
PEEP
THIS IS RE-ALLY BAD!! I USE THE CREDIT CARD A LOT BECAUSE IT'S CONVE-NIENT...
...BUT I LOSE ALL TRACK OF HOW MUCH I SPENT!!
I'm really, really going to have to reign myself in!

SOMEONE WITH GOOD COMMON-SENSE WHO NEVER SEEMS TO CATCH A BREAK

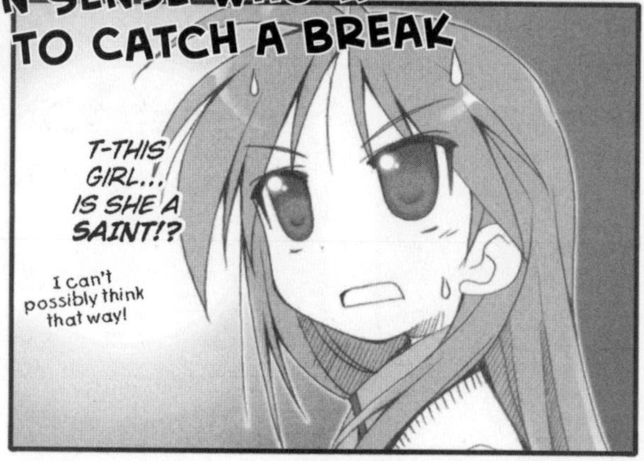
T-THIS GIRL...! IS SHE A SAINT!?
I can't possibly think that way!

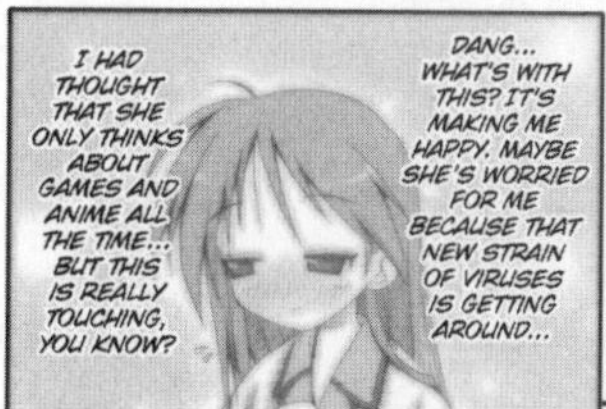
DANG... WHAT'S WITH THIS? IT'S MAKING ME HAPPY. MAYBE SHE'S WORRIED FOR ME BECAUSE THAT NEW STRAIN OF VIRUSES IS GETTING AROUND...
I HAD THOUGHT THAT SHE ONLY THINKS ABOUT GAMES AND ANIME ALL THE TIME... BUT THIS IS REALLY TOUCHING, YOU KNOW?

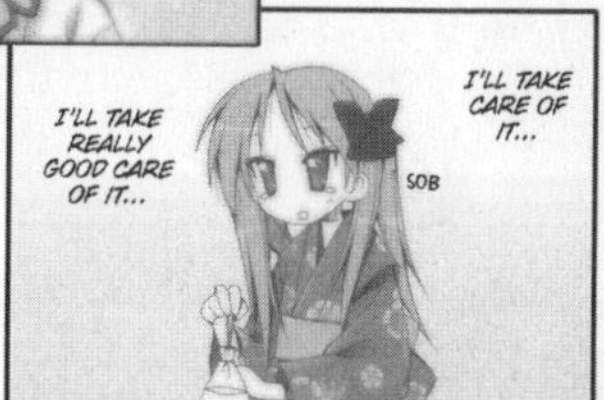
I'LL TAKE CARE OF IT...
SOB
I'LL TAKE REALLY GOOD CARE OF IT...

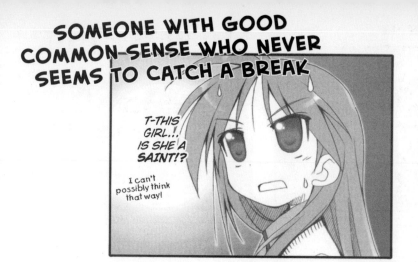

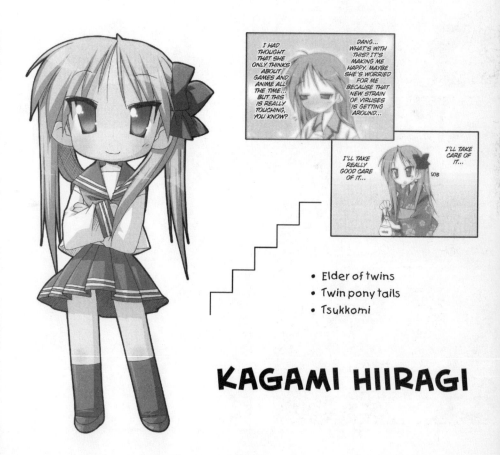

- Elder of twins
- Twin pony tails
- Tsukkomi

KAGAMI HIIRAGI

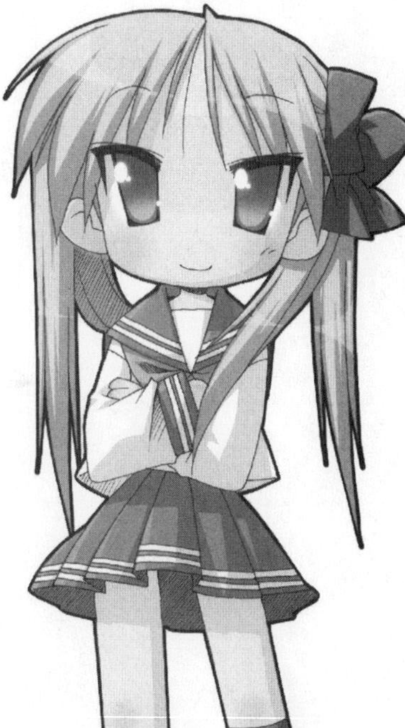

Lucky☆Star

episode 128
effective advertising

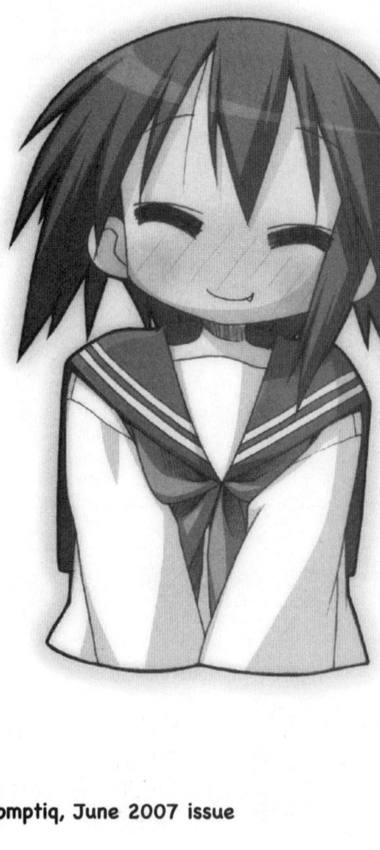

● Comptiq, June 2007 issue

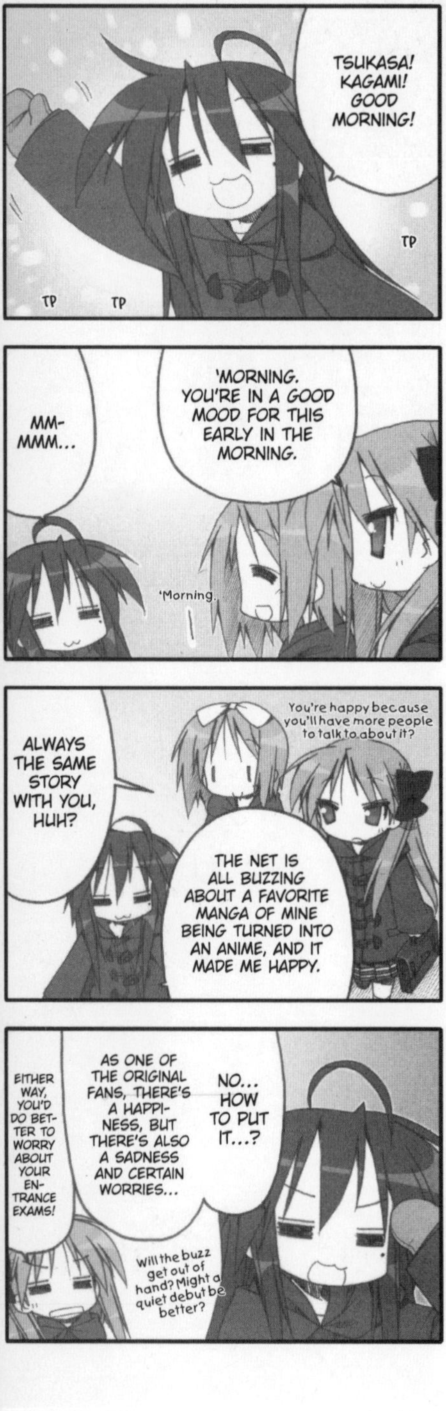
TSUKASA! KAGAMI! GOOD MORNING!
TP
TP
TP
'MORNING. YOU'RE IN A GOOD MOOD FOR THIS EARLY IN THE MORNING.
MM-MMM...
'Morning.
You're happy because you'll have more people to talk to about it?
ALWAYS THE SAME STORY WITH YOU, HUH?
THE NET IS ALL BUZZING ABOUT A FAVORITE MANGA OF MINE BEING TURNED INTO AN ANIME, AND IT MADE ME HAPPY.
NO... HOW TO PUT IT...?
AS ONE OF THE ORIGINAL FANS, THERE'S A HAPPI-NESS, BUT THERE'S ALSO A SADNESS AND CERTAIN WORRIES...
EITHER WAY, YOU'D DO BET-TER TO WORRY ABOUT YOUR EN-TRANCE EXAMS!
Will the buzz get out of hand? Might a quiet debut be better?

a truly trivial matter

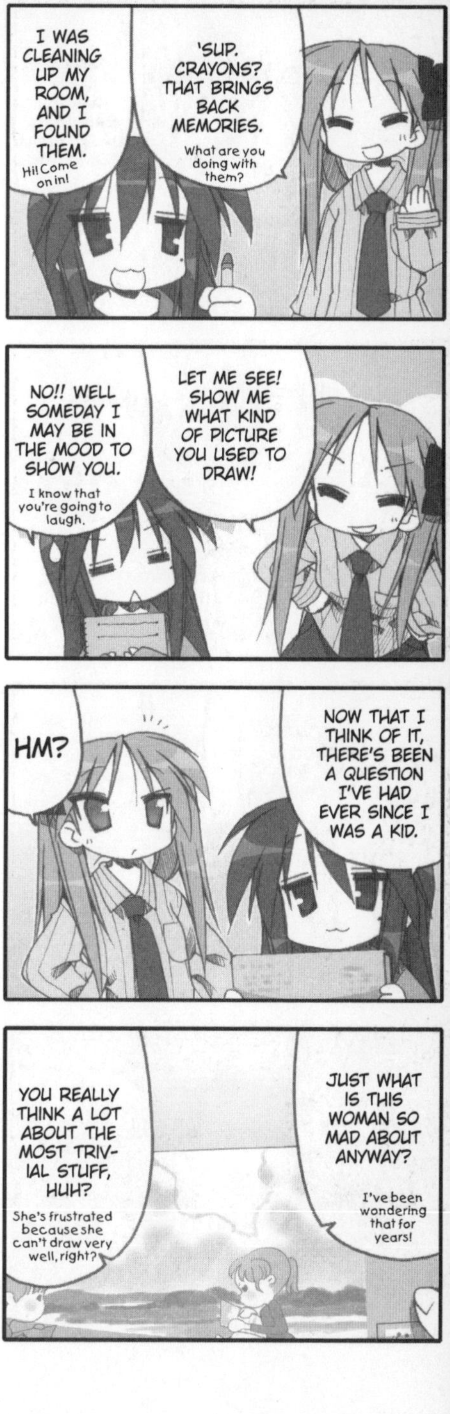
'SUP. CRAYONS? THAT BRINGS BACK MEMORIES.
What are you doing with them?
I WAS CLEANING UP MY ROOM, AND I FOUND THEM.
Hi! Come on in!
LET ME SEE! SHOW ME WHAT KIND OF PICTURE YOU USED TO DRAW!
NO!! WELL SOMEDAY I MAY BE IN THE MOOD TO SHOW YOU.
I know that you're going to laugh.
NOW THAT I THINK OF IT, THERE'S BEEN A QUESTION I'VE HAD EVER SINCE I WAS A KID.
HM?
JUST WHAT IS THIS WOMAN SO MAD ABOUT ANYWAY?
I've been wondering that for years!
YOU REALLY THINK A LOT ABOUT THE MOST TRIV-IAL STUFF, HUH?
She's frustrated because she can't draw very well, right?

status

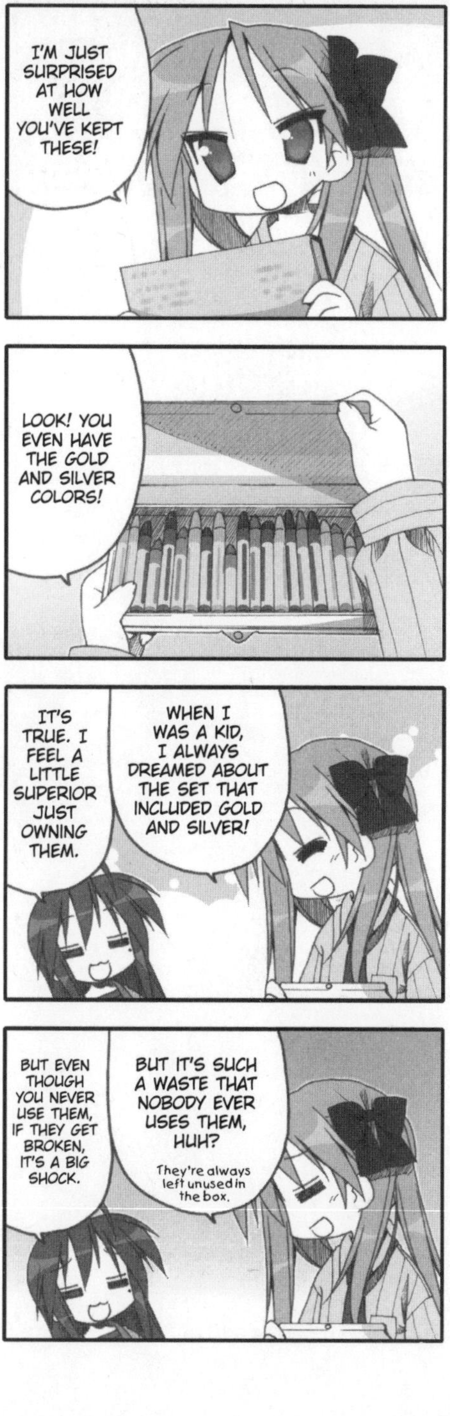
I'M JUST SURPRISED AT HOW WELL YOU'VE KEPT THESE!
LOOK! YOU EVEN HAVE THE GOLD AND SILVER COLORS!
WHEN I WAS A KID, I ALWAYS DREAMED ABOUT THE SET THAT INCLUDED GOLD AND SILVER!
IT'S TRUE. I FEEL A LITTLE SUPERIOR JUST OWNING THEM.
BUT IT'S SUCH A WASTE THAT NOBODY EVER USES THEM, HUH?
They're always left unused in the box.
BUT EVEN THOUGH YOU NEVER USE THEM, IF THEY GET BROKEN, IT'S A BIG SHOCK.

on the bandwagon

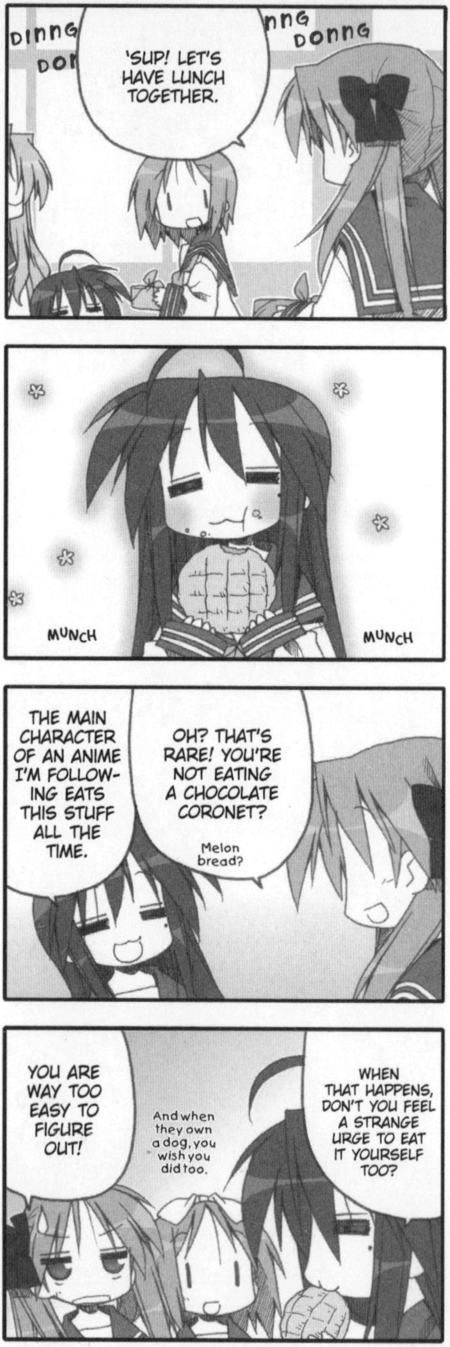
nnG
DONNG
'SUP! LET'S HAVE LUNCH TOGETHER.
DINNG
DON
MUNCH
MUNCH
OH? THAT'S RARE! YOU'RE NOT EATING A CHOCOLATE CORONET?
Melon bread?
THE MAIN CHARACTER OF AN ANIME I'M FOLLOWING EATS THIS STUFF ALL THE TIME.
WHEN THAT HAPPENS, DON'T YOU FEEL A STRANGE URGE TO EAT IT YOURSELF TOO?
And when they own a dog, you wish you did too.
YOU ARE WAY TOO EASY TO FIGURE OUT!

missing the train

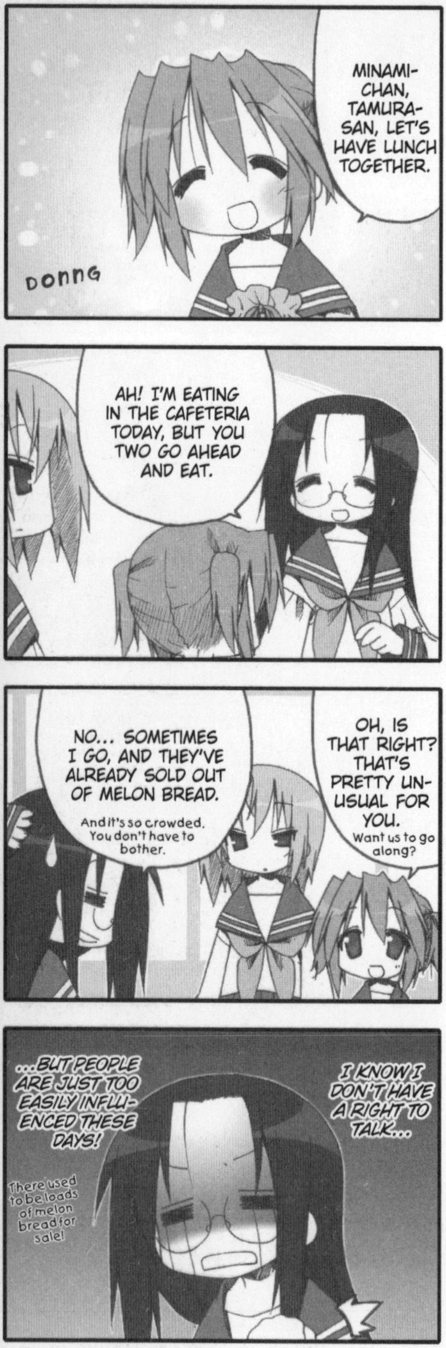
MINAMI-CHAN, TAMURA-SAN, LET'S HAVE LUNCH TOGETHER.
DONNG
AH! I'M EATING IN THE CAFETERIA TODAY, BUT YOU TWO GO AHEAD AND EAT.
OH, IS THAT RIGHT? THAT'S PRETTY UNUSUAL FOR YOU.
Want us to go along?
NO... SOMETIMES I GO, AND THEY'VE ALREADY SOLD OUT OF MELON BREAD.
And it's so crowded. You don't have to bother.
I KNOW I DON'T HAVE A RIGHT TO TALK...
...BUT PEOPLE ARE JUST TOO EASILY INFLUENCED THESE DAYS!
There used to be loads of melon bread for sale!

THE UNSUNG HERO

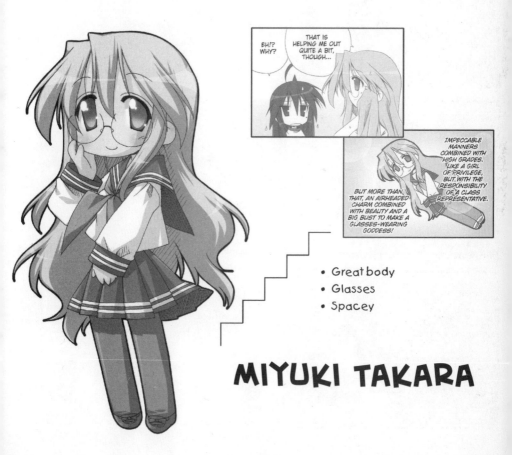

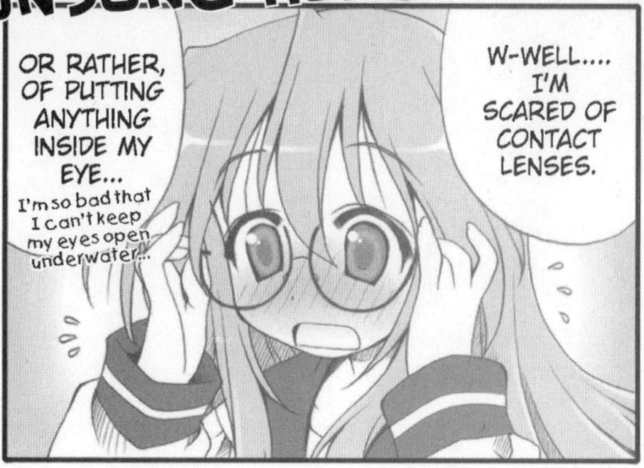
W-WELL.... I'M SCARED OF CONTACT LENSES.
OR RATHER, OF PUTTING ANYTHING INSIDE MY EYE...
I'm so bad that I can't keep my eyes open underwater...

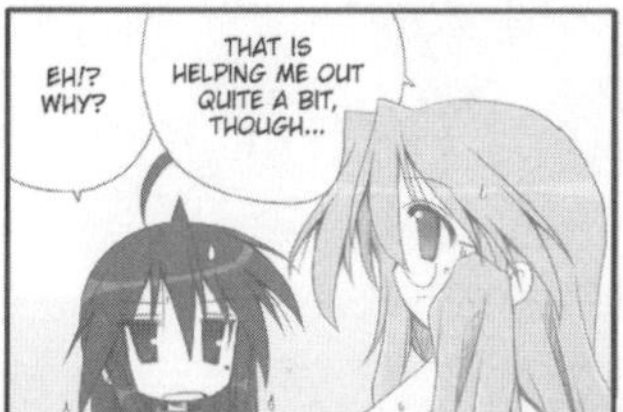
THAT IS HELPING ME OUT QUITE A BIT, THOUGH...
EH!? WHY?

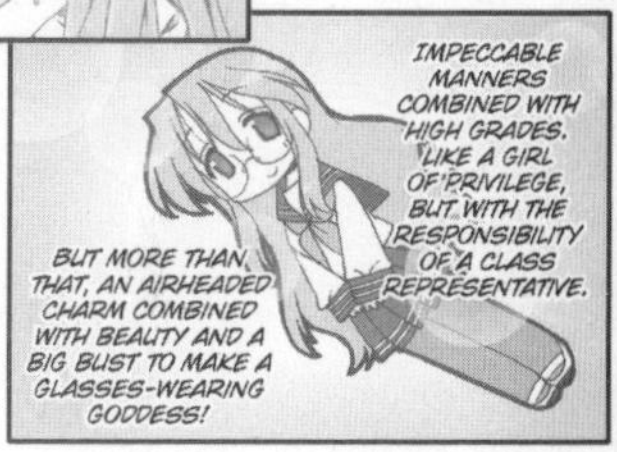
IMPECCABLE MANNERS COMBINED WITH HIGH GRADES. LIKE A GIRL OF PRIVILEGE, BUT WITH THE RESPONSIBILITY OF A CLASS REPRESENTATIVE.
BUT MORE THAN THAT, AN AIRHEADED CHARM COMBINED WITH BEAUTY AND A BIG BUST TO MAKE A GLASSES-WEARING GODDESS!

- Great body
- Glasses
- Spacey

MIYUKI TAKARA

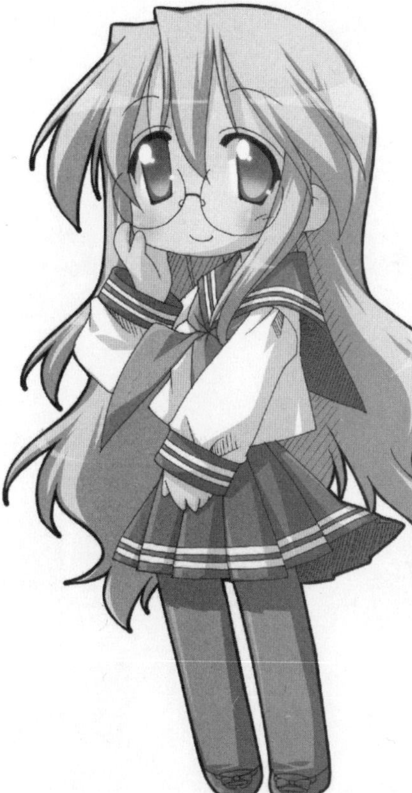

Lucky☆Star

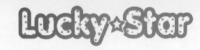

episode 129
comfortably warm weather

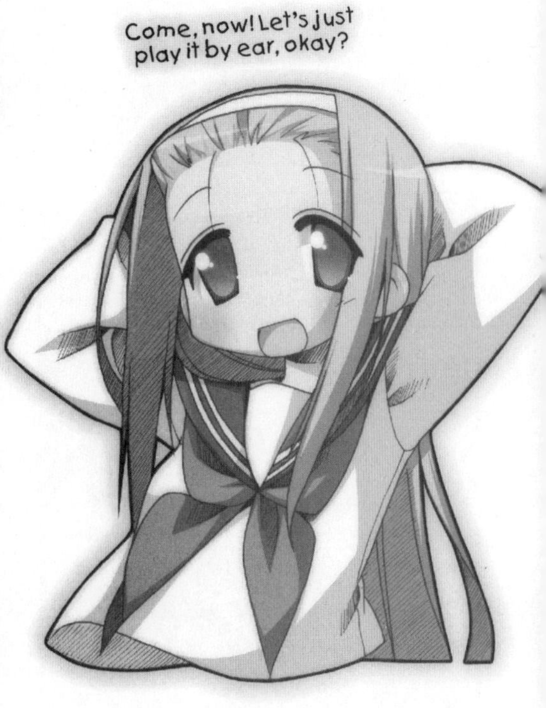

Come, now! Let's just play it by ear, okay?

● Comptiq, June 2007 issue

principles governing behavior

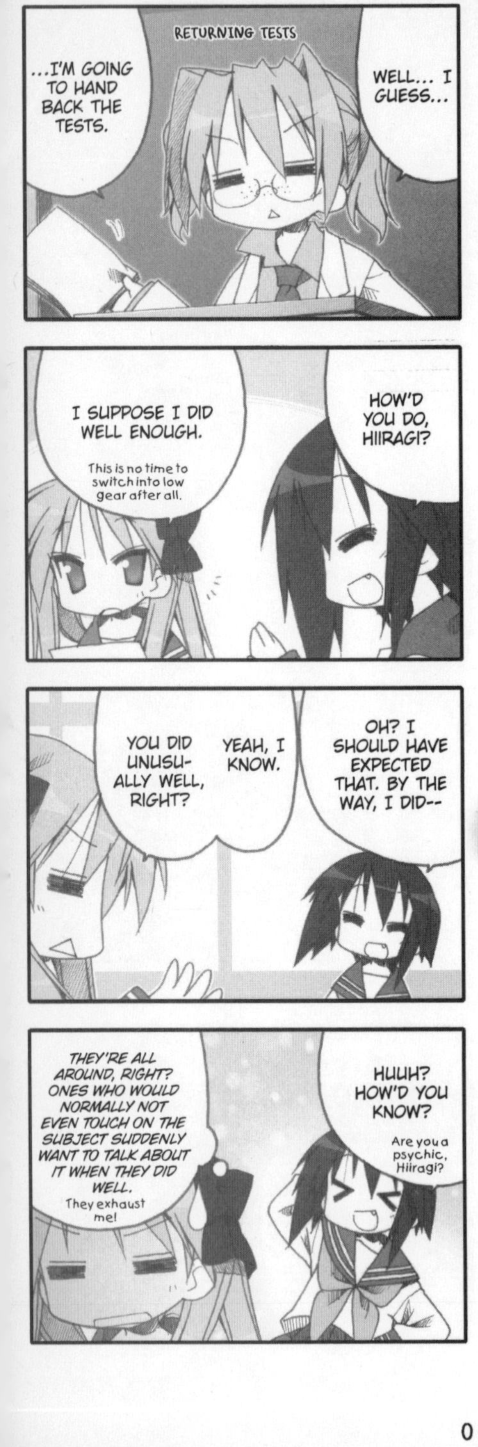

RETURNING TESTS
WELL... I GUESS...
...I'M GOING TO HAND BACK THE TESTS.
HOW'D YOU DO, HIIRAGI?
I SUPPOSE I DID WELL ENOUGH.
This is no time to switch into low gear after all.
OH? I SHOULD HAVE EXPECTED THAT. BY THE WAY, I DID--
YEAH, I KNOW.
YOU DID UNUSU-ALLY WELL, RIGHT?
HUUH? HOW'D YOU KNOW?
Are you a psychic, Hiiragi?
THEY'RE ALL AROUND, RIGHT? ONES WHO WOULD NORMALLY NOT EVEN TOUCH ON THE SUBJECT SUDDENLY WANT TO TALK ABOUT IT WHEN THEY DID WELL.
They exhaust me!

the moment of bliss

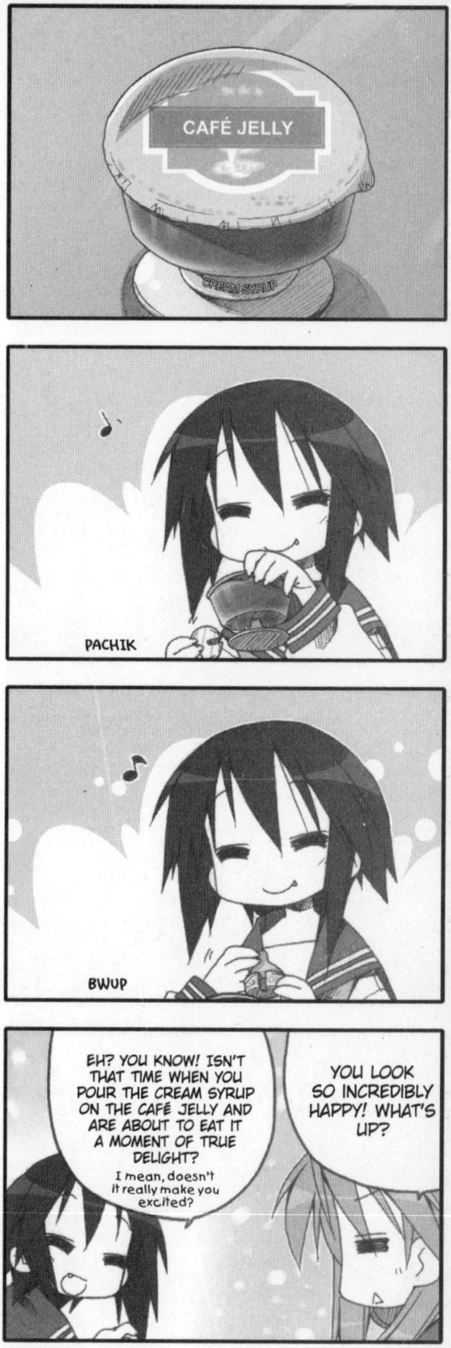
CAFÉ JELLY
CREAM SYRUP
PACHIK
BWUP
YOU LOOK SO INCREDIBLY HAPPY! WHAT'S UP?
EH? YOU KNOW! ISN'T THAT TIME WHEN YOU POUR THE CREAM SYRUP ON THE CAFÉ JELLY AND ARE ABOUT TO EAT IT A MOMENT OF TRUE DELIGHT?
I mean, doesn't it really make you excited?

a simple question

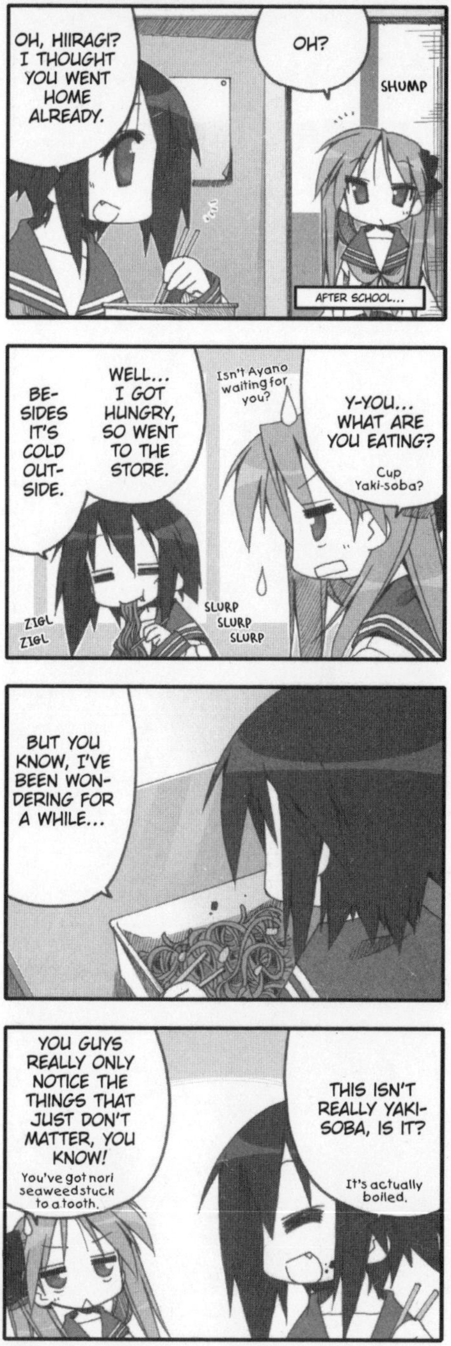
SHUMP
OH?
OH, HIIRAGI? I THOUGHT YOU WENT HOME ALREADY.
AFTER SCHOOL...
Y-YOU... WHAT ARE YOU EATING?
Cup Yaki-soba?
Isn't Ayano waiting for you?
WELL... I GOT HUNGRY, SO WENT TO THE STORE.
BE-SIDES IT'S COLD OUT-SIDE.
SLURP SLURP SLURP
ZIGL ZIGL
BUT YOU KNOW, I'VE BEEN WON-DERING FOR A WHILE...
THIS ISN'T REALLY YAKI-SOBA, IS IT?
It's actually boiled.
YOU GUYS REALLY ONLY NOTICE THE THINGS THAT JUST DON'T MATTER, YOU KNOW!
You've got nori seaweed stuck to a tooth.

the weapon that is never used

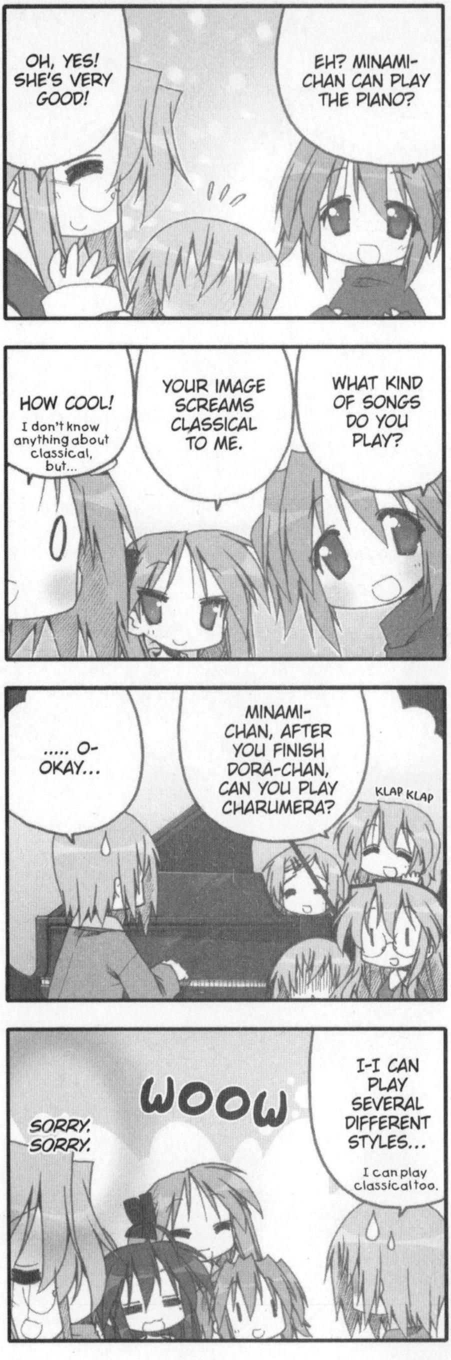
EH? MINAMI-CHAN CAN PLAY THE PIANO?
OH, YES! SHE'S VERY GOOD!
WHAT KIND OF SONGS DO YOU PLAY?
YOUR IMAGE SCREAMS CLASSICAL TO ME.
HOW COOL!
I don't know anything about classical, but...
MINAMI-CHAN, AFTER YOU FINISH DORA-CHAN, CAN YOU PLAY CHARUMERA?
KLAP KLAP
..... O-OKAY...
I-I CAN PLAY SEVERAL DIFFERENT STYLES...
I can play classical too.
WOOW
SORRY. SORRY.

wasn't necessary

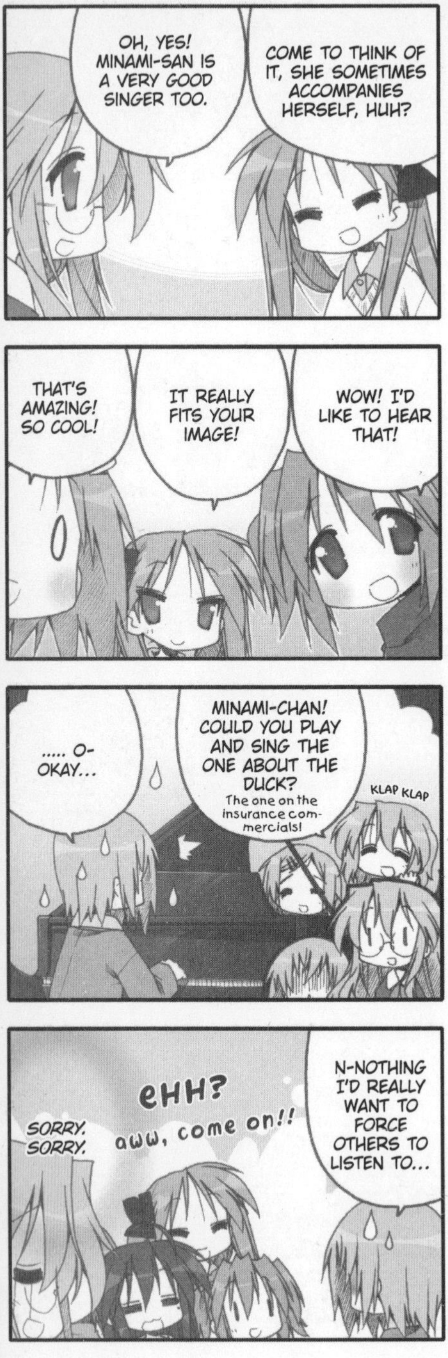
COME TO THINK OF IT, SHE SOMETIMES ACCOMPANIES HERSELF, HUH?
OH, YES! MINAMI-SAN IS A VERY GOOD SINGER TOO.
WOW! I'D LIKE TO HEAR THAT!
IT REALLY FITS YOUR IMAGE!
THAT'S AMAZING! SO COOL!
MINAMI-CHAN! COULD YOU PLAY AND SING THE ONE ABOUT THE DUCK?
The one on the insurance commercials!
KLAP KLAP
..... O-OKAY...
N-NOTHING I'D REALLY WANT TO FORCE OTHERS TO LISTEN TO...
eHH?
aww, come on!!
SORRY. SORRY.

AN ATHLETIC TYPE WHO LOOKS BEST WHEN SMILING

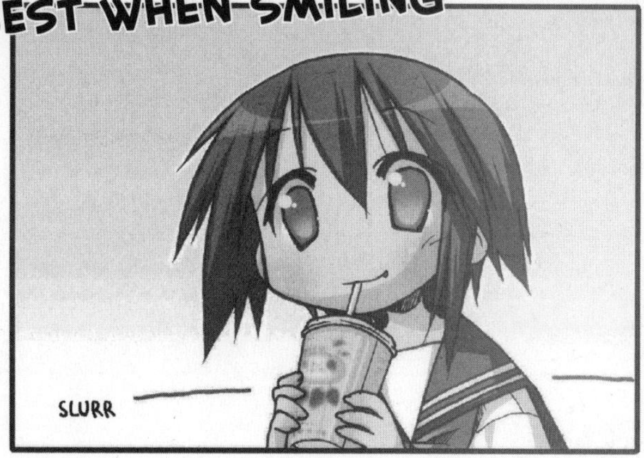
SLURR

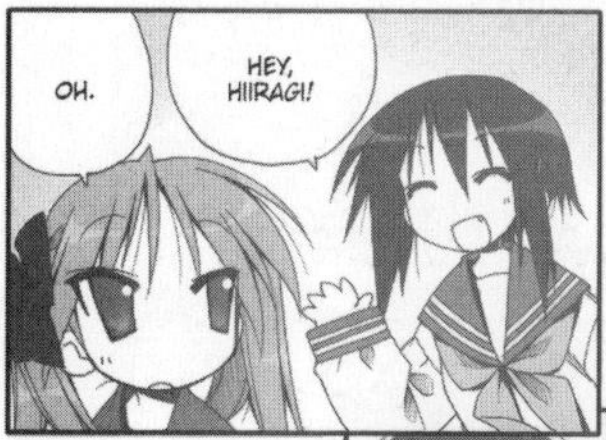
HEY, HIIRAGI!
OH.

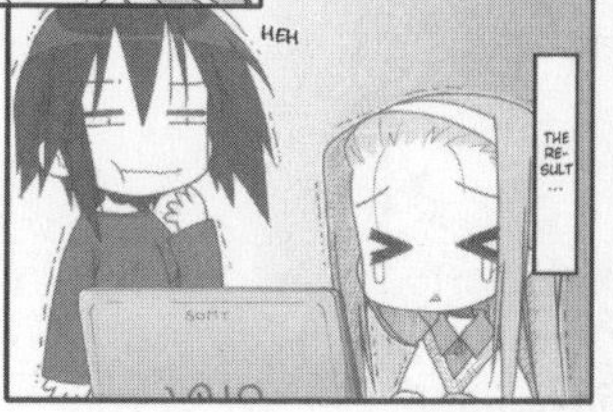
THE RE- SULT ...
HEH

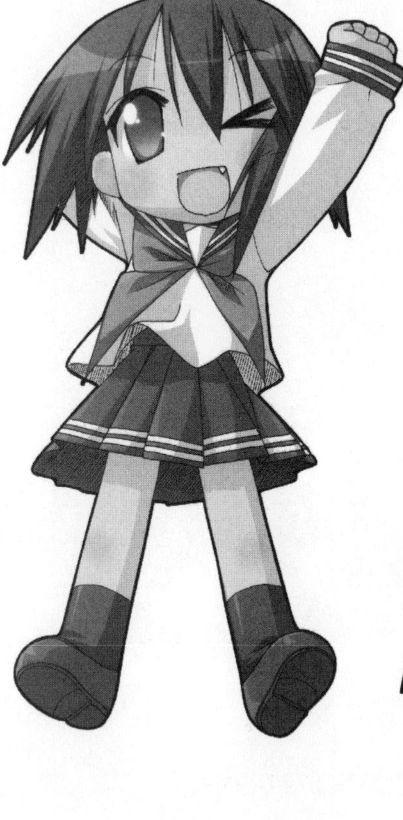

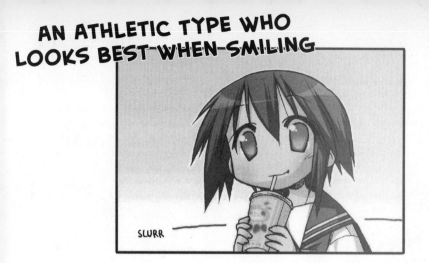

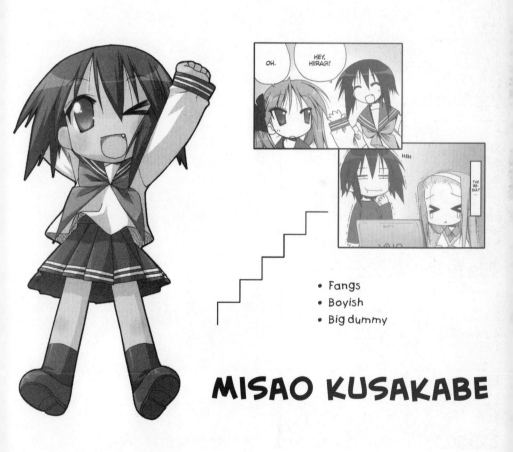

- Fangs
- Boyish
- Big dummy

MISAO KUSAKABE

Lucky☆Star

episode 130
let's take a break

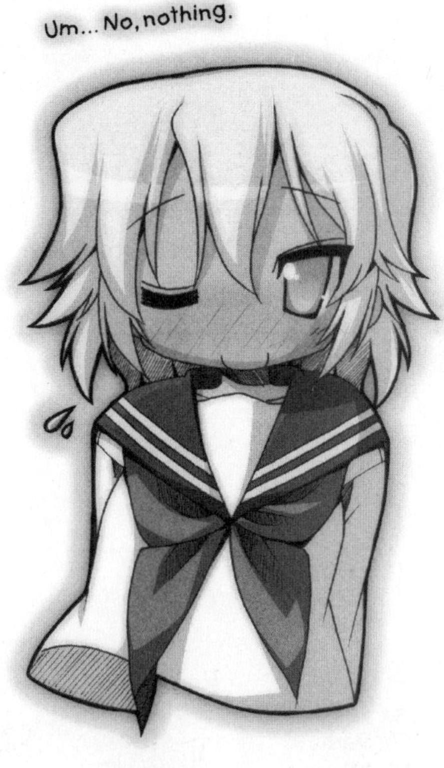
Um... No, nothing.

● Comptiq, June 2007 issue

over too quickly

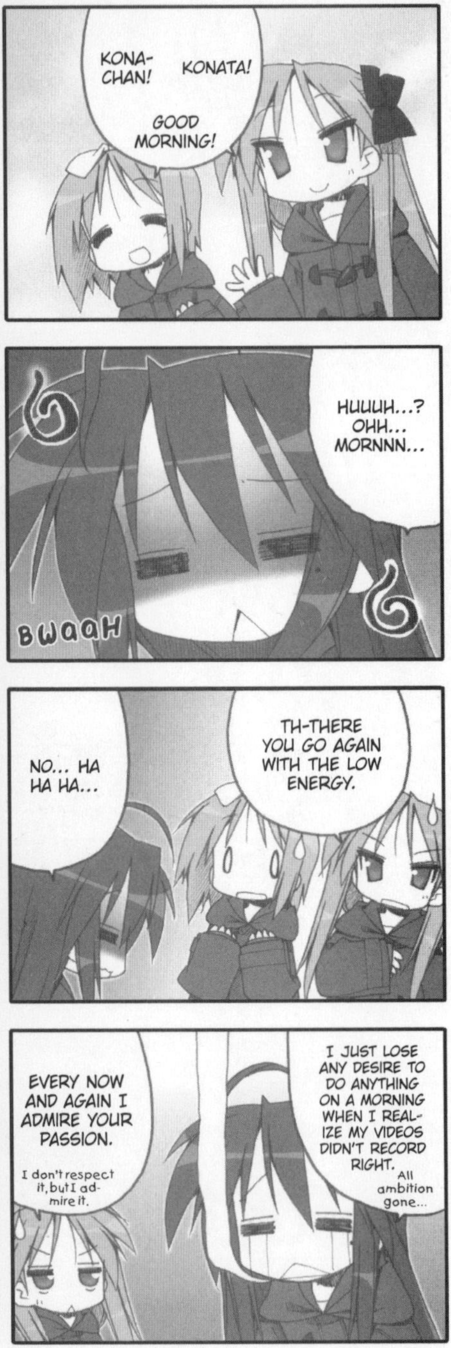
KONATA!
KONA-CHAN!
GOOD MORNING!
HUUUH...? OHH... MORNNN...
BWaaH
TH-THERE YOU GO AGAIN WITH THE LOW ENERGY.
NO... HA HA HA...
I JUST LOSE ANY DESIRE TO DO ANYTHING ON A MORNING WHEN I REAL-IZE MY VIDEOS DIDN'T RECORD RIGHT.
All ambition gone...
EVERY NOW AND AGAIN I ADMIRE YOUR PASSION.
I don't respect it, but I ad-mire it.

can't give up

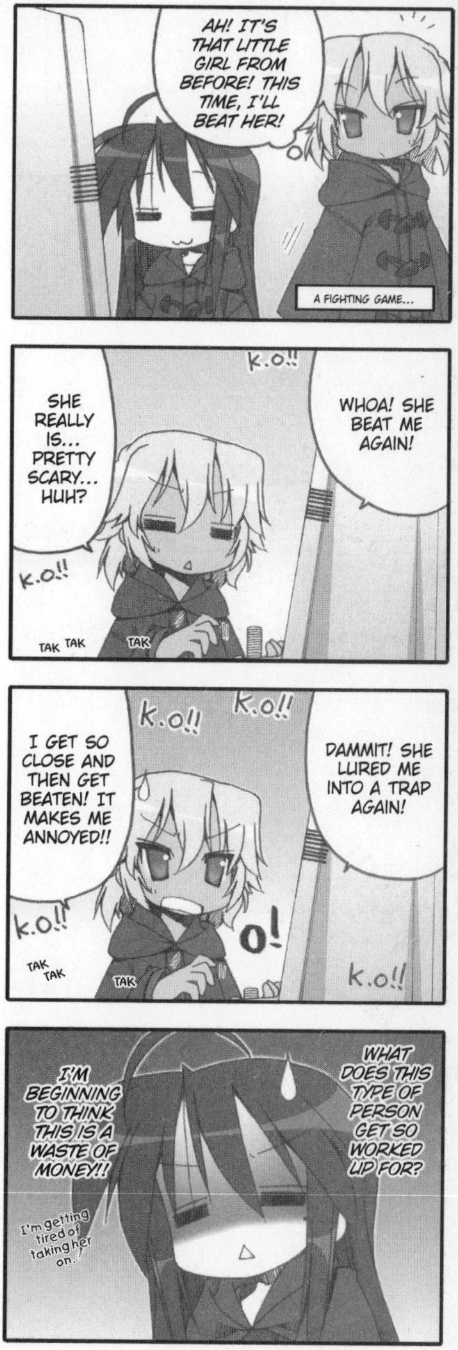
AH! IT'S THAT LITTLE GIRL FROM BEFORE! THIS TIME, I'LL BEAT HER!
A FIGHTING GAME...
K.O!!
WHOA! SHE BEAT ME AGAIN!
SHE REALLY IS... PRETTY SCARY... HUH?
K.O!!
TAK TAK
TAK
K.O!!
DAMMIT! SHE LURED ME INTO A TRAP AGAIN!
K.O!!
I GET SO CLOSE AND THEN GET BEATEN! IT MAKES ME ANNOYED!!
K.O!!
O!
TAK TAK
TAK
K.O!!
WHAT DOES THIS TYPE OF PERSON GET SO WORKED UP FOR?
I'M BEGINNING TO THINK THIS IS A WASTE OF MONEY!!
I'm getting tired of taking her on.

until she wins

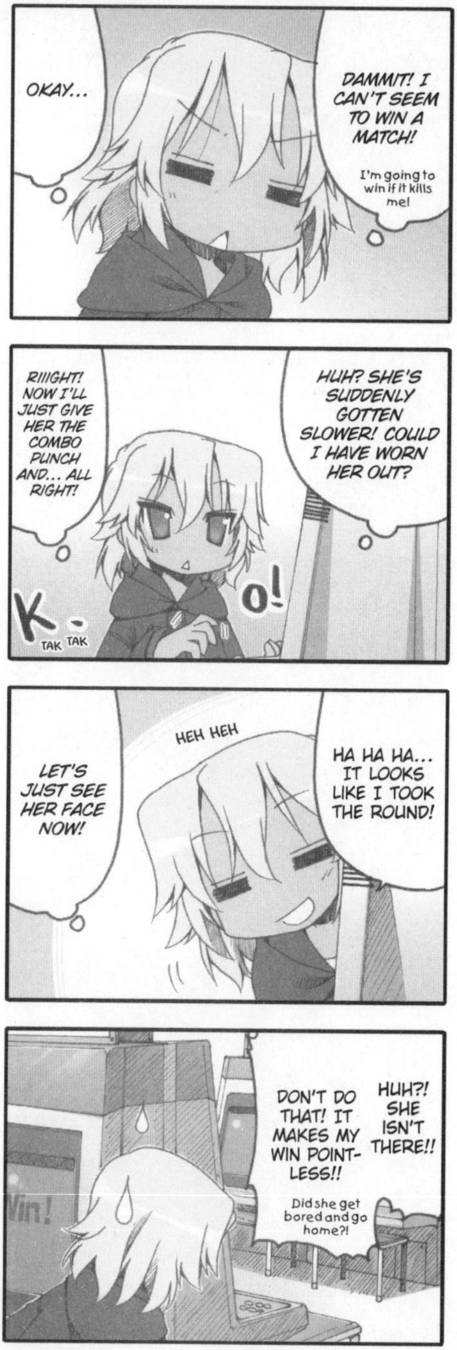
DAMMIT! I CAN'T SEEM TO WIN A MATCH!
I'm going to win if it kills me!
OKAY...
HUH? SHE'S SUDDENLY GOTTEN SLOWER! COULD I HAVE WORN HER OUT?
RIIIGHT! NOW I'LL JUST GIVE HER THE COMBO PUNCH AND... ALL RIGHT!
O!
K-
TAK TAK
HA HA HA... IT LOOKS LIKE I TOOK THE ROUND!
HEH HEH
LET'S JUST SEE HER FACE NOW!
HUH?! SHE ISN'T THERE!!
DON'T DO THAT! IT MAKES MY WIN POINT-LESS!!
Did she get bored and go home?!
Win!

in reality

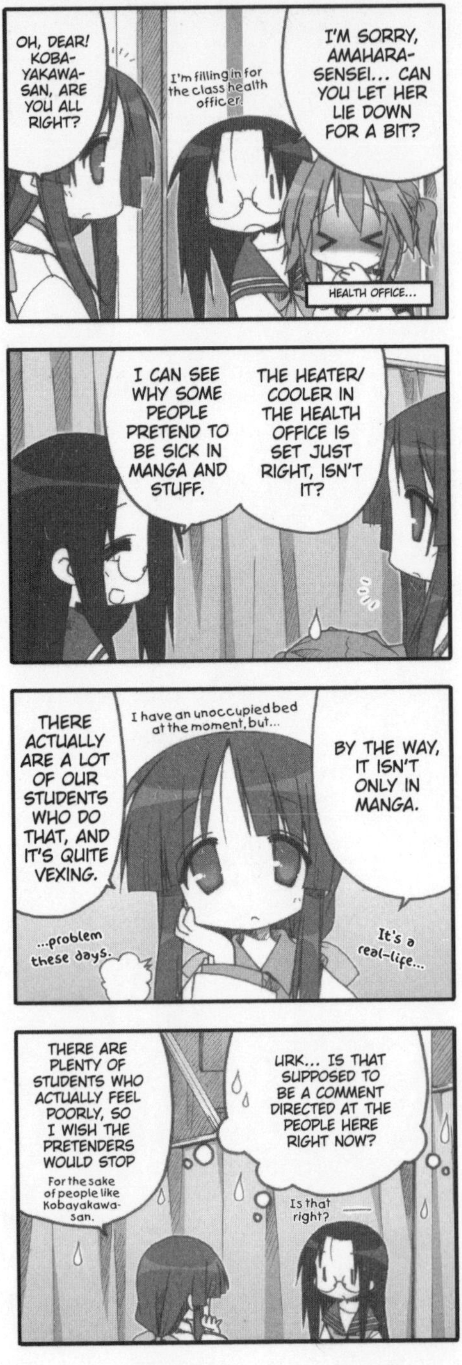
I'M SORRY, AMAHARA-SENSEI... CAN YOU LET HER LIE DOWN FOR A BIT?
I'm filling in for the class health officer.
OH, DEAR! KOBAYAKAWA-SAN, ARE YOU ALL RIGHT?
HEALTH OFFICE...
THE HEATER/COOLER IN THE HEALTH OFFICE IS SET JUST RIGHT, ISN'T IT?
I CAN SEE WHY SOME PEOPLE PRETEND TO BE SICK IN MANGA AND STUFF.
BY THE WAY, IT ISN'T ONLY IN MANGA.
I have an unoccupied bed at the moment, but...
THERE ACTUALLY ARE A LOT OF OUR STUDENTS WHO DO THAT, AND IT'S QUITE VEXING.
It's a real-life...
...problem these days.
URK... IS THAT SUPPOSED TO BE A COMMENT DIRECTED AT THE PEOPLE HERE RIGHT NOW?
Is that right?
THERE ARE PLENTY OF STUDENTS WHO ACTUALLY FEEL POORLY, SO I WISH THE PRETENDERS WOULD STOP
For the sake of people like Kobayakawa-san.

for a smile

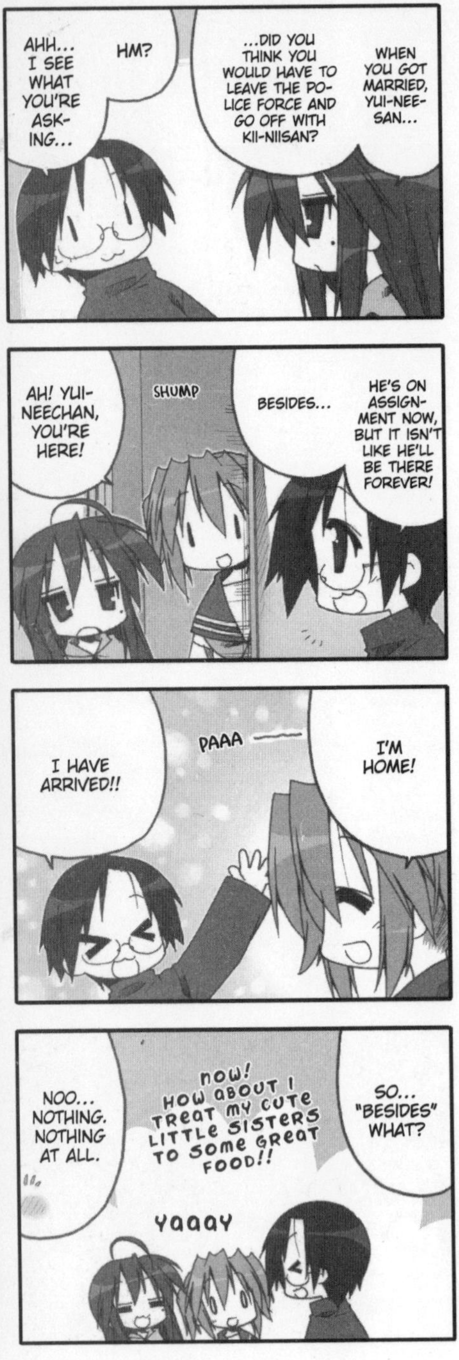
WHEN YOU GOT MARRIED, YUI-NEE-SAN...
...DID YOU THINK YOU WOULD HAVE TO LEAVE THE POLICE FORCE AND GO OFF WITH KII-NIISAN?
HM?
AHH... I SEE WHAT YOU'RE ASKING...
HE'S ON ASSIGNMENT NOW, BUT IT ISN'T LIKE HE'LL BE THERE FOREVER!
BESIDES...
SHUMP
AH! YUI-NEECHAN, YOU'RE HERE!
I'M HOME!
PAAA
I HAVE ARRIVED!!
SO... "BESIDES" WHAT?
NOW! HOW ABOUT I TREAT MY CUTE LITTLE SISTERS TO SOME GREAT FOOD!!
NOO... NOTHING. NOTHING AT ALL.
yaaay

THE RELIABLE CLASSMATE

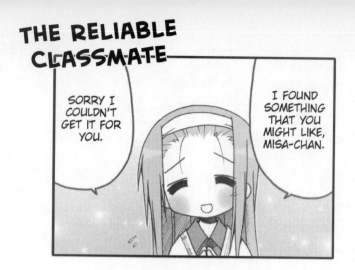

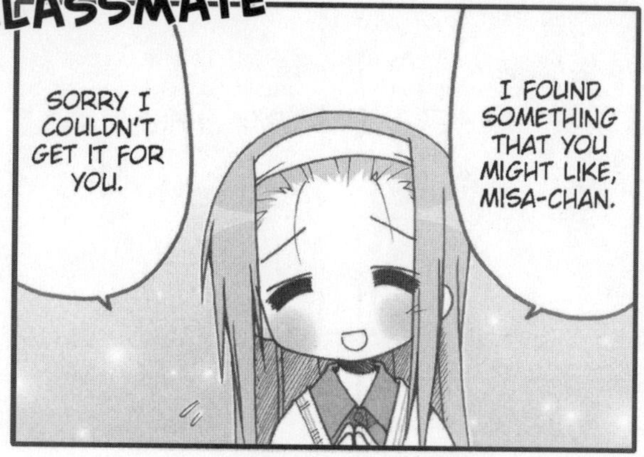
I FOUND SOMETHING THAT YOU MIGHT LIKE, MISA-CHAN.
SORRY I COULDN'T GET IT FOR YOU.

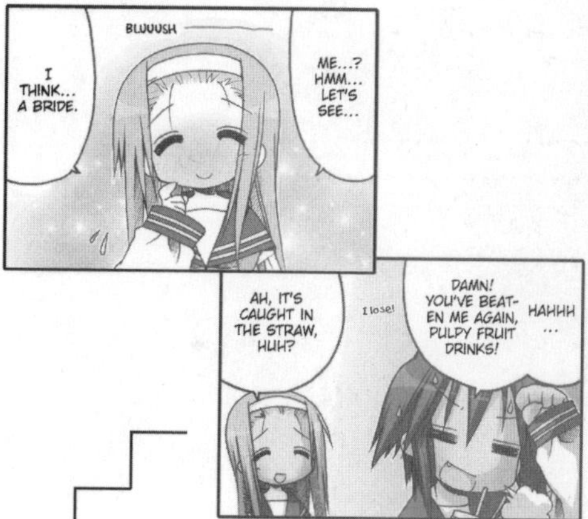
ME...? HMM... LET'S SEE...
BLUUUSH
I THINK... A BRIDE.
HAHHH ...
DAMN! YOU'VE BEAT-EN ME AGAIN, PULPY FRUIT DRINKS!
I lose!
AH, IT'S CAUGHT IN THE STRAW, HUH?

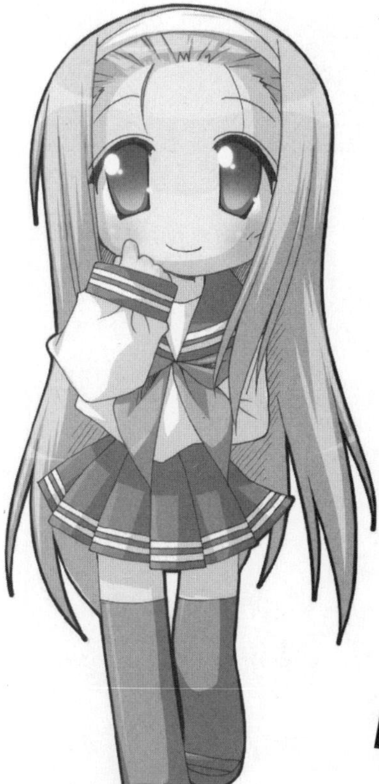

- Forehead
- Thigh Gal
- Domestic

AYANO MINEGISHI

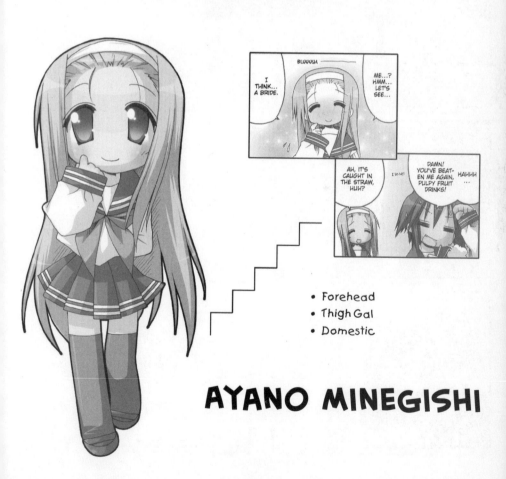

episode 131
life in the damp

● Comptiq, July 2007 issue

the love bombshell

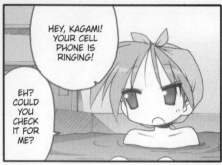

HEY, KAGAMI! YOUR CELL PHONE IS RINGING!
EH? COULD YOU CHECK IT FOR ME?
AH! IT LOOKS LIKE A TEXT MESSAGE.
OH. THANK YOU.
"I REALLY HOPE YOU TWO GIRLIES COME BY AND PLAY AGAIN SOMETIME!" IS WHAT IT SAYS IN THE SUBJECT LINE! IS IT A GUY?
HEHN HEHN
KACHIK
?!
KONATA, DIDN'T YOU SAY YOU WERE NEVER GOING TO WRITE THOSE WEIRD SUBJECTS ON YOUR TEXTS EVER AGAIN? Do you have any idea how much they hounded me after that?
HEY, KAGAMI! I'M JUST TRYING TO MAKE YOUR SCHOOL DAYS MORE COLORFUL!

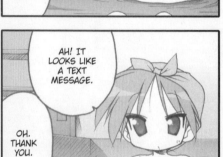

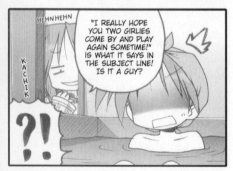

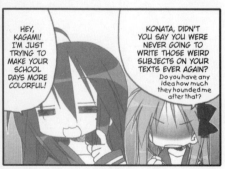

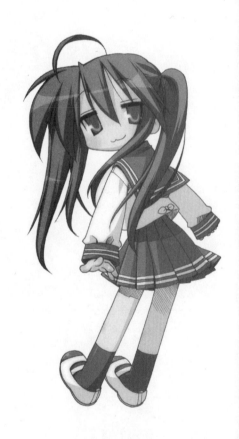

the speed of pain

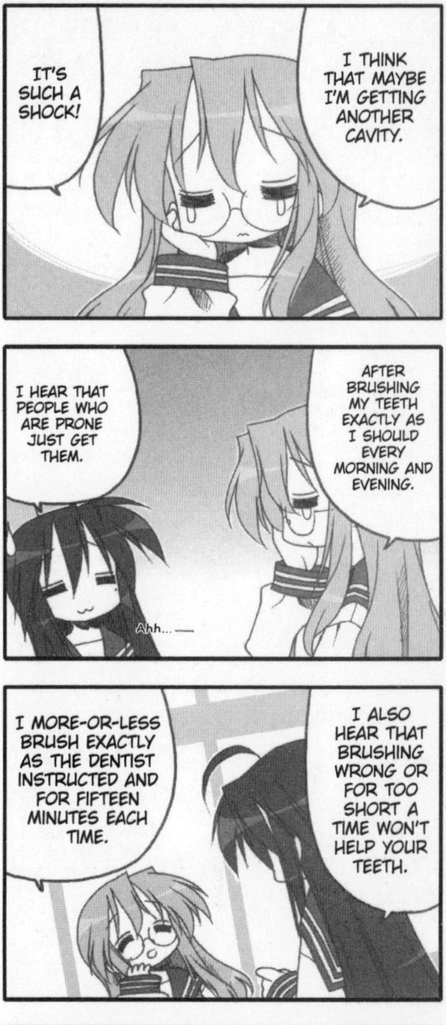
I THINK THAT MAYBE I'M GETTING ANOTHER CAVITY.
IT'S SUCH A SHOCK!
AFTER BRUSHING MY TEETH EXACTLY AS I SHOULD EVERY MORNING AND EVENING.
I HEAR THAT PEOPLE WHO ARE PRONE JUST GET THEM.
Ahh...
I ALSO HEAR THAT BRUSHING WRONG OR FOR TOO SHORT A TIME WON'T HELP YOUR TEETH.
I MORE-OR-LESS BRUSH EXACTLY AS THE DENTIST INSTRUCTED AND FOR FIFTEEN MINUTES EACH TIME.
..... HUH? SUPER-WOMAN HERE BRUSHES FOR THAT LONG EACH TIME...?
AS BEST AS I CAN REMEMBER, BRUSHING FOR FIVE MINUTES IN THE MORNING SEEMS LIKE AN EXTREMELY LONG TIME...
Fifteen minutes?!
But even so, I get cavities, huh?

the filter effect

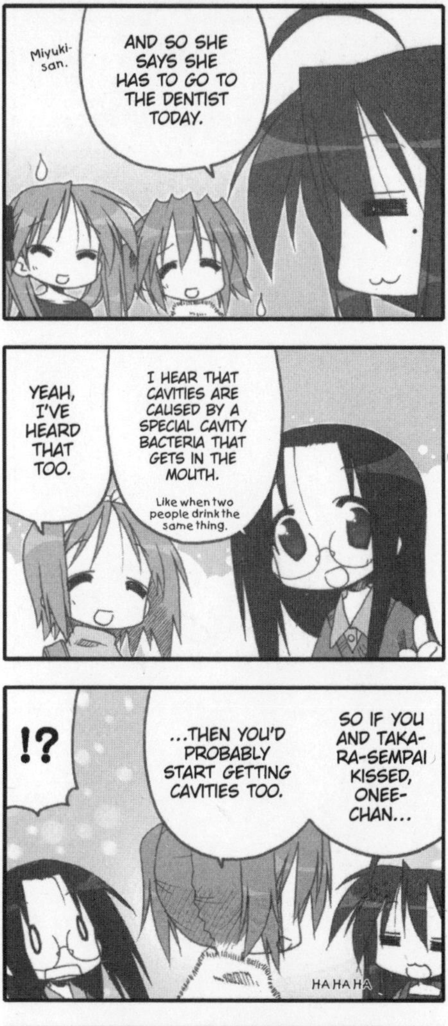
AND SO SHE SAYS SHE HAS TO GO TO THE DENTIST TODAY.
Miyuki-san.
I HEAR THAT CAVITIES ARE CAUSED BY A SPECIAL CAVITY BACTERIA THAT GETS IN THE MOUTH.
Like when two people drink the same thing.
YEAH, I'VE HEARD THAT TOO.
SO IF YOU AND TAKA-RA-SEMPAI KISSED, ONEE-CHAN...
...THEN YOU'D PROBABLY START GETTING CAVITIES TOO.
!?
HA HA HA
What can one little kiss hurt?
STOP SAYING THAT!!
Oh, I'm so embarrassed!
DON'T GO MAKING ME ANY WORSE THAN I ALREADY AM!
I'm already bad enough!
UUUN
AFUU

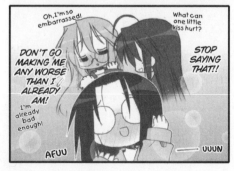

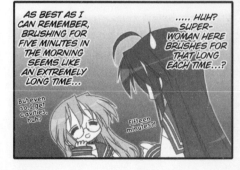

without thinking

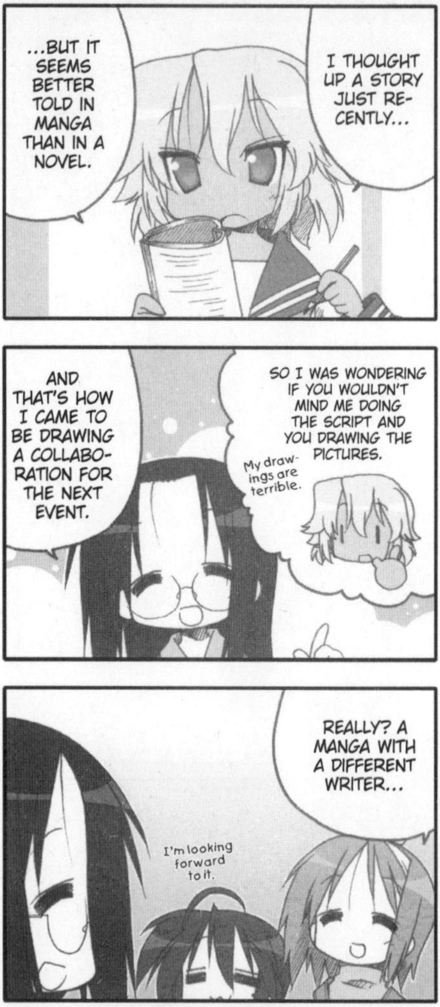
I THOUGHT UP A STORY JUST RE-CENTLY...
...BUT IT SEEMS BETTER TOLD IN MANGA THAN IN A NOVEL.
SO I WAS WONDERING IF YOU WOULDN'T MIND ME DOING THE SCRIPT AND YOU DRAWING THE PICTURES.
My drawings are terrible.
AND THAT'S HOW I CAME TO BE DRAWING A COLLABORATION FOR THE NEXT EVENT.
REALLY? A MANGA WITH A DIFFERENT WRITER...
I'm looking forward to it.
EXCITEMENT EXPECTATIONS
OH, NO!!
IT'S ALMOST LIKE...I JUST STEPPED ON A LANDMINE.

that! that!

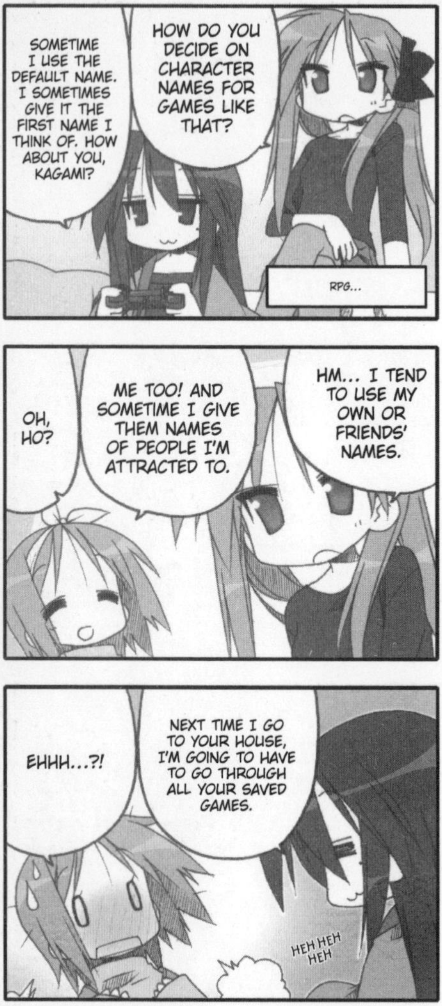
HOW DO YOU DECIDE ON CHARACTER NAMES FOR GAMES LIKE THAT?
SOMETIME I USE THE DEFAULT NAME. I SOMETIMES GIVE IT THE FIRST NAME I THINK OF. HOW ABOUT YOU, KAGAMI?
RPG...
HM... I TEND TO USE MY OWN OR FRIENDS' NAMES.
ME TOO! AND SOMETIME I GIVE THEM NAMES OF PEOPLE I'M ATTRACTED TO.
OH, HO?
NEXT TIME I GO TO YOUR HOUSE, I'M GOING TO HAVE TO GO THROUGH ALL YOUR SAVED GAMES.
EHHH...?!
HEH HEH HEH
THAT! HIIRAGI-SEMPAI!!
BWAAAAAA
THAT'S EXACTLY WHAT I WANT TO SEE!!
Not some plot that you've thought up for me.

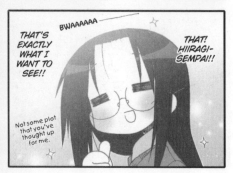

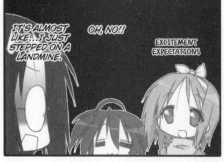

THE TRUE TALENT(?) COMING ALONG FOR THE RIDE

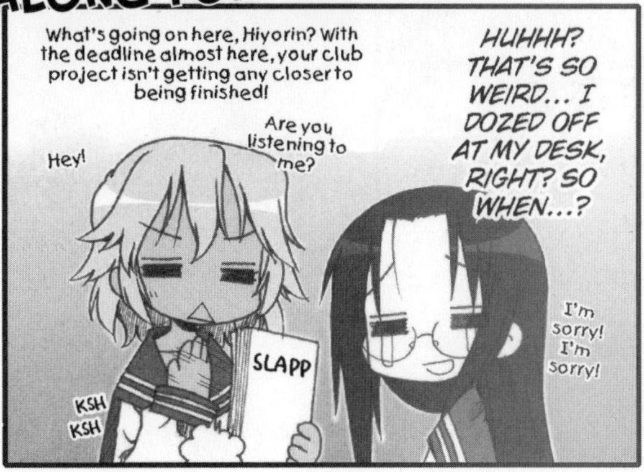
HUHHH? THAT'S SO WEIRD... I DOZED OFF AT MY DESK, RIGHT? SO WHEN...?
What's going on here, Hiyorin? With the deadline almost here, your club project isn't getting any closer to being finished!
Are you listening to me?
Hey!
I'm sorry! I'm sorry!
SLAPP
KSH KSH

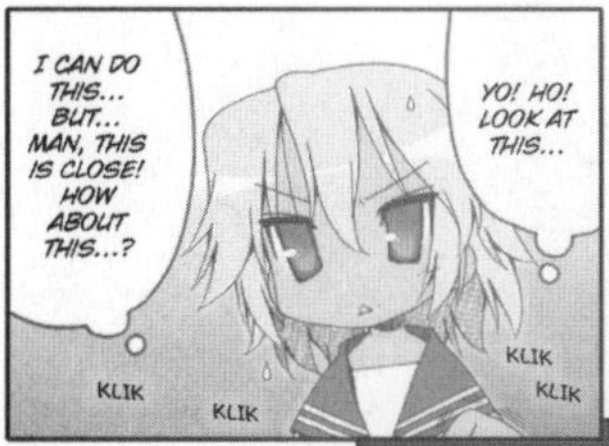
YO! HO! LOOK AT THIS...
I CAN DO THIS... BUT... MAN, THIS IS CLOSE! HOW ABOUT THIS...?
KLIK
KLIK
KLIK
KLIK

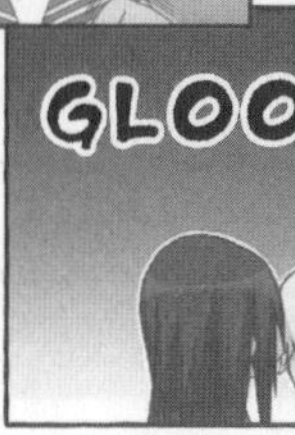
GLOOOOM
I guess so...

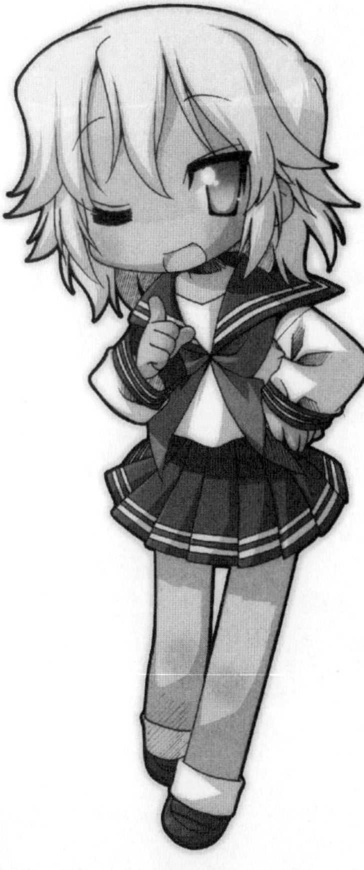

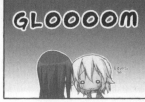

- Gamer
- Likes gambling
- Good at looking after others

KOU YASAKA

Lucky☆Star

episode 132
slightly out of whack

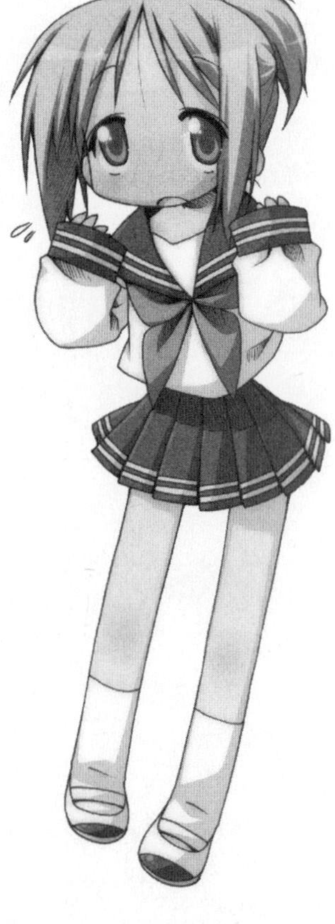

● Comptiq, July 2007 issue

sparkling eyes

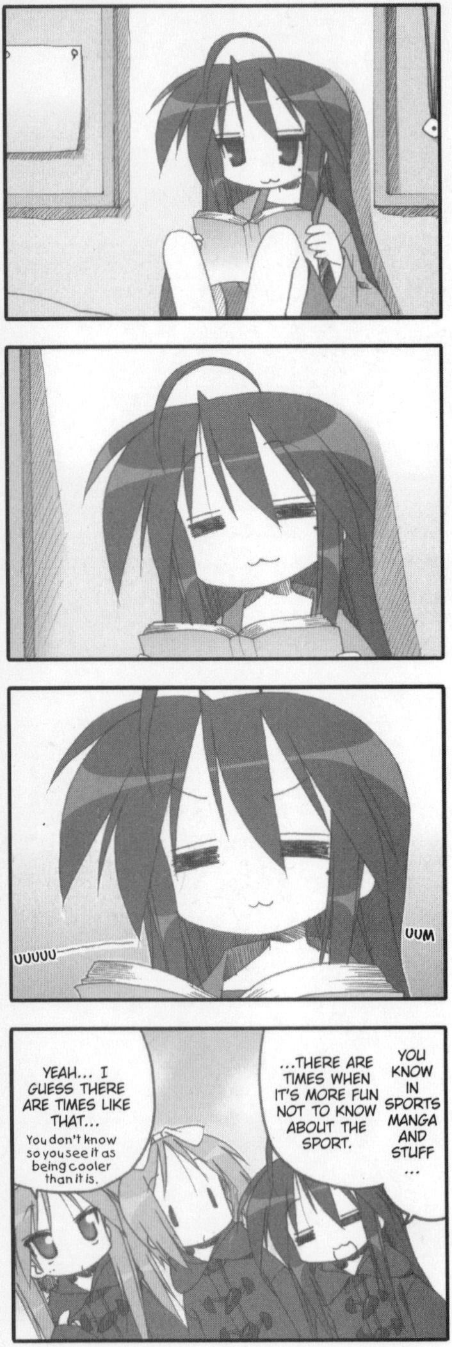
UUUUU——
UUM
YOU KNOW IN SPORTS MANGA AND STUFF...
...THERE ARE TIMES WHEN IT'S MORE FUN NOT TO KNOW ABOUT THE SPORT.
YEAH... I GUESS THERE ARE TIMES LIKE THAT...
You don't know so you see it as being cooler than it is.

the cause of a driving fail

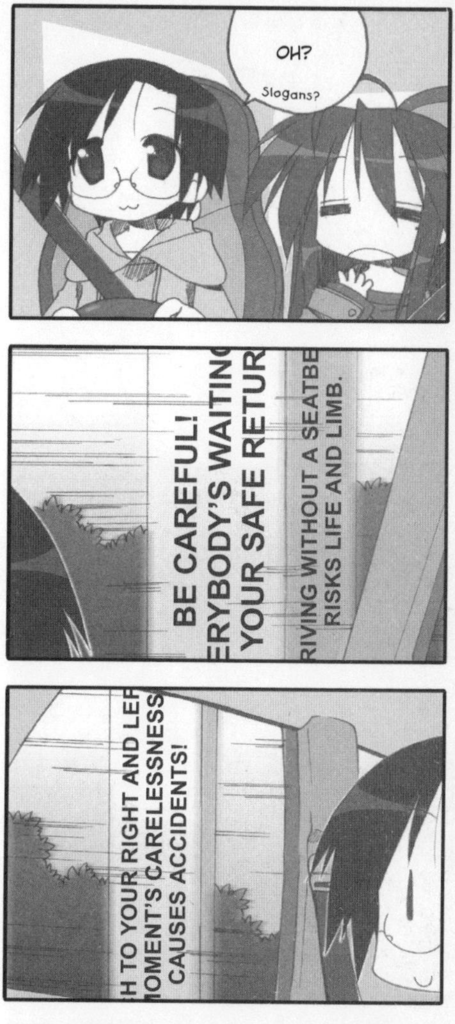
OH?
Slogans?
BE CAREFUL!
ERYBODY'S WAITIN
YOUR SAFE RETUR
RIVING WITHOUT A SEATBE
RISKS LIFE AND LIMB.
H TO YOUR RIGHT AND LEF
OMENT'S CARELESSNES
CAUSES ACCIDENTS!
AAAAH! NEE-SAN! EYES FRONT! EYES FRONT!!
SKReeeCH
UWAAAAH!!

could just die

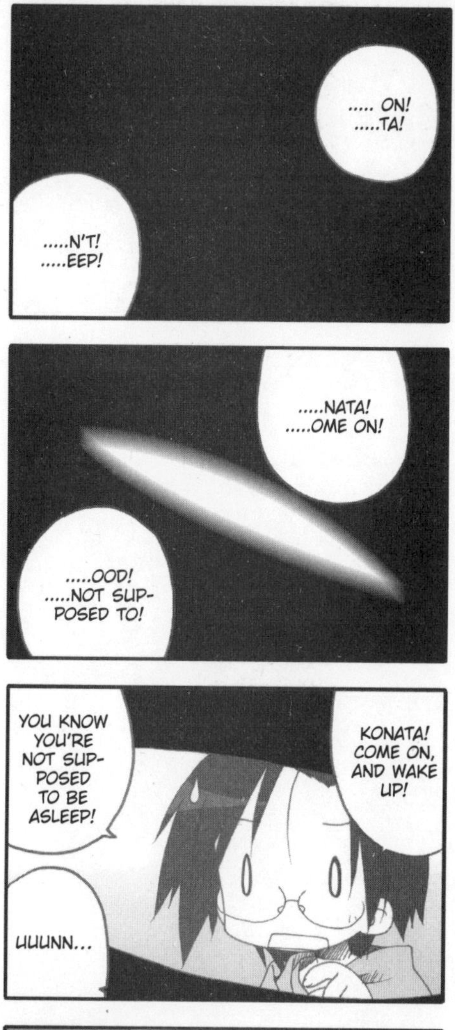
..... ON! .....TA!
.....N'T! .....EEP!
.....NATA! .....OME ON!
.....OOD! .....NOT SUP-POSED TO!
KONATA! COME ON, AND WAKE UP!
YOU KNOW YOU'RE NOT SUP-POSED TO BE ASLEEP!
UUUNN...
YAAAWN! SORRY... IT'S JUST THAT I HAD A LATE NIGHT LAST NIGHT.
Playing my net games.
WITH YOU SLEEPING IN THE PASSEN-GER SEAT, IT MAKES ME SO SLEEPY TOO!

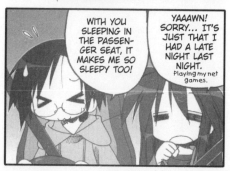

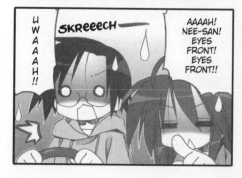

festive color

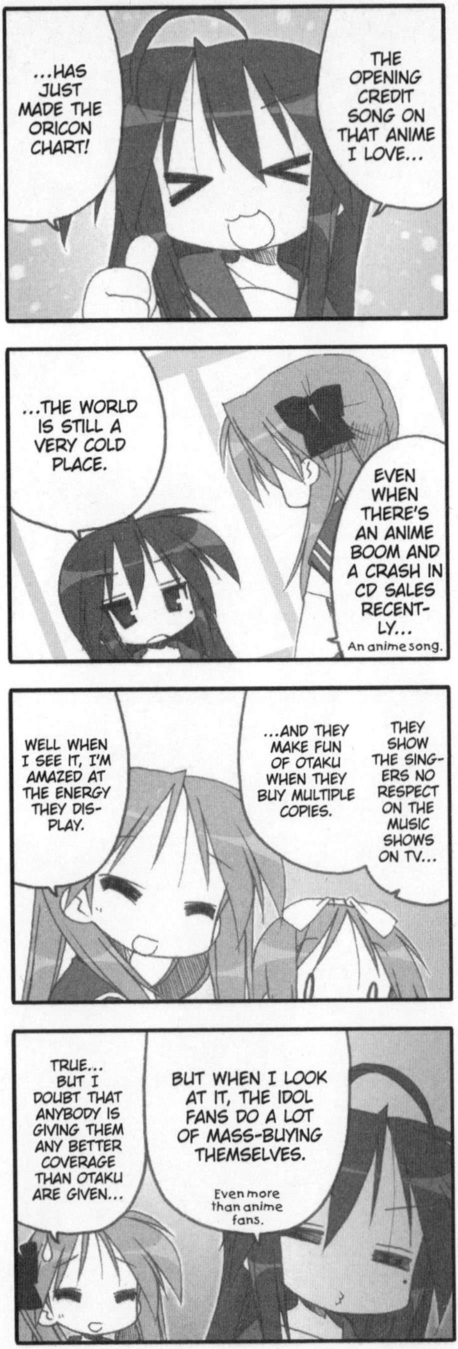
THE OPENING CREDIT SONG ON THAT ANIME I LOVE...
...HAS JUST MADE THE ORICON CHART!
EVEN WHEN THERE'S AN ANIME BOOM AND A CRASH IN CD SALES RECENTLY...
An anime song.
...THE WORLD IS STILL A VERY COLD PLACE.
THEY SHOW THE SINGERS NO RESPECT ON THE MUSIC SHOWS ON TV...
...AND THEY MAKE FUN OF OTAKU WHEN THEY BUY MULTIPLE COPIES.
WELL WHEN I SEE IT, I'M AMAZED AT THE ENERGY THEY DISPLAY.
BUT WHEN I LOOK AT IT, THE IDOL FANS DO A LOT OF MASS-BUYING THEMSELVES.
Even more than anime fans.
TRUE... BUT I DOUBT THAT ANYBODY IS GIVING THEM ANY BETTER COVERAGE THAN OTAKU ARE GIVEN...

graven images

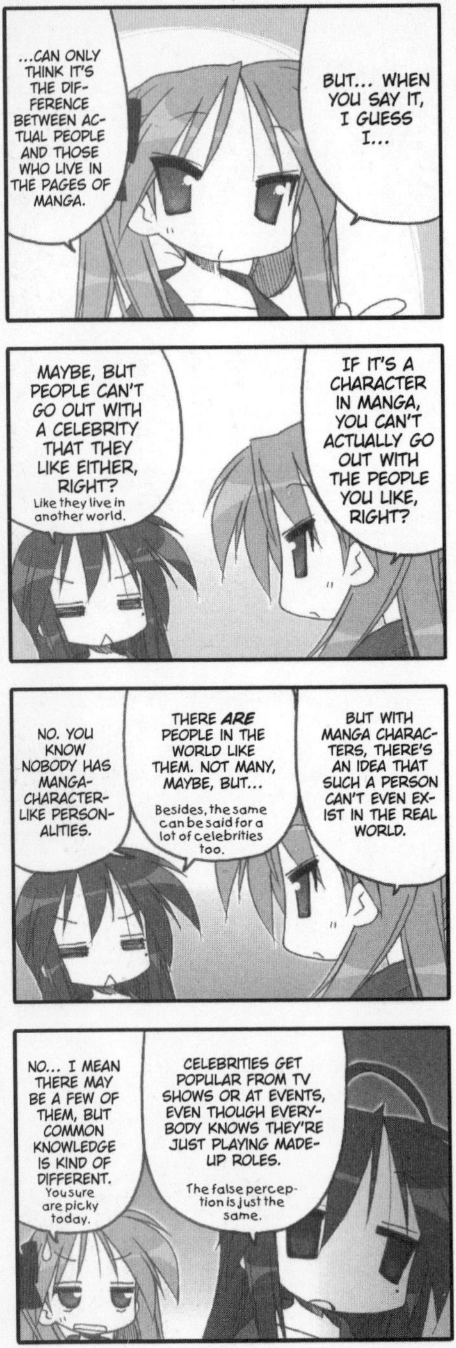
BUT... WHEN YOU SAY IT, I GUESS I...
...CAN ONLY THINK IT'S THE DIFFERENCE BETWEEN ACTUAL PEOPLE AND THOSE WHO LIVE IN THE PAGES OF MANGA.
IF IT'S A CHARACTER IN MANGA, YOU CAN'T ACTUALLY GO OUT WITH THE PEOPLE YOU LIKE, RIGHT?
MAYBE, BUT PEOPLE CAN'T GO OUT WITH A CELEBRITY THAT THEY LIKE EITHER, RIGHT?
Like they live in another world.
BUT WITH MANGA CHARACTERS, THERE'S AN IDEA THAT SUCH A PERSON CAN'T EVEN EXIST IN THE REAL WORLD.
THERE *ARE* PEOPLE IN THE WORLD LIKE THEM. NOT MANY, MAYBE, BUT...
Besides, the same can be said for a lot of celebrities too.
NO. YOU KNOW NOBODY HAS MANGA-CHARACTER-LIKE PERSONALITIES.
CELEBRITIES GET POPULAR FROM TV SHOWS OR AT EVENTS, EVEN THOUGH EVERYBODY KNOWS THEY'RE JUST PLAYING MADE-UP ROLES.
The false perception is just the same.
NO... I MEAN THERE MAY BE A FEW OF THEM, BUT COMMON KNOWLEDGE IS KIND OF DIFFERENT.
You sure are picky today.

AN ELEMENT OF WALKING MOE

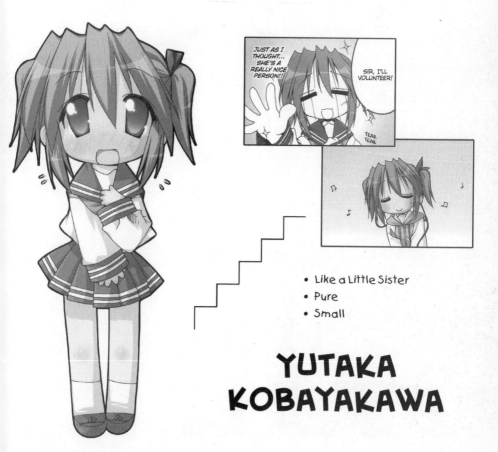

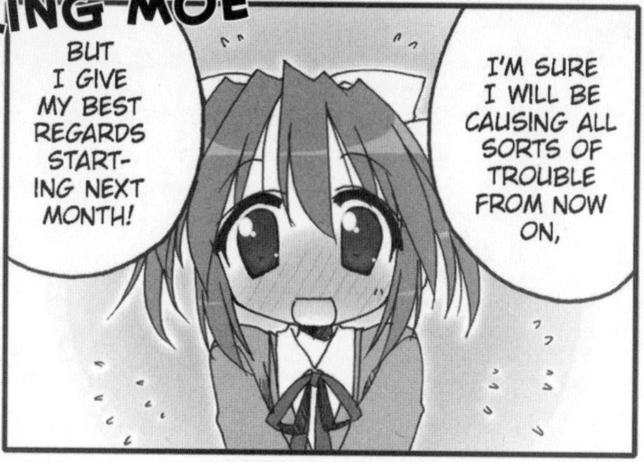
I'M SURE I WILL BE CAUSING ALL SORTS OF TROUBLE FROM NOW ON,
BUT I GIVE MY BEST REGARDS STARTING NEXT MONTH!

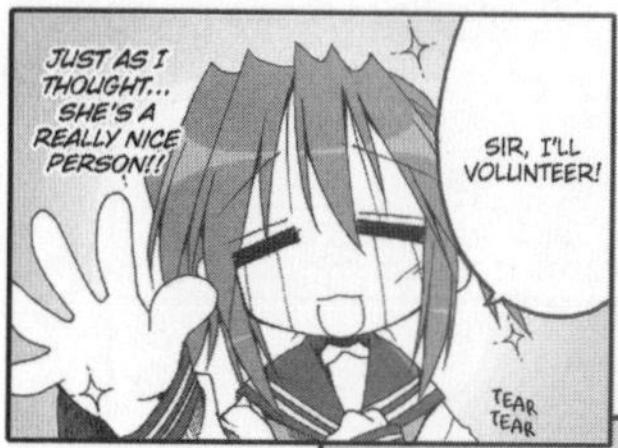
SIR, I'LL VOLUNTEER!
JUST AS I THOUGHT... SHE'S A REALLY NICE PERSON!!
TEAR TEAR

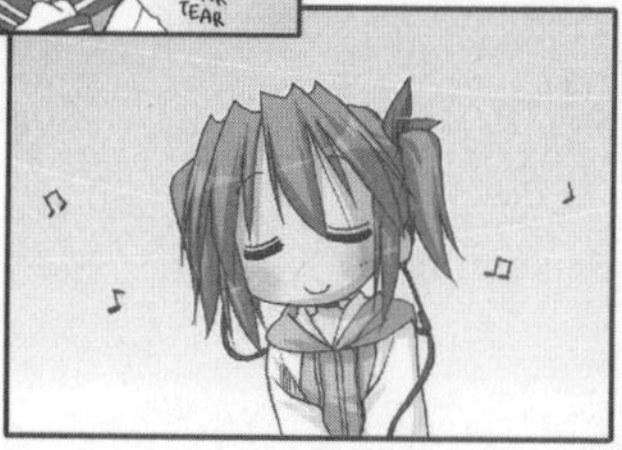

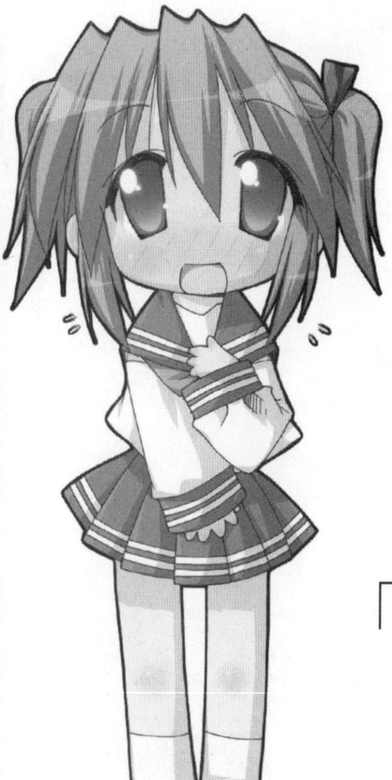

- Like a Little Sister
- Pure
- Small

YUTAKA KOBAYAKAWA

Lucky☆Star

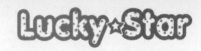

episode 133
instant trap

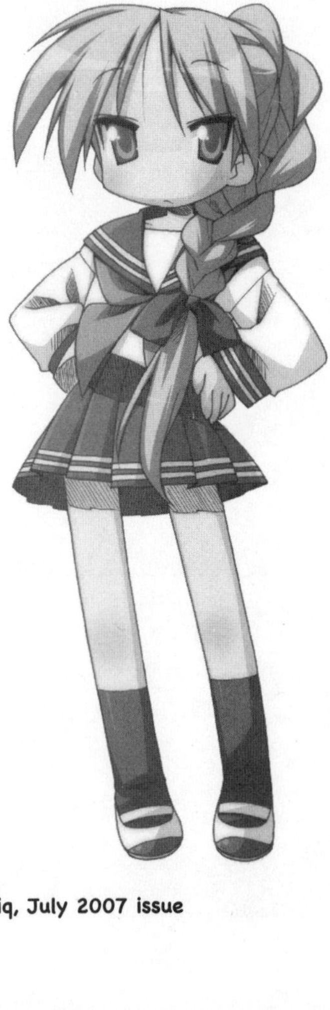

● Comptiq, July 2007 issue

too heavy or too frail

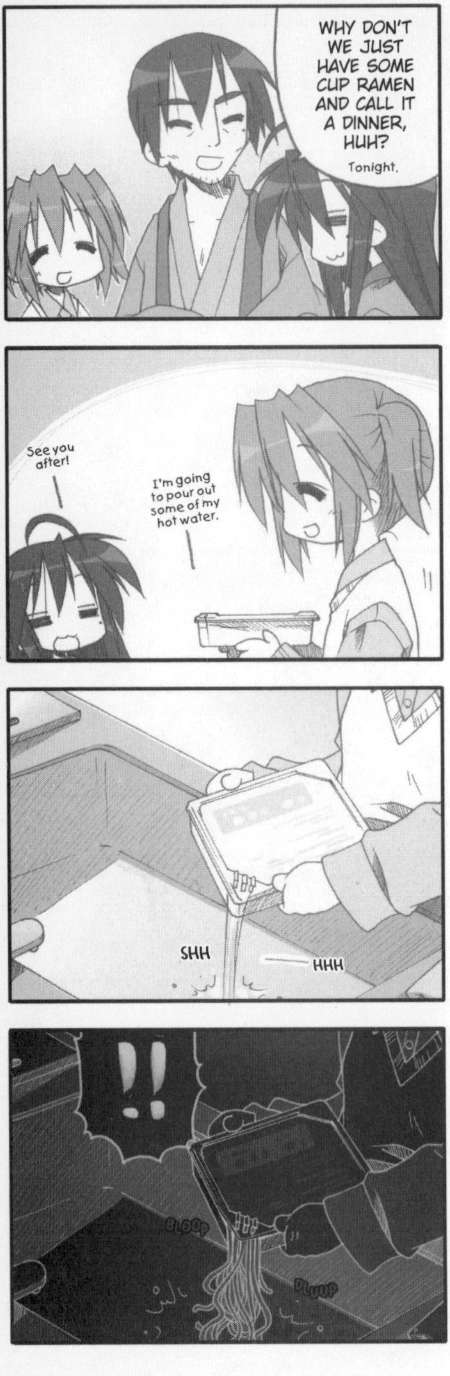
WHY DON'T WE JUST HAVE SOME CUP RAMEN AND CALL IT A DINNER, HUH?
Tonight.
I'm going to pour out some of my hot water.
See you after!
SHH
HHH
!!
BLOOP
BLUUP

the person who doesn't read

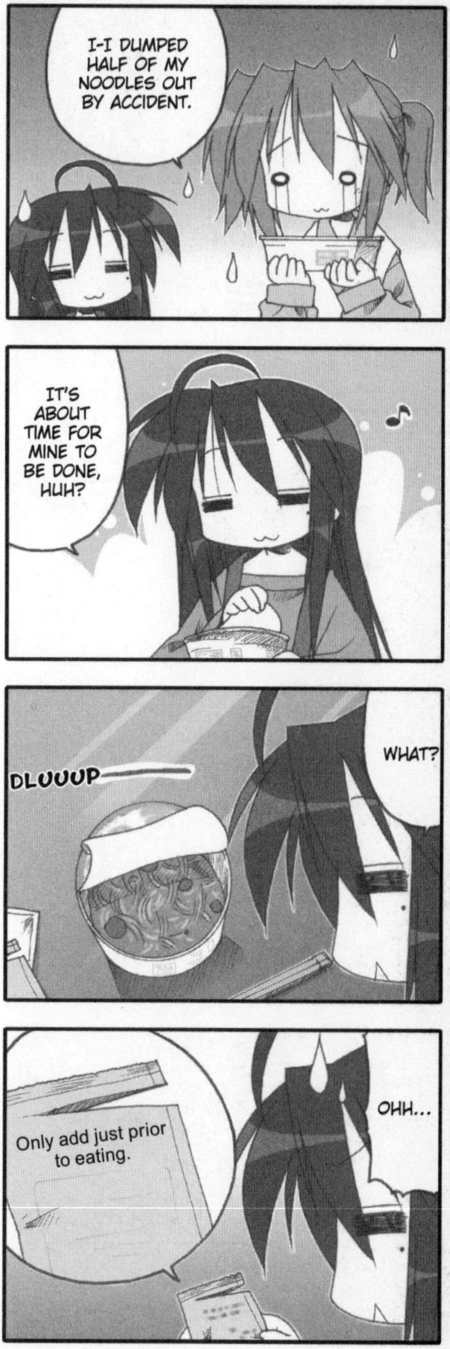
I-I DUMPED HALF OF MY NOODLES OUT BY ACCIDENT.
IT'S ABOUT TIME FOR MINE TO BE DONE, HUH?
WHAT?
DLUUUP
OHH...
Only add just prior to eating.

hide and seek

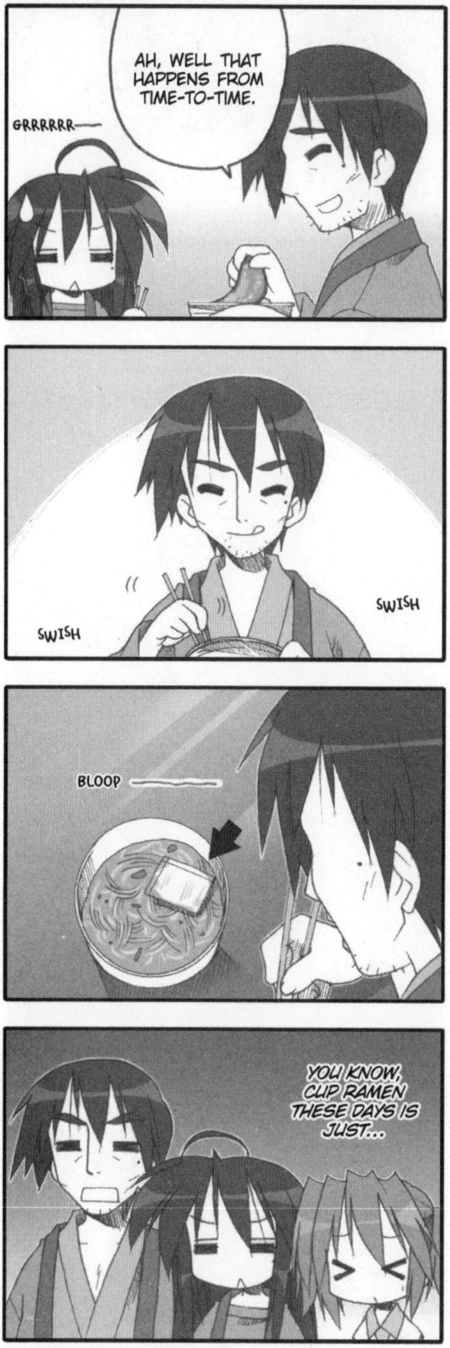
AH, WELL THAT HAPPENS FROM TIME-TO-TIME.
GRRRRRR
SWISH
SWISH
BLOOP
YOU KNOW, CUP RAMEN THESE DAYS IS JUST...

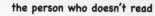

production costs

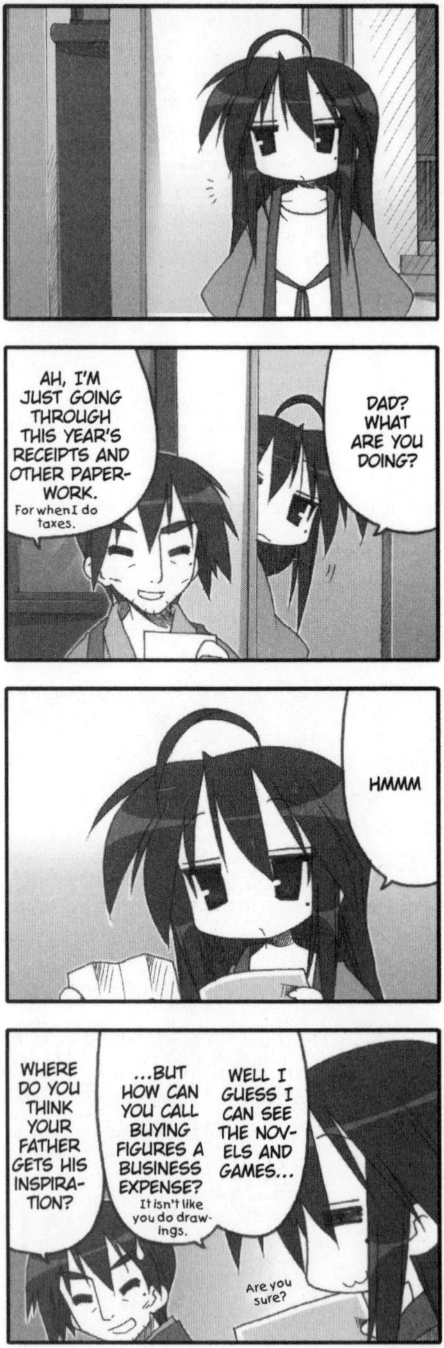
DAD? WHAT ARE YOU DOING?
AH, I'M JUST GOING THROUGH THIS YEAR'S RECEIPTS AND OTHER PAPER-WORK.
For when I do taxes.
HMMM
WELL I GUESS I CAN SEE THE NOV-ELS AND GAMES...
...BUT HOW CAN YOU CALL BUYING FIGURES A BUSINESS EXPENSE?
It isn't like you do draw-ings.
WHERE DO YOU THINK YOUR FATHER GETS HIS INSPIRA-TION?
Are you sure?

as in fainting

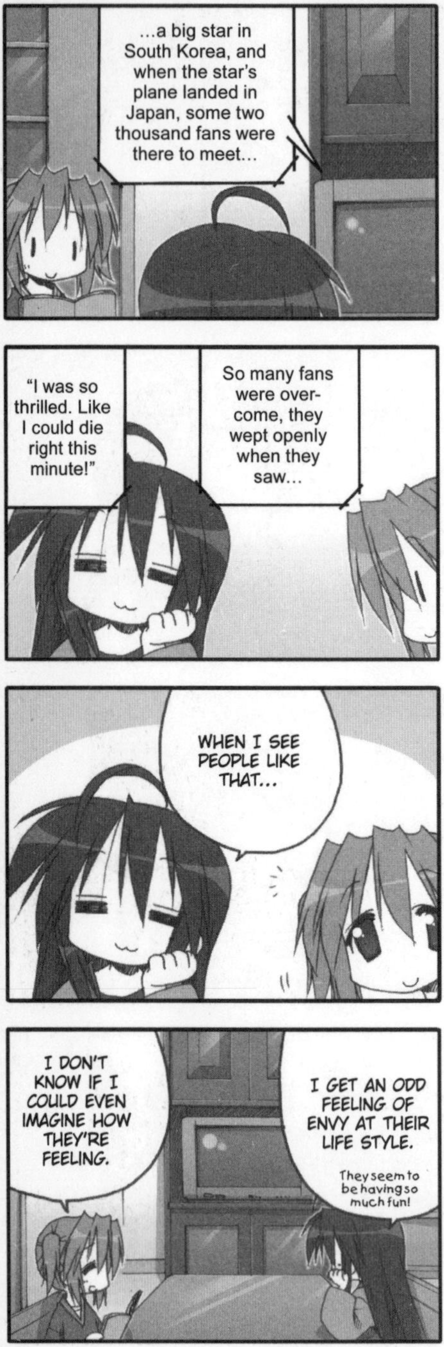
...a big star in South Korea, and when the star's plane landed in Japan, some two thousand fans were there to meet...
So many fans were over-come, they wept openly when they saw...
"I was so thrilled. Like I could die right this minute!"
WHEN I SEE PEOPLE LIKE THAT...
I GET AN ODD FEELING OF ENVY AT THEIR LIFE STYLE.
They seem to be having so much fun!
I DON'T KNOW IF I COULD EVEN IMAGINE HOW THEY'RE FEELING.

THE PERFECT PERSON ASIDE FROM HER BUST LINE

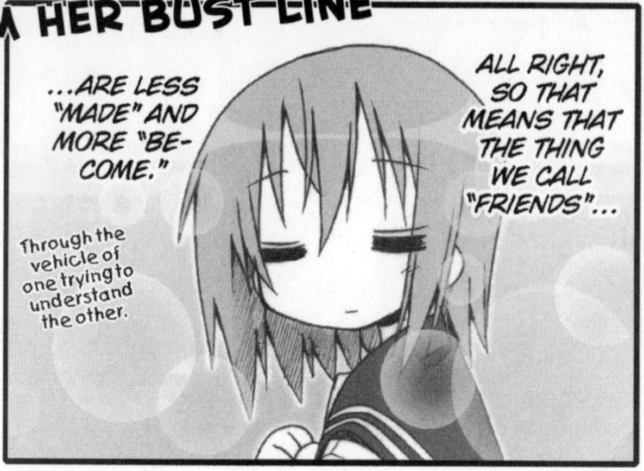
ALL RIGHT, SO THAT MEANS THAT THE THING WE CALL "FRIENDS"...
...ARE LESS "MADE" AND MORE "BE-COME."
Through the vehicle of one trying to understand the other.

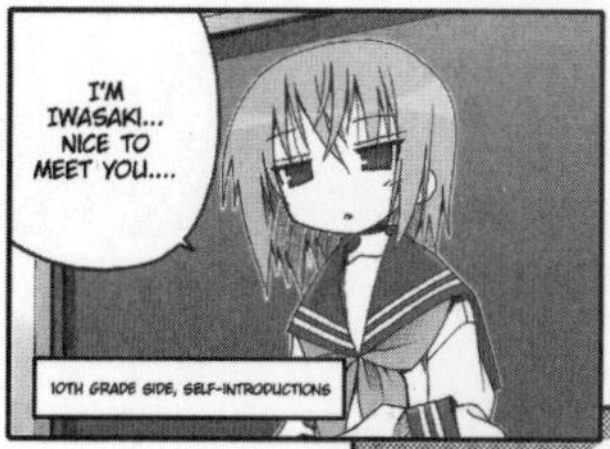
I'M IWASAKI... NICE TO MEET YOU....
10TH GRADE SIDE, SELF-INTRODUCTIONS

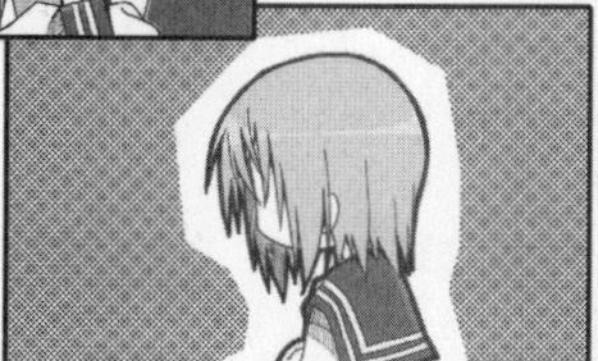
TOUCH
TOUCH

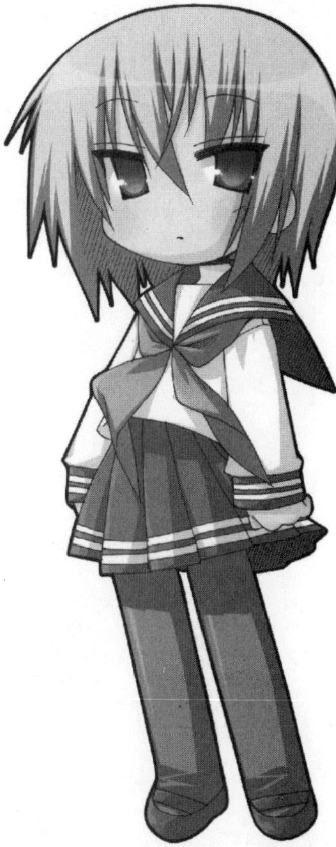

- Silent
- Flat
- Other people's toy

MINAMI IWASAKI

Lucky☆Star

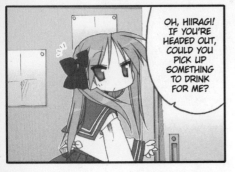

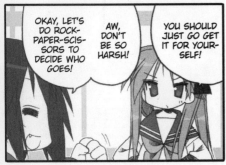

episode 134
loved one

● Comptiq, August 2007 issue

cornered

OH, HIIRAGI! IF YOU'RE HEADED OUT, COULD YOU PICK UP SOMETHING TO DRINK FOR ME?
YOU SHOULD JUST GO GET IT FOR YOUR-SELF!
AW, DON'T BE SO HARSH!
OKAY, LET'S DO ROCK-PAPER-SCIS-SORS TO DECIDE WHO GOES!
......
......
THAT MEANS YOU SHOULDN'T ORDER PEOPLE AROUND AND JUST GO GET IT YOURSELF, RIGHT?
HEH HEH HEH
B-- BUT THIS TIME THE RULE WAS THAT THE WINNER GOES TO GET THE DRINKS!
WHAT? ARE WE SIX YEARS OLD OR SOME-THING?!

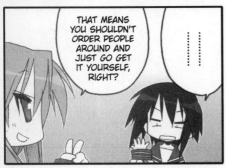

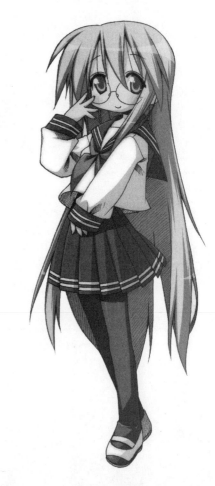

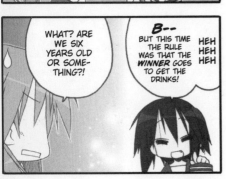

stamp your little foot

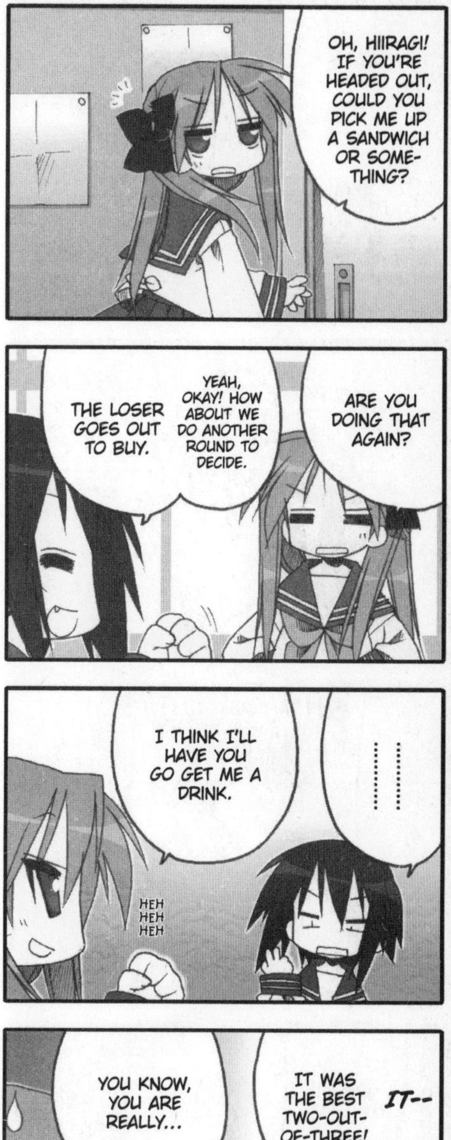
OH, HIIRAGI! IF YOU'RE HEADED OUT, COULD YOU PICK ME UP A SANDWICH OR SOME-THING?
ARE YOU DOING THAT AGAIN?
YEAH, OKAY! HOW ABOUT WE DO ANOTHER ROUND TO DECIDE.
THE LOSER GOES OUT TO BUY.
......
I THINK I'LL HAVE YOU GO GET ME A DRINK.
HEH HEH HEH
IT--
IT WAS THE BEST TWO-OUT-OF-THREE!
YOU KNOW, YOU ARE REALLY...

that's how you are

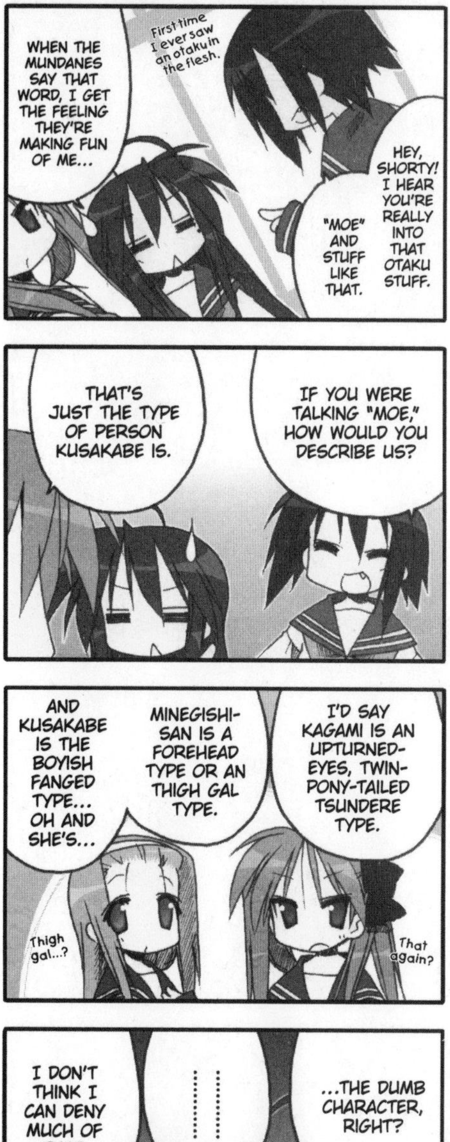
HEY, SHORTY! I HEAR YOU'RE REALLY INTO THAT OTAKU STUFF.
"MOE" AND STUFF LIKE THAT.
First time I ever saw an otaku in the flesh.
WHEN THE MUNDANES SAY THAT WORD, I GET THE FEELING THEY'RE MAKING FUN OF ME...
IF YOU WERE TALKING "MOE," HOW WOULD YOU DESCRIBE US?
THAT'S JUST THE TYPE OF PERSON KUSAKABE IS.
I'D SAY KAGAMI IS AN UPTURNED-EYES, TWIN-PONY-TAILED TSUNDERE TYPE.
That again?
MINEGISHI-SAN IS A FOREHEAD TYPE OR AN THIGH GAL TYPE.
Thigh gal...?
AND KUSAKABE IS THE BOYISH FANGED TYPE... OH AND SHE'S...
...THE DUMB CHARACTER, RIGHT?
......
I DON'T THINK I CAN DENY MUCH OF THAT.
She pretty much just described us.

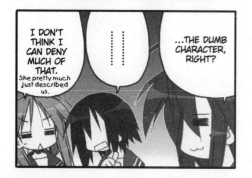

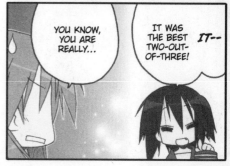

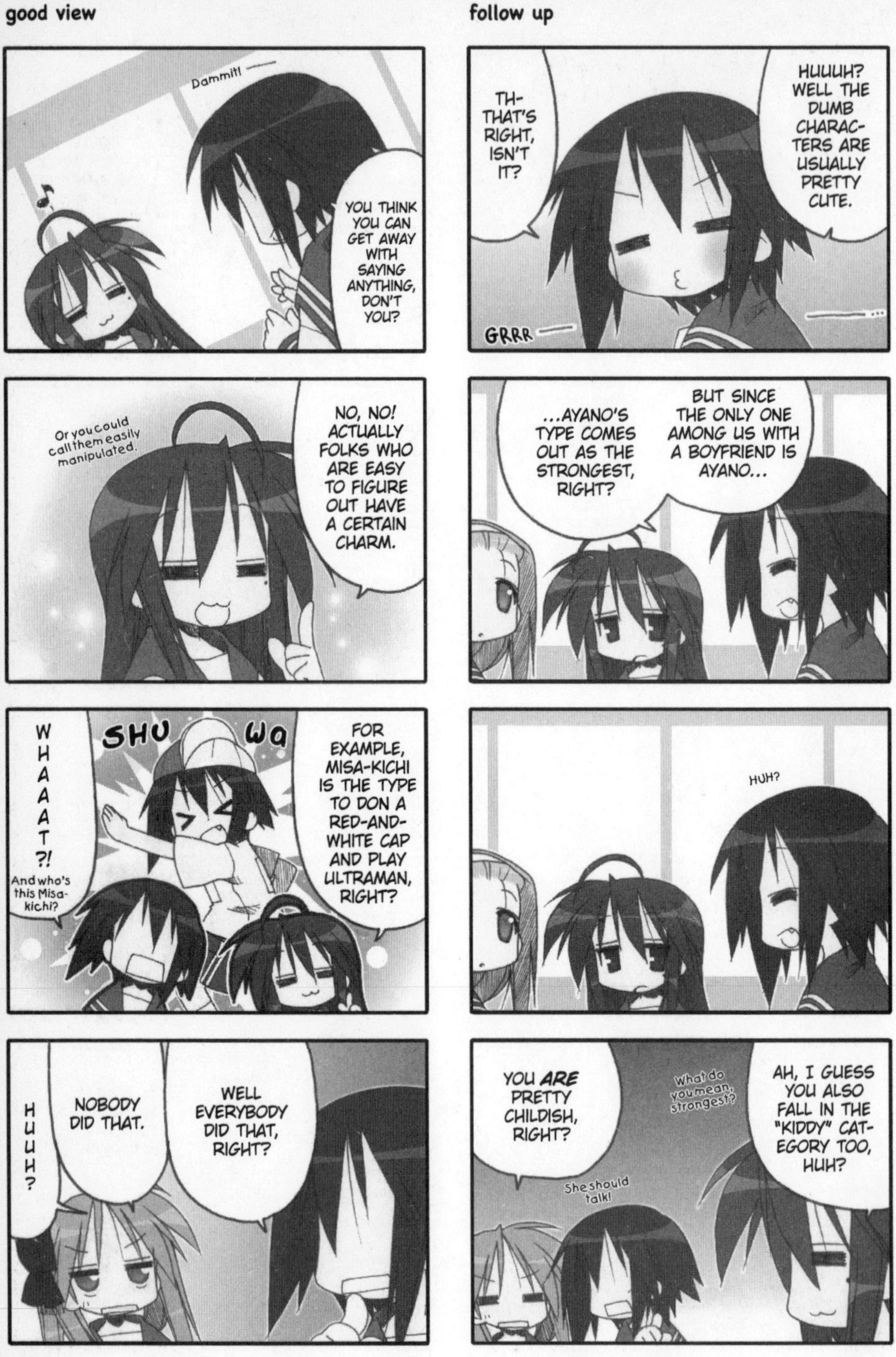
follow up
HUUUH? WELL THE DUMB CHARACTERS ARE USUALLY PRETTY CUTE.
TH-THAT'S RIGHT, ISN'T IT?
——...
GRRR——
BUT SINCE THE ONLY ONE AMONG US WITH A BOYFRIEND IS AYANO...
...AYANO'S TYPE COMES OUT AS THE STRONGEST, RIGHT?
HUH?
AH, I GUESS YOU ALSO FALL IN THE "KIDDY" CATEGORY TOO, HUH?
What do you mean, strongest?
YOU ARE PRETTY CHILDISH, RIGHT?
She should talk!
good view
Dammit! ——
YOU THINK YOU CAN GET AWAY WITH SAYING ANYTHING, DON'T YOU?
NO, NO! ACTUALLY FOLKS WHO ARE EASY TO FIGURE OUT HAVE A CERTAIN CHARM.
Or you could call them easily manipulated.
FOR EXAMPLE, MISA-KICHI IS THE TYPE TO DON A RED-AND-WHITE CAP AND PLAY ULTRAMAN, RIGHT?
SHU Wa
WHAAAAT?!
And who's this Misa-kichi?
WELL EVERYBODY DID THAT, RIGHT?
NOBODY DID THAT.
HUUUH?

A WIDE-RANGING ALL-ROUNDER

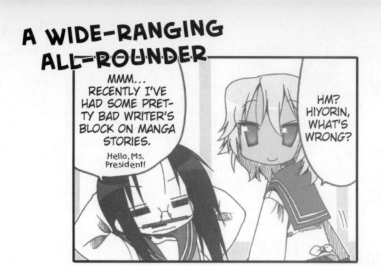

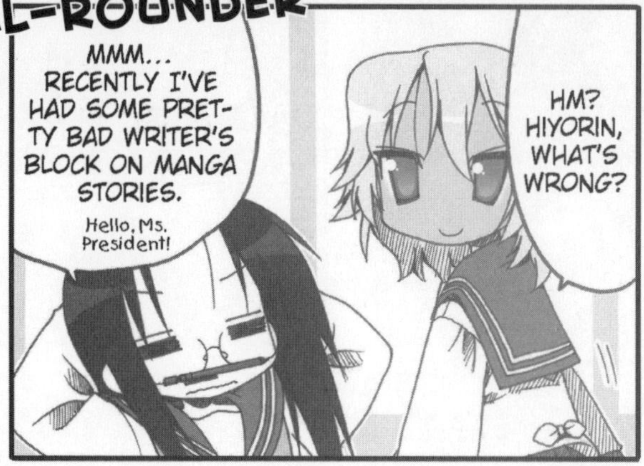
HM? HIYORIN, WHAT'S WRONG?
MMM... RECENTLY I'VE HAD SOME PRET-TY BAD WRITER'S BLOCK ON MANGA STORIES.
Hello, Ms. President!

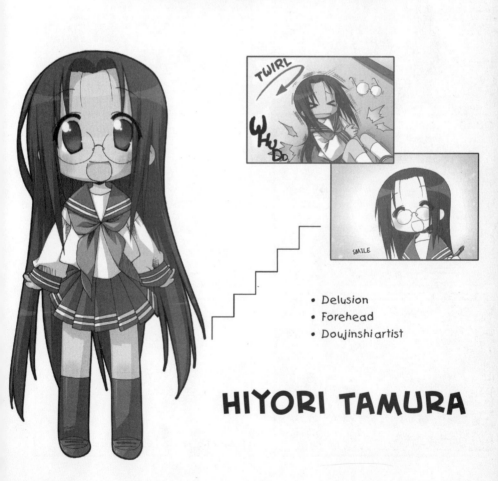

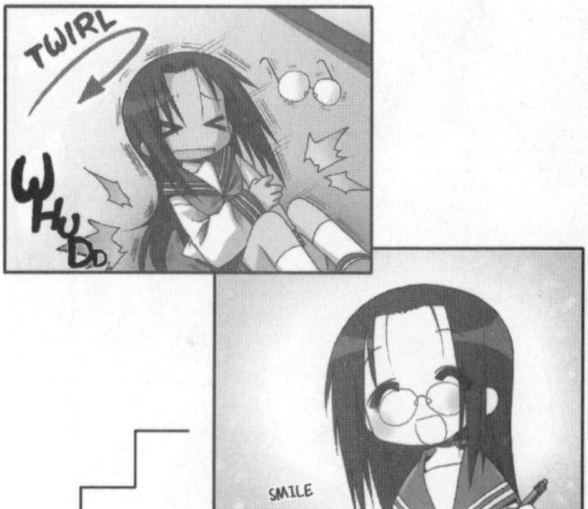
TWIRL
WHUDD
SMILE

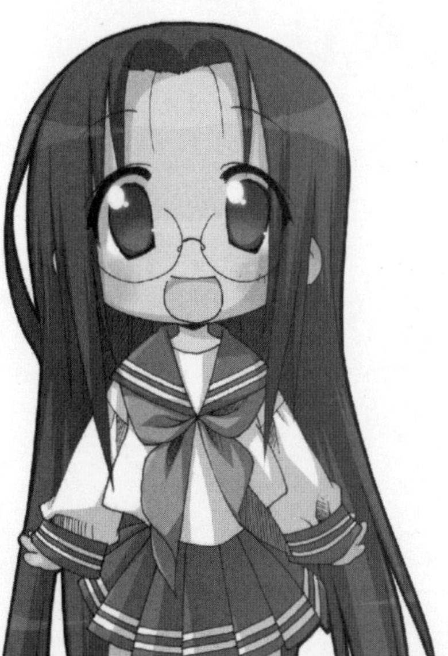

- Delusion
- Forehead
- Doujinshi artist

HIYORI TAMURA

Lucky☆Star

episode 135
inevitable 2

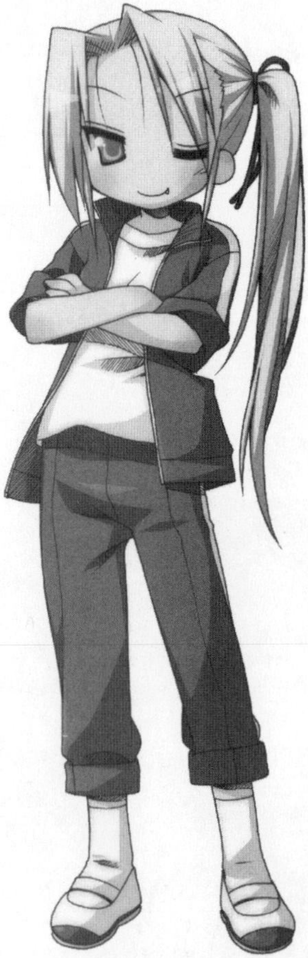

● Comptiq, August 2007 issue

the conclusion

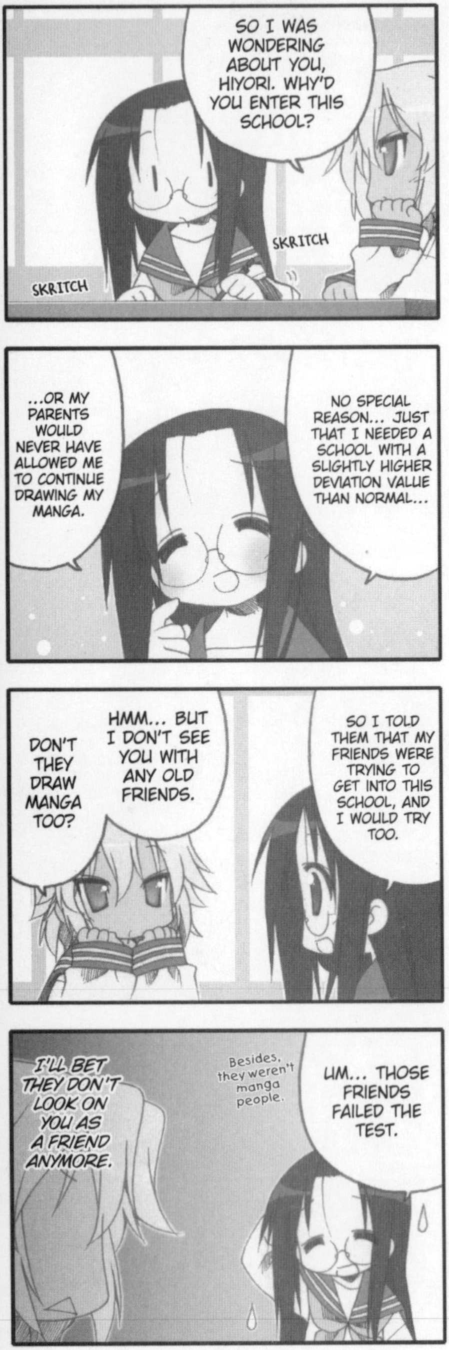
SO I WAS WONDERING ABOUT YOU, HIYORI. WHY'D YOU ENTER THIS SCHOOL?
SKRITCH
SKRITCH
NO SPECIAL REASON... JUST THAT I NEEDED A SCHOOL WITH A SLIGHTLY HIGHER DEVIATION VALUE THAN NORMAL...
...OR MY PARENTS WOULD NEVER HAVE ALLOWED ME TO CONTINUE DRAWING MY MANGA.
SO I TOLD THEM THAT MY FRIENDS WERE TRYING TO GET INTO THIS SCHOOL, AND I WOULD TRY TOO.
HMM... BUT I DON'T SEE YOU WITH ANY OLD FRIENDS.
DON'T THEY DRAW MANGA TOO?
UM... THOSE FRIENDS FAILED THE TEST.
Besides, they weren't manga people.
I'LL BET THEY DON'T LOOK ON YOU AS A FRIEND ANYMORE.

line of sight

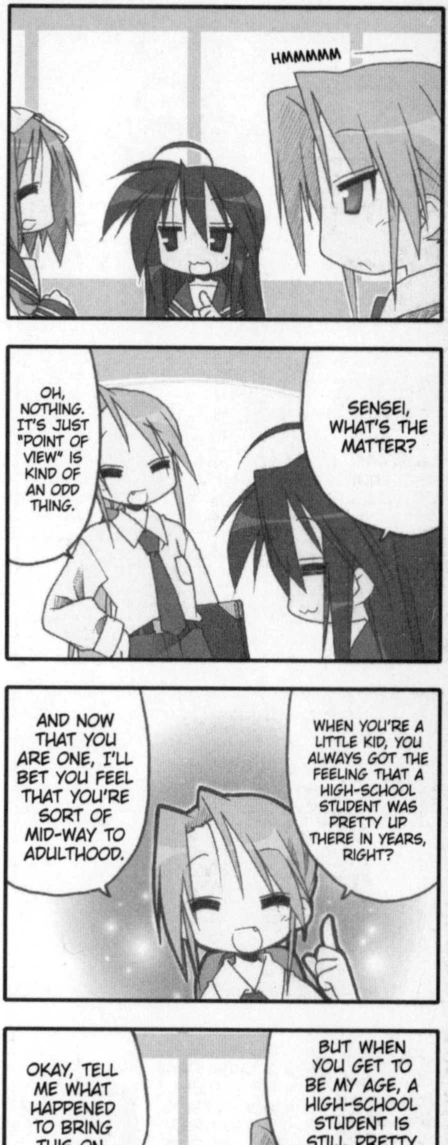
HMMMMM —
SENSEI, WHAT'S THE MATTER?
OH, NOTHING. IT'S JUST "POINT OF VIEW" IS KIND OF AN ODD THING.
WHEN YOU'RE A LITTLE KID, YOU ALWAYS GOT THE FEELING THAT A HIGH-SCHOOL STUDENT WAS PRETTY UP THERE IN YEARS, RIGHT?
AND NOW THAT YOU ARE ONE, I'LL BET YOU FEEL THAT YOU'RE SORT OF MID-WAY TO ADULTHOOD.
BUT WHEN YOU GET TO BE MY AGE, A HIGH-SCHOOL STUDENT IS STILL PRETTY MUCH A BRAT KID.
OKAY, TELL ME WHAT HAPPENED TO BRING THIS ON.

something just tugs on you

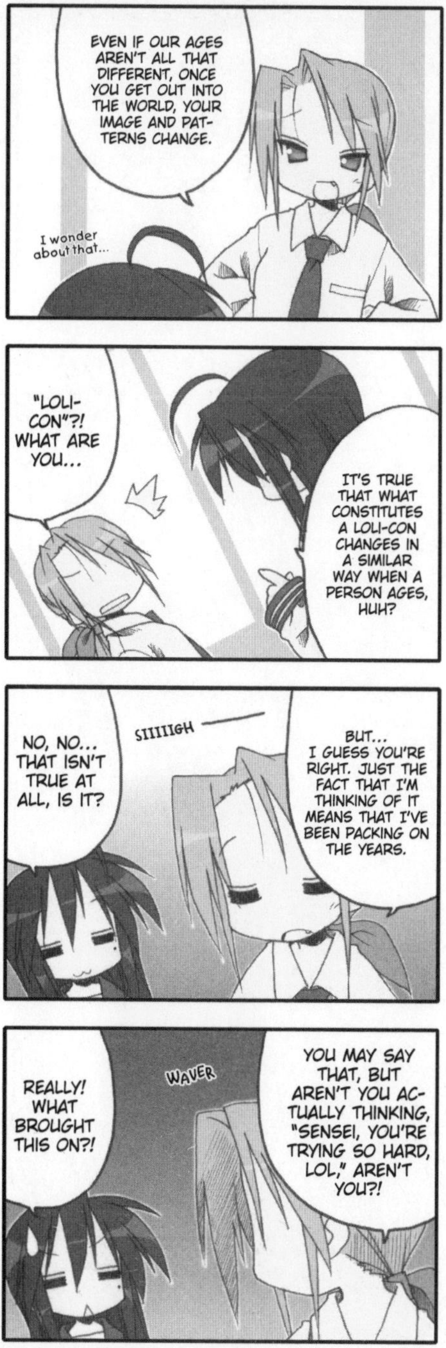
EVEN IF OUR AGES AREN'T ALL THAT DIFFERENT, ONCE YOU GET OUT INTO THE WORLD, YOUR IMAGE AND PAT-TERNS CHANGE.
I wonder about that...
IT'S TRUE THAT WHAT CONSTITUTES A LOLI-CON CHANGES IN A SIMILAR WAY WHEN A PERSON AGES, HUH?
"LOLI-CON"?! WHAT ARE YOU...
BUT... I GUESS YOU'RE RIGHT. JUST THE FACT THAT I'M THINKING OF IT MEANS THAT I'VE BEEN PACKING ON THE YEARS.
SIIIIIGH —
NO, NO... THAT ISN'T TRUE AT ALL, IS IT?
YOU MAY SAY THAT, BUT AREN'T YOU AC-TUALLY THINKING, "SENSEI, YOU'RE TRYING SO HARD, LOL," AREN'T YOU?!
WAVER
REALLY! WHAT BROUGHT THIS ON?!

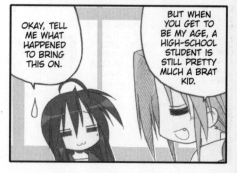

the point that irritates

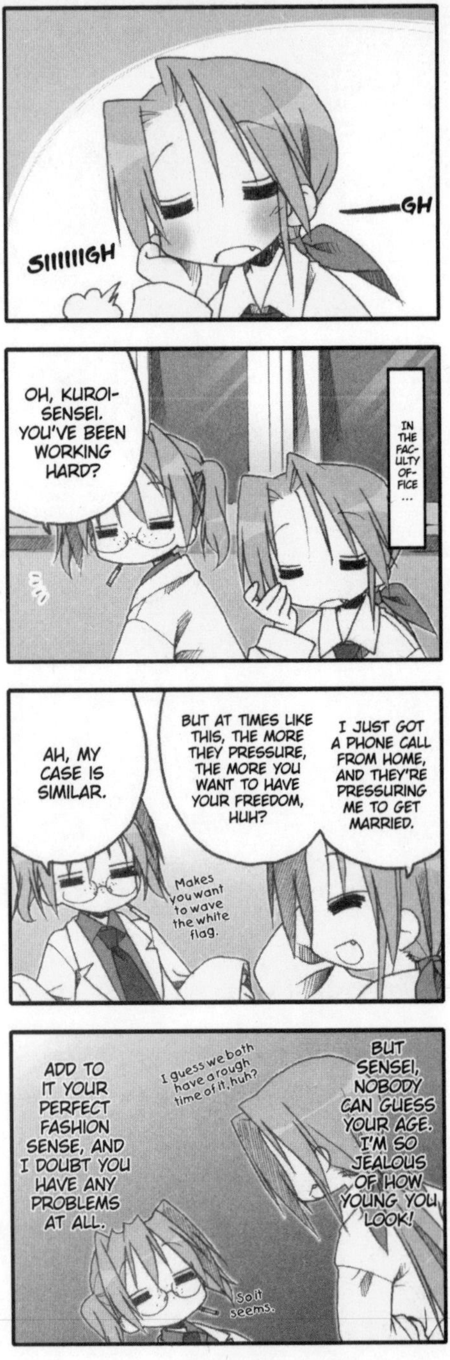
—GH
SIIIIIIGH
IN THE FACULTY OFFICE...
OH, KUROI-SENSEI. YOU'VE BEEN WORKING HARD?
I JUST GOT A PHONE CALL FROM HOME, AND THEY'RE PRESSURING ME TO GET MARRIED.
BUT AT TIMES LIKE THIS, THE MORE THEY PRESSURE, THE MORE YOU WANT TO HAVE YOUR FREEDOM, HUH?
AH, MY CASE IS SIMILAR.
Makes you want to wave the white flag.
BUT SENSEI, NOBODY CAN GUESS YOUR AGE. I'M SO JEALOUS OF HOW YOUNG YOU LOOK!
I guess we both have a rough time of it, huh?
ADD TO IT YOUR PERFECT FASHION SENSE, AND I DOUBT YOU HAVE ANY PROBLEMS AT ALL.
So it seems.

temperament

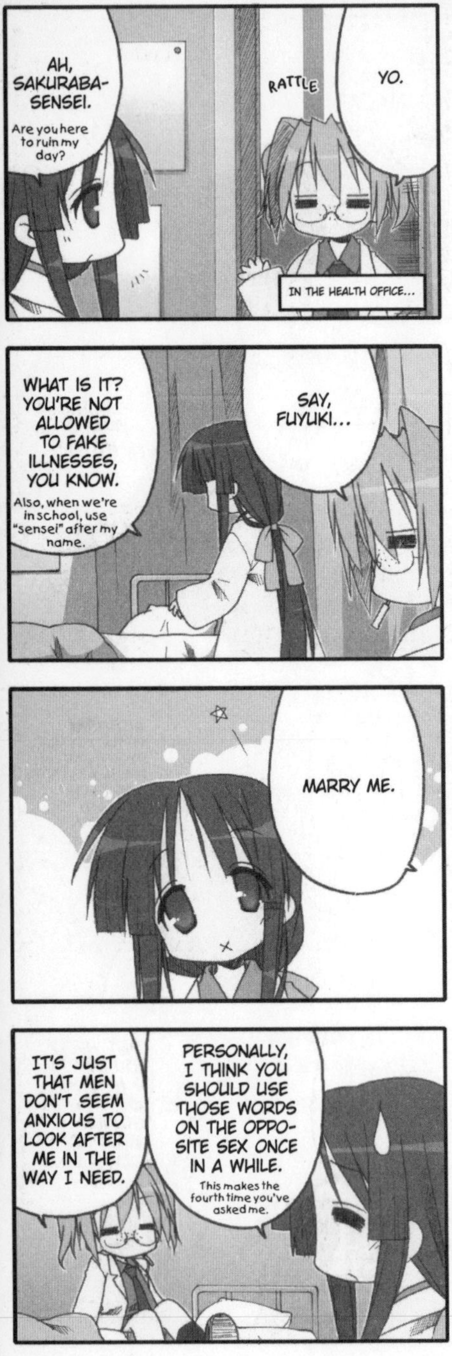
YO.
RATTLE
AH, SAKURABA-SENSEI.
Are you here to ruin my day?
IN THE HEALTH OFFICE...
SAY, FUYUKI...
WHAT IS IT? YOU'RE NOT ALLOWED TO FAKE ILLNESSES, YOU KNOW.
Also, when we're in school, use "sensei" after my name.
MARRY ME.
PERSONALLY, I THINK YOU SHOULD USE THOSE WORDS ON THE OPPOSITE SEX ONCE IN A WHILE.
This makes the fourth time you've asked me.
IT'S JUST THAT MEN DON'T SEEM ANXIOUS TO LOOK AFTER ME IN THE WAY I NEED.

A GIRL WITH CULTURAL MISCONCEPTIONS IN HIGH GEAR

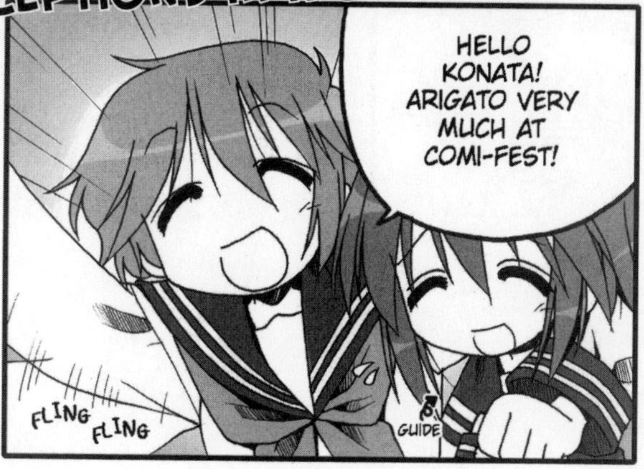
HELLO KONATA! ARIGATO VERY MUCH AT COMI-FEST!
GUIDE
FLING FLING

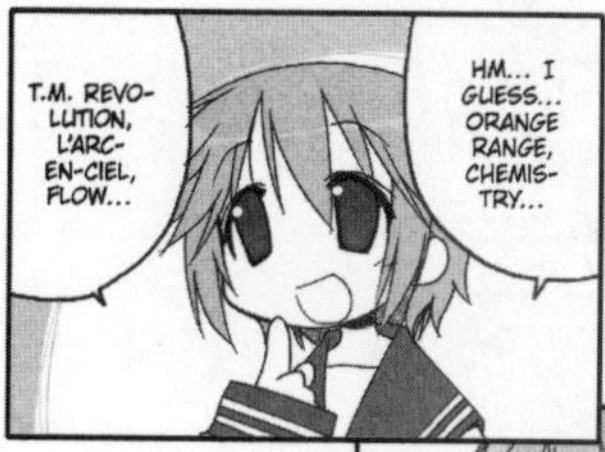
HM... I GUESS... ORANGE RANGE, CHEMISTRY...
T.M. REVOLUTION, L'ARC-EN-CIEL, FLOW...

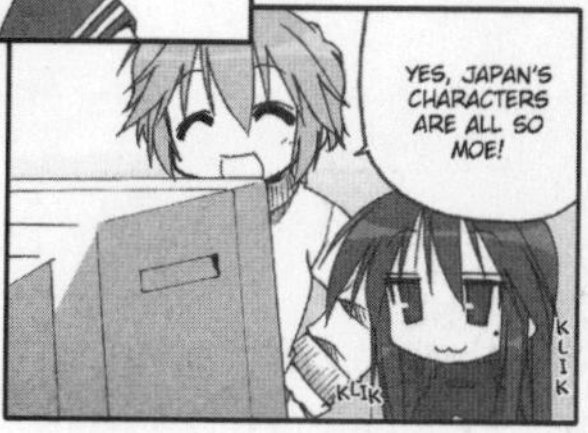
YES, JAPAN'S CHARACTERS ARE ALL SO MOE!
KLIK
KLIK

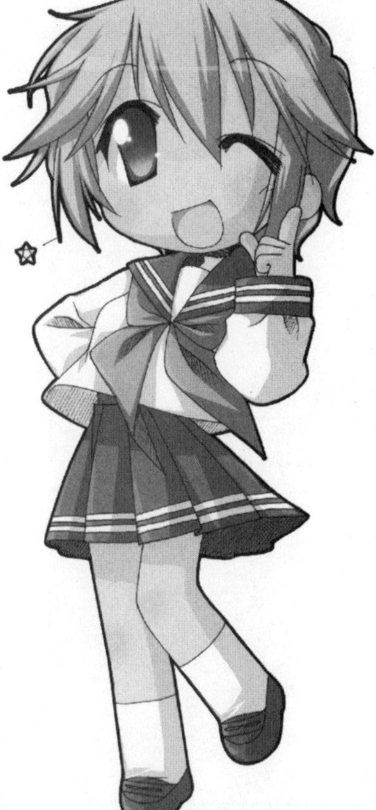

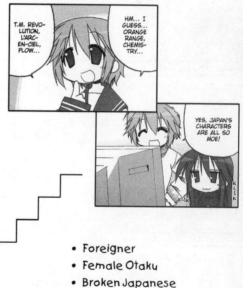

- Foreigner
- Female Otaku
- Broken Japanese

PATRICIA MARTIN

Lucky☆Star

episode 136
a casual happiness

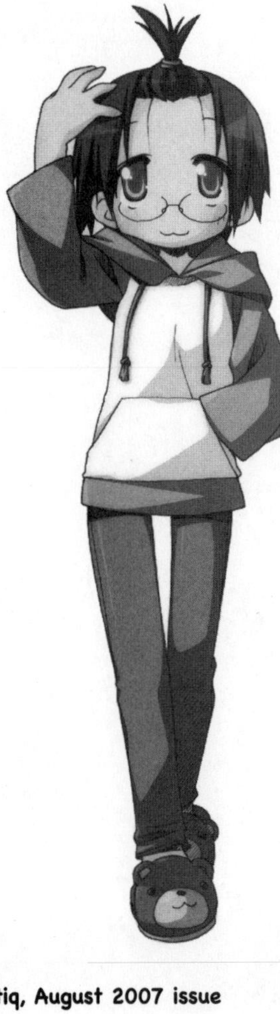

● Comptiq, August 2007 issue

mutual understanding

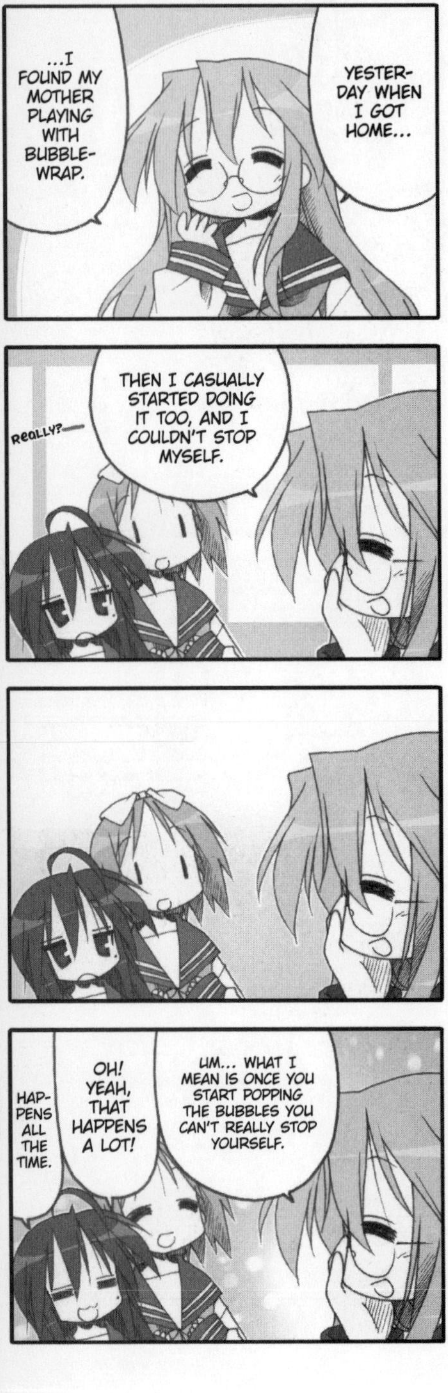

YESTER-DAY WHEN I GOT HOME...
...I FOUND MY MOTHER PLAYING WITH BUBBLE-WRAP.
THEN I CASUALLY STARTED DOING IT TOO, AND I COULDN'T STOP MYSELF.
Really?
UM... WHAT I MEAN IS ONCE YOU START POPPING THE BUBBLES YOU CAN'T REALLY STOP YOURSELF.
OH! YEAH, THAT HAPPENS A LOT!
HAP-PENS ALL THE TIME.

irreverence

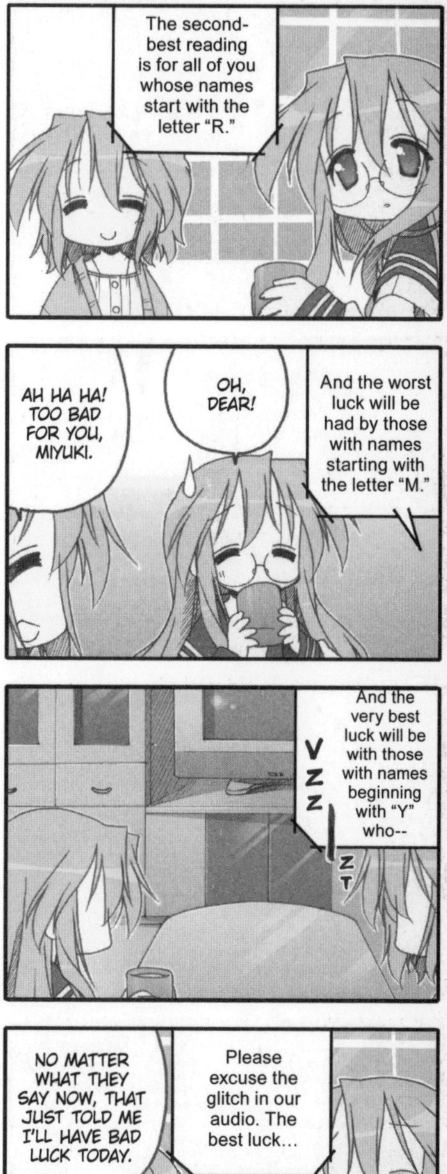
The second-best reading is for all of you whose names start with the letter "R."
And the worst luck will be had by those with names starting with the letter "M."
OH, DEAR!
AH HA HA! TOO BAD FOR YOU, MIYUKI.
And the very best luck will be with those with names beginning with "Y" who--
VZZ
ZZT
Please excuse the glitch in our audio. The best luck...
NO MATTER WHAT THEY SAY NOW, THAT JUST TOLD ME I'LL HAVE BAD LUCK TODAY.

have it or don't have it

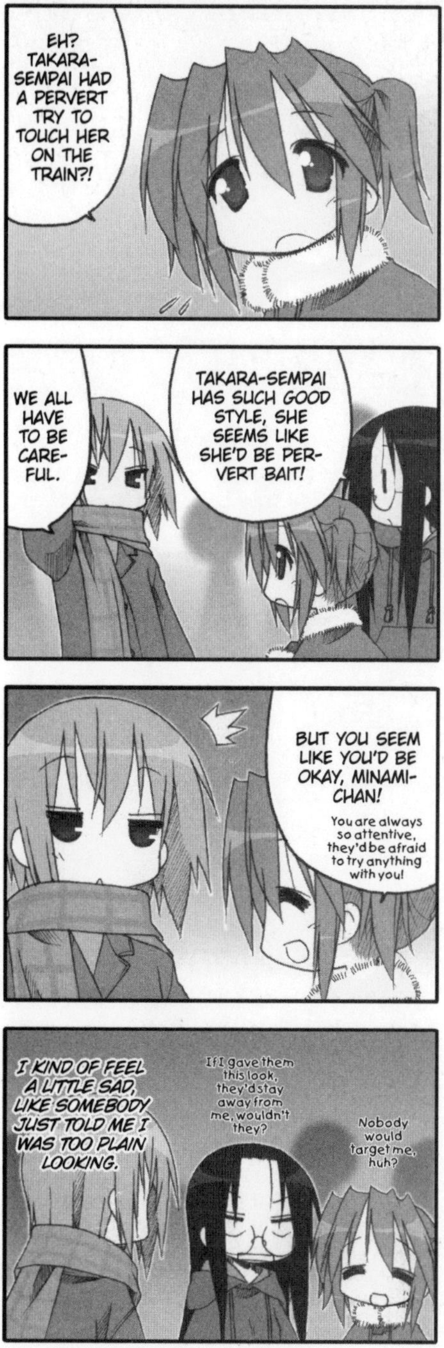
EH? TAKARA-SEMPAI HAD A PERVERT TRY TO TOUCH HER ON THE TRAIN?!
TAKARA-SEMPAI HAS SUCH GOOD STYLE, SHE SEEMS LIKE SHE'D BE PERVERT BAIT!
WE ALL HAVE TO BE CAREFUL.
BUT YOU SEEM LIKE YOU'D BE OKAY, MINAMI-CHAN!
You are always so attentive, they'd be afraid to try anything with you!
Nobody would target me, huh?
If I gave them this look, they'd stay away from me, wouldn't they?
I KIND OF FEEL A LITTLE SAD, LIKE SOMEBODY JUST TOLD ME I WAS TOO PLAIN LOOKING.

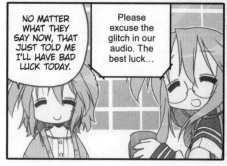

self-awareness

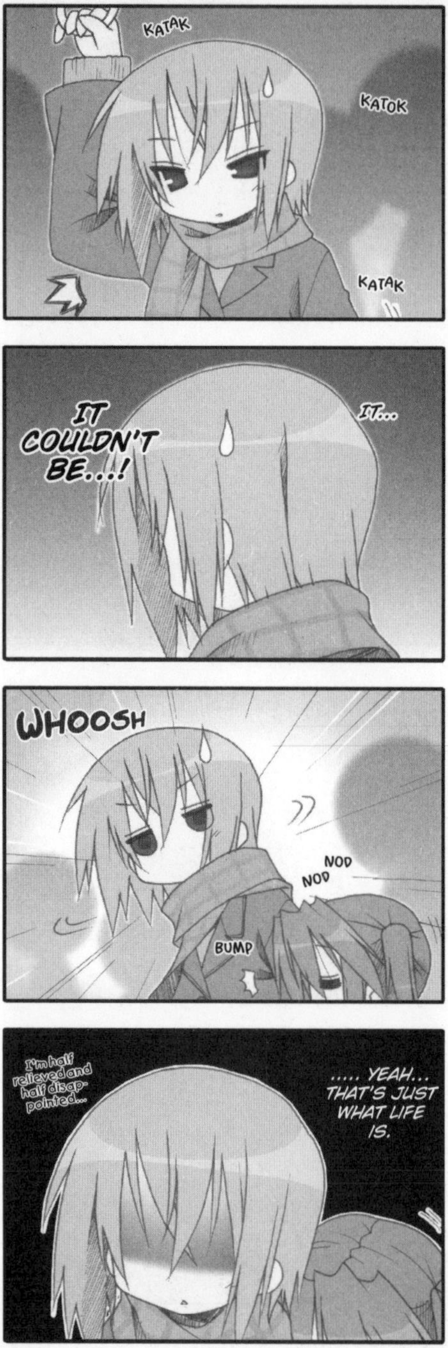
KATAK
KATOK
KATAK
IT...
IT COULDN'T BE...!
WHOOSH
NOD
NOD
BUMP
..... YEAH... THAT'S JUST WHAT LIFE IS.
I'm half relieved and half disappointed...

that kind of atmosphere

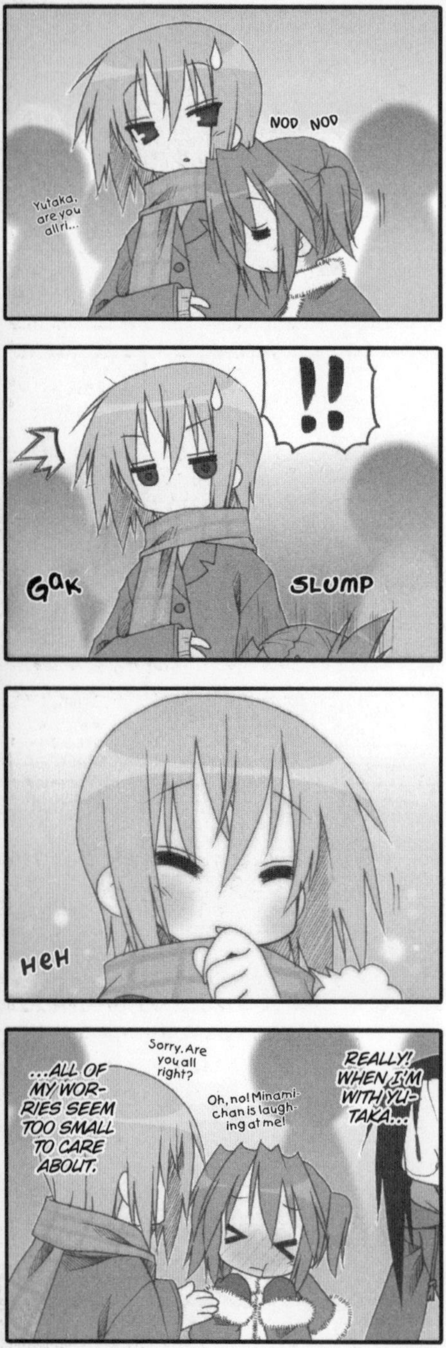
NOD NOD
Yutaka, are you all ri...
!!
GAK
SLUMP
HEH
REALLY! WHEN I'M WITH YU-TAKA...
Sorry. Are you all right?
Oh, no! Minami-chan is laughing at me!
...ALL OF MY WOR-RIES SEEM TOO SMALL TO CARE ABOUT.

A RUNAWAY CAR THAT OBEYS THE SPEED LIMIT

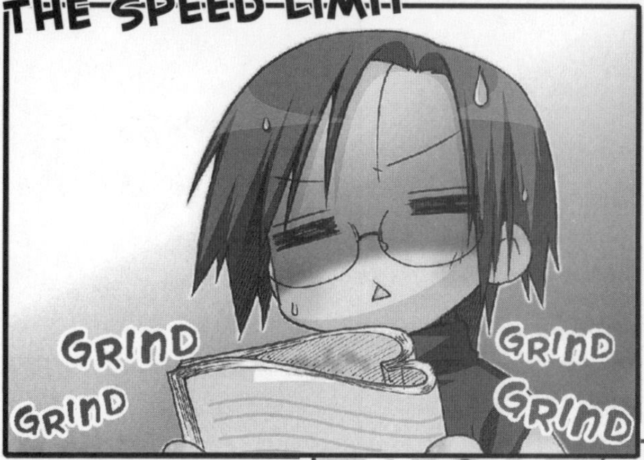
GRIND
GRIND
GRIND
GRIND

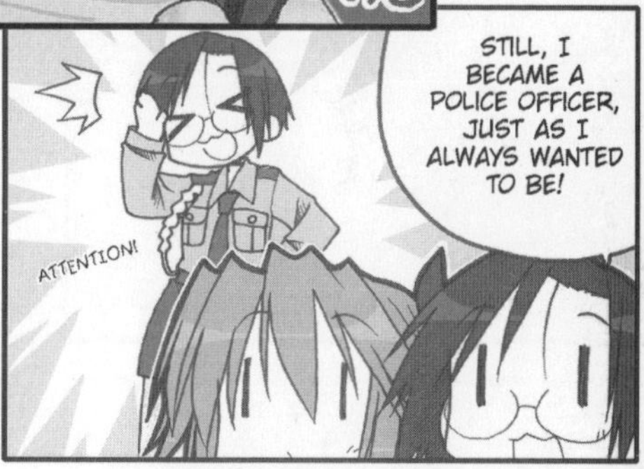
STILL, I BECAME A POLICE OFFICER, JUST AS I ALWAYS WANTED TO BE!
ATTENTION!

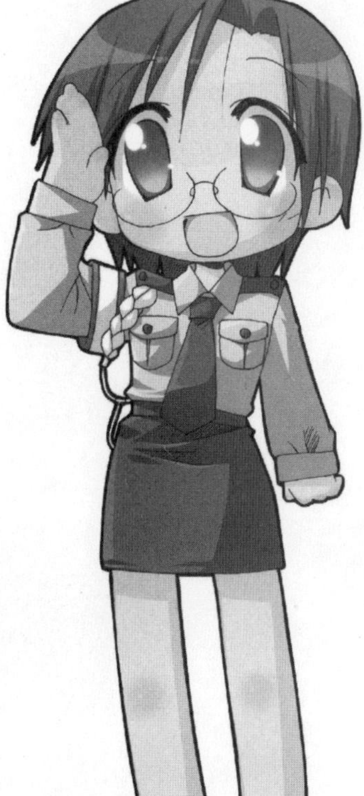

- Police officer
- Lots of energy
- Wife

YUI NARUMI

Lucky☆Star

episode 137
the unbalanced scales

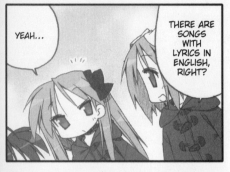

● Comptiq, September 2007 issue

THERE ARE SONGS WITH LYRICS IN ENGLISH, RIGHT?
YEAH...
DO THE PEOPLE WHO LISTEN TO WESTERN MUSIC ALL THE TIME KNOW WHAT THE LYRICS MEAN?
I really wonder!
HM... I CAN'T REALLY SAY.
I guess some of them translate the lyrics for themselves.
HA HA HA! YOU KNOW THAT SONGS ARE THINGS THAT RESONATE IN ONE'S SOUL!
TSK TSK TSK
HM... THAT'S AN UNUSUALLY CORRECT AND NORMAL THOUGHT FOR YOU.
WELL, THERE ARE SO MANY ANIME SONGS WHERE I HAVE NO IDEA WHAT IT IS THEY'RE SINGING THESE DAYS.
If the album doesn't have the lyrics printed, I have no idea!
AND IN THE END, IT ALWAYS COMES DOWN TO THAT, HUH?

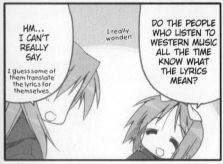

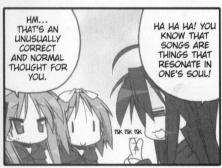

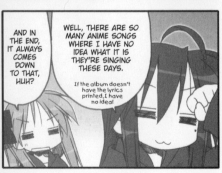

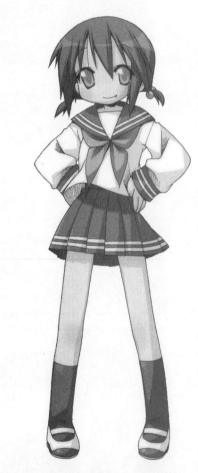

beyond the window

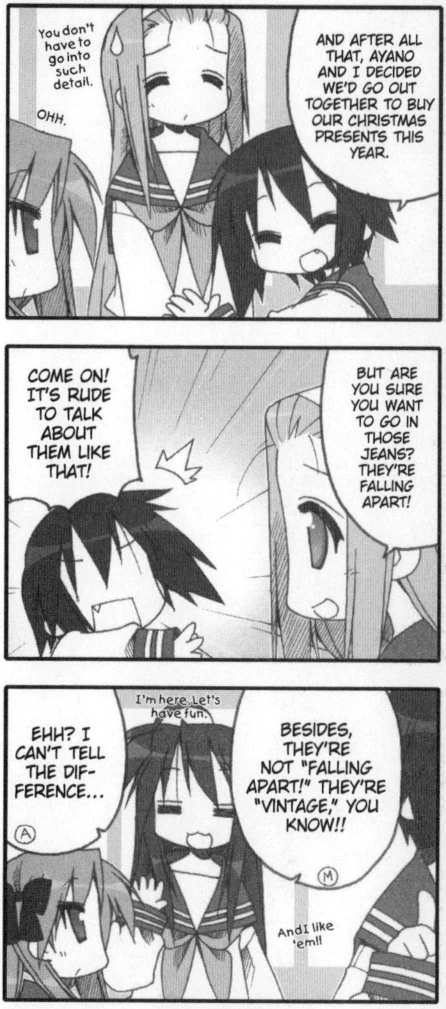
AND AFTER ALL THAT, AYANO AND I DECIDED WE'D GO OUT TOGETHER TO BUY OUR CHRISTMAS PRESENTS THIS YEAR.
You don't have to go into such detail.
OHH.
BUT ARE YOU SURE YOU WANT TO GO IN THOSE JEANS? THEY'RE FALLING APART!
COME ON! IT'S RUDE TO TALK ABOUT THEM LIKE THAT!
BESIDES, THEY'RE NOT "FALLING APART!" THEY'RE "VINTAGE," YOU KNOW!!
I'm here. Let's have fun.
EHH? I CAN'T TELL THE DIFFERENCE...
And I like 'em!!
OH, SHORTY!! NOW I CAN UNDERSTAND A LITTLE HOW IT FEELS WHEN OTHERS MISUNDERSTAND YOUR TASTES!!
I'M NOT SURE WHAT BROUGHT THIS ON, BUT NATURALLY A PERSON'S TASTES IS AN AREA OF LITTLE CONCERN FROM OTHER PEOPLE'S POINTS OF VIEW.
But why are you addressing that at me?

on-target percentage

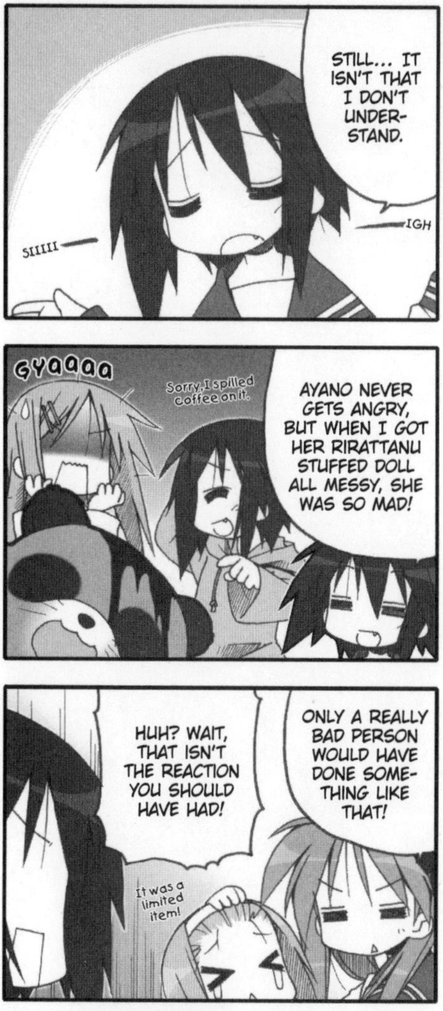
STILL... IT ISN'T THAT I DON'T UNDERSTAND.
SIIIII— —IGH
AYANO NEVER GETS ANGRY, BUT WHEN I GOT HER RIRATTANU STUFFED DOLL ALL MESSY, SHE WAS SO MAD!
Sorry, I spilled coffee on it.
GYaaaa
ONLY A REALLY BAD PERSON WOULD HAVE DONE SOMETHING LIKE THAT!
HUH? WAIT, THAT ISN'T THE REACTION YOU SHOULD HAVE HAD!
It was a limited item!
BY THE WAY, TASTE IS JUST ONE WORD, BUT...
...THERE ARE THINGS THE WORLD FINDS UNDERSTANDABLE AND THINGS IT FINDS EASY TO CONDEMN.
DON'T YOU GET THE FEELING THE WORLD IS REALLY UNFAIR?!
WAAAAAAAH!

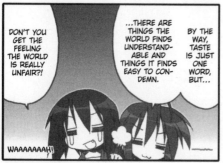

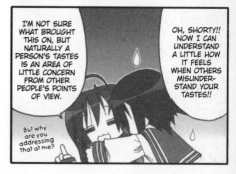

the word of god

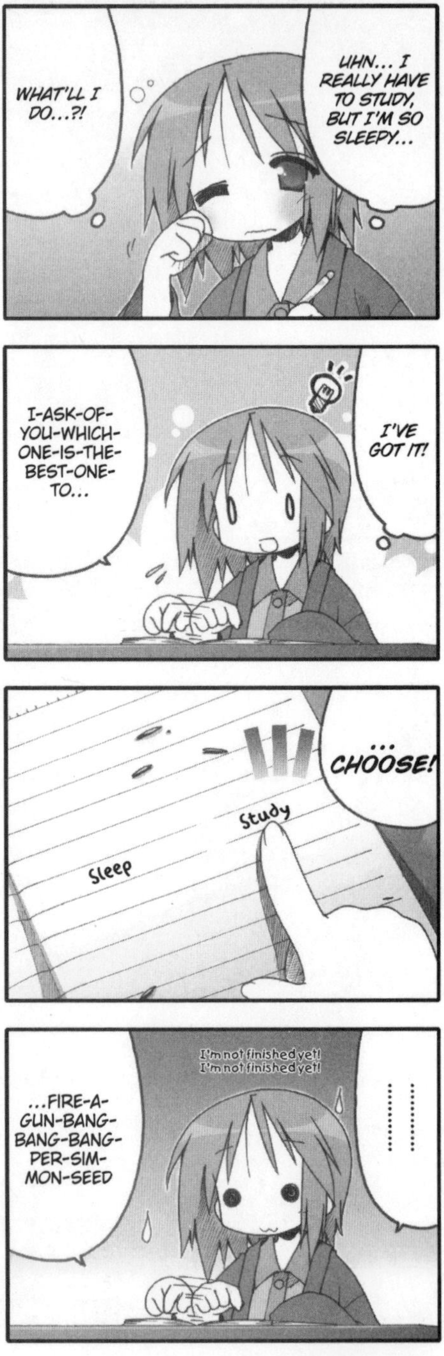
UHN... I REALLY HAVE TO STUDY, BUT I'M SO SLEEPY...
WHAT'LL I DO...?!
I'VE GOT IT!
I-ASK-OF-YOU-WHICH-ONE-IS-THE-BEST-ONE-TO...
...CHOOSE!
Study
Sleep
......
I'm not finished yet! I'm not finished yet!
...FIRE-A-GUN-BANG-BANG-BANG-PER-SIM-MON-SEED

court of appeals

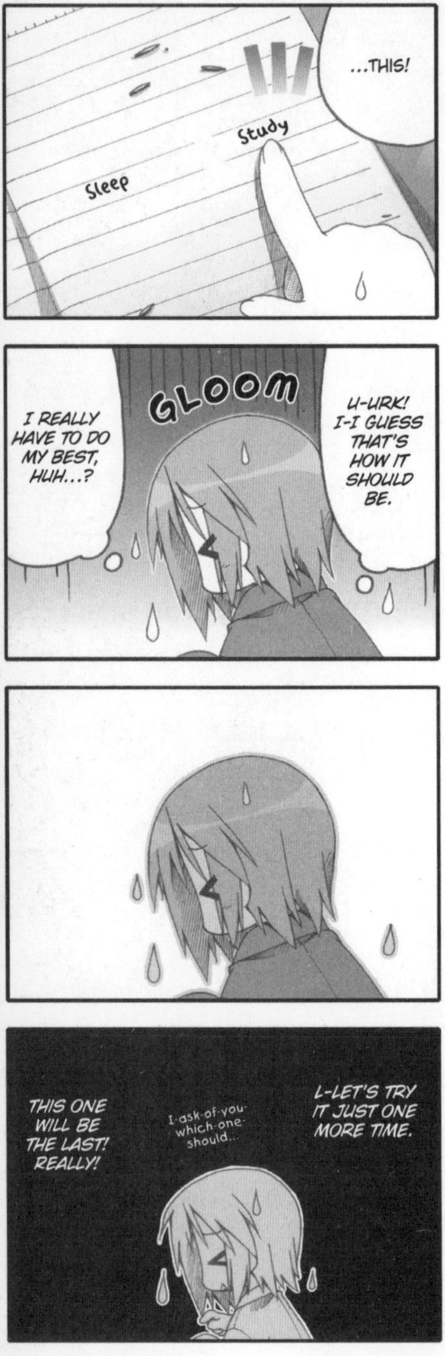
...THIS!
Study
Sleep
U-URK! I-I GUESS THAT'S HOW IT SHOULD BE.
GLOOM
I REALLY HAVE TO DO MY BEST, HUH...?
L-LET'S TRY IT JUST ONE MORE TIME.
I-ask-of-you-which-one-should...
THIS ONE WILL BE THE LAST! REALLY!

RYOUOU'S "FRIEND" TEACHER

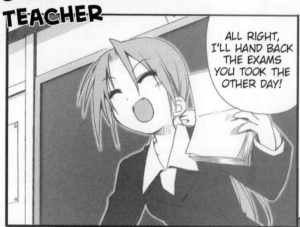

ALL RIGHT, I'LL HAND BACK THE EXAMS YOU TOOK THE OTHER DAY!

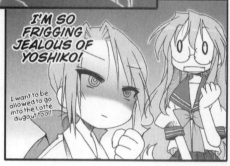

I'M SO FRIGGING JEALOUS OF YOSHIKO!

I want to be allowed to go into the Lotte dugout too!!

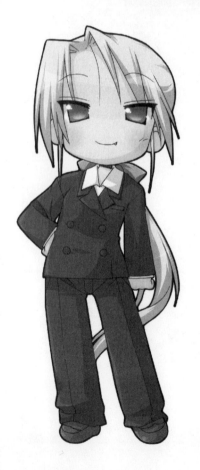

- Loves baseball
- Loves net games
- Fake Kansai accent

NANAKO KUROI

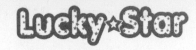

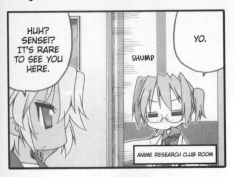

Lucky☆Star

episode 138
falling on deaf ears

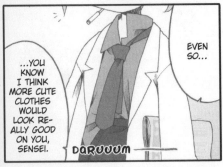

● Comptiq, September 2007 issue

the grass is brown on both sides

YO.
SHUMP
HUH? SENSEI? IT'S RARE TO SEE YOU HERE.
ANIME RESEARCH CLUB ROOM
EVEN SO...
...YOU KNOW I THINK MORE CUTE CLOTHES WOULD LOOK RE-ALLY GOOD ON YOU, SENSEI.
DARUUUM
YOU ALREADY HAVE THE SHORT-CUTE THING GOING, SO IT'S REALLY A WASTE!
IT DOESN'T MATTER. WHAT'S REALLY IMPORTANT FOR PEOPLE IS WHAT'S INSIDE.
FSHH
"INSIDE?" SENSEI, HERE IN JAPAN THEY SAY, "IF YOUR CLOTHES ARE MESSY, SO IS YOUR SOUL!"
YEAH? YOU REALLY DON'T KNOW WHEN TO SHUT UP, DO YOU?

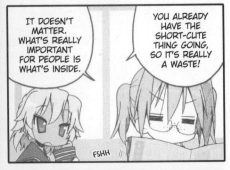

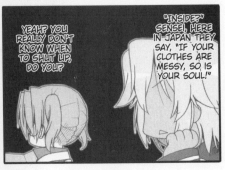

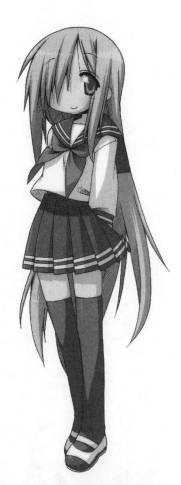

the voice from behind

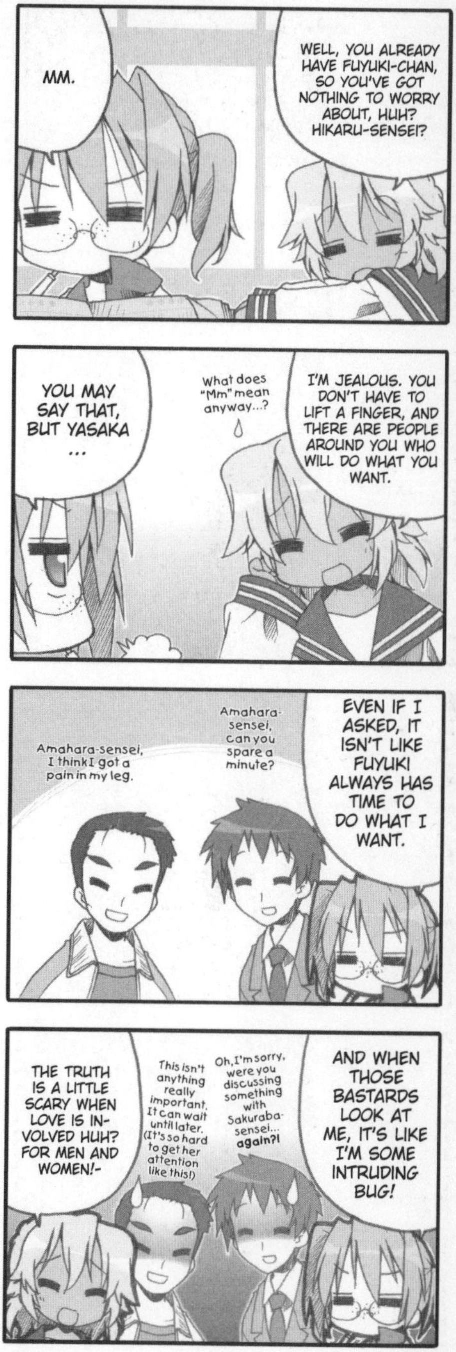
WELL, YOU ALREADY HAVE FUYUKI-CHAN, SO YOU'VE GOT NOTHING TO WORRY ABOUT, HUH? HIKARU-SENSEI?
MM.
I'M JEALOUS. YOU DON'T HAVE TO LIFT A FINGER, AND THERE ARE PEOPLE AROUND YOU WHO WILL DO WHAT YOU WANT.
What does "Mm" mean anyway...?
YOU MAY SAY THAT, BUT YASAKA ...
EVEN IF I ASKED, IT ISN'T LIKE FUYUKI ALWAYS HAS TIME TO DO WHAT I WANT.
Amahara-sensei, can you spare a minute?
Amahara-sensei, I think I got a pain in my leg.
AND WHEN THOSE BASTARDS LOOK AT ME, IT'S LIKE I'M SOME INTRUDING BUG!
Oh, I'm sorry, were you discussing something with Sakuraba-sensei... again?!
This isn't anything really important. It can wait until later. (It's so hard to get her attention like this!)
THE TRUTH IS A LITTLE SCARY WHEN LOVE IS INVOLVED HUH? FOR MEN AND WOMEN!-

plumb bob

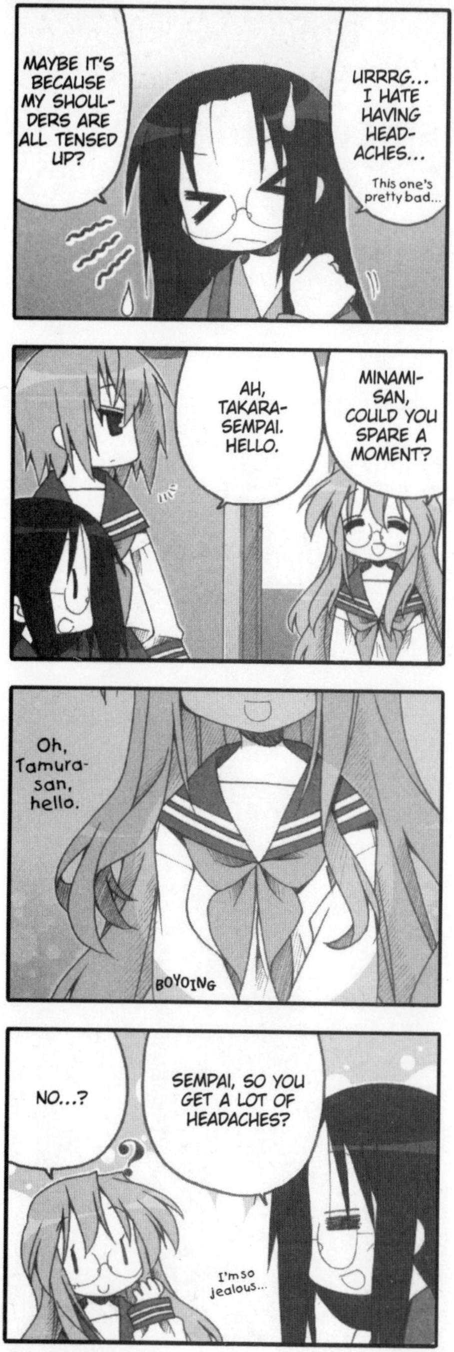
URRRG... I HATE HAVING HEADACHES...
This one's pretty bad...
MAYBE IT'S BECAUSE MY SHOULDERS ARE ALL TENSED UP?
MINAMI-SAN, COULD YOU SPARE A MOMENT?
AH, TAKARA-SEMPAI. HELLO.
Oh, Tamura-san, hello.
BOYOING
SEMPAI, SO YOU GET A LOT OF HEADACHES?
NO...?
I'm so jealous...

she's no good

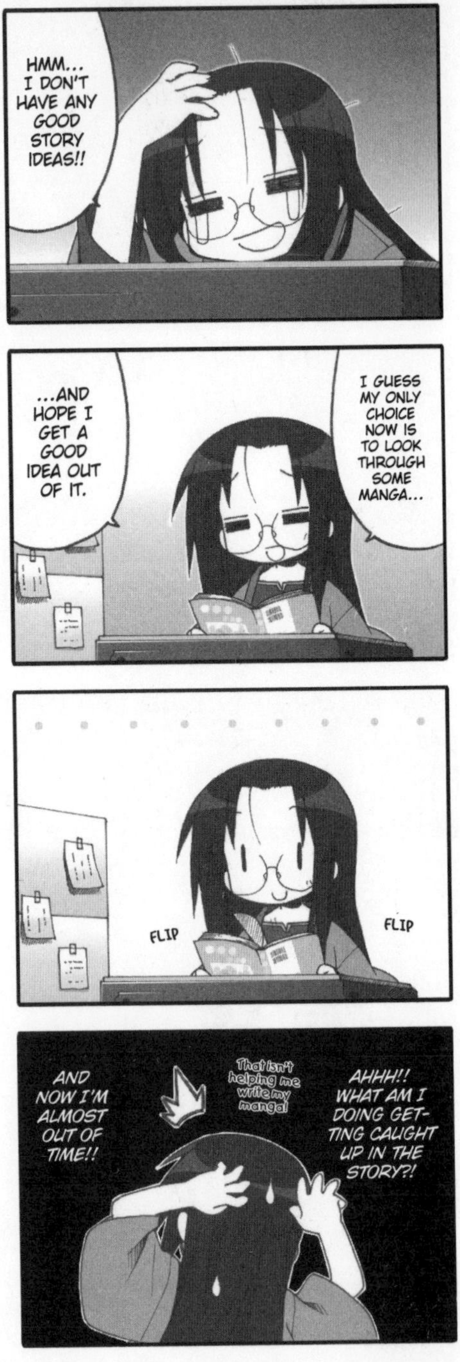
HMM... I DON'T HAVE ANY GOOD STORY IDEAS!!
I GUESS MY ONLY CHOICE NOW IS TO LOOK THROUGH SOME MANGA...
...AND HOPE I GET A GOOD IDEA OUT OF IT.
FLIP
FLIP
AHHH!! WHAT AM I DOING GET-TING CAUGHT UP IN THE STORY?!
That isn't helping me write my manga!
AND NOW I'M ALMOST OUT OF TIME!!

plans are unplanned

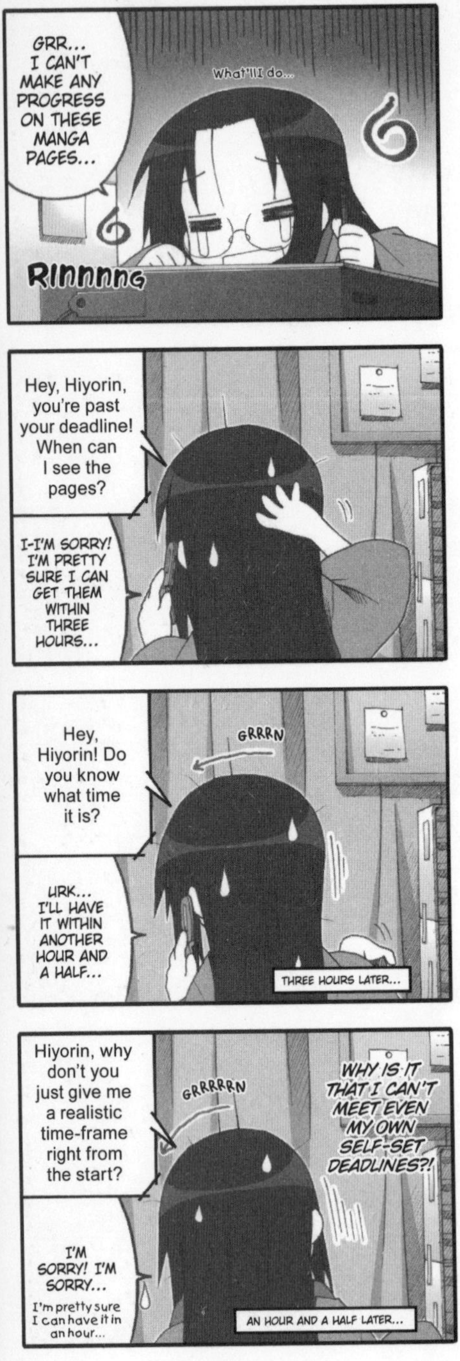
What'll I do...
GRR... I CAN'T MAKE ANY PROGRESS ON THESE MANGA PAGES...
RINNNNG
Hey, Hiyorin, you're past your deadline! When can I see the pages?
I-I'M SORRY! I'M PRETTY SURE I CAN GET THEM WITHIN THREE HOURS...
GRRRN
Hey, Hiyorin! Do you know what time it is?
URK... I'LL HAVE IT WITHIN ANOTHER HOUR AND A HALF...
THREE HOURS LATER...
WHY IS IT THAT I CAN'T MEET EVEN MY OWN SELF-SET DEADLINES?!
GRRRRRN
Hiyorin, why don't you just give me a realistic time-frame right from the start?
I'M SORRY! I'M SORRY...
I'm pretty sure I can have it in an hour...
AN HOUR AND A HALF LATER...

RYOUOU'S SAMURAI

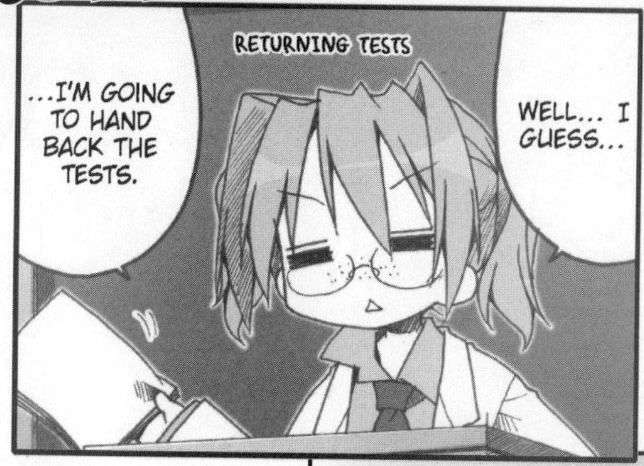
RETURNING TESTS
WELL... I GUESS...
...I'M GOING TO HAND BACK THE TESTS.

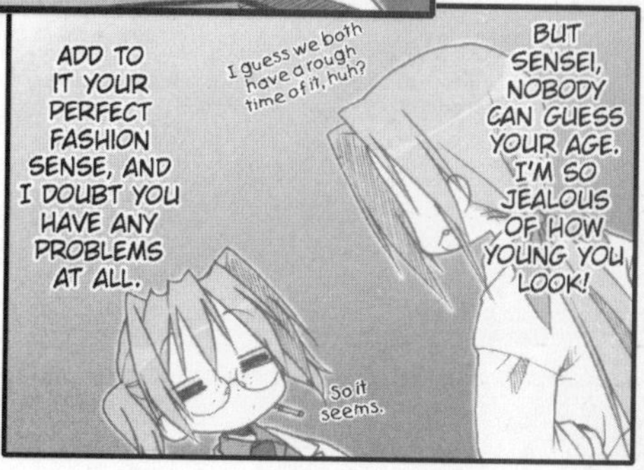
BUT SENSEI, NOBODY CAN GUESS YOUR AGE. I'M SO JEALOUS OF HOW YOUNG YOU LOOK!
I guess we both have a rough time of it, huh?
ADD TO IT YOUR PERFECT FASHION SENSE, AND I DOUBT YOU HAVE ANY PROBLEMS AT ALL.
So it seems.

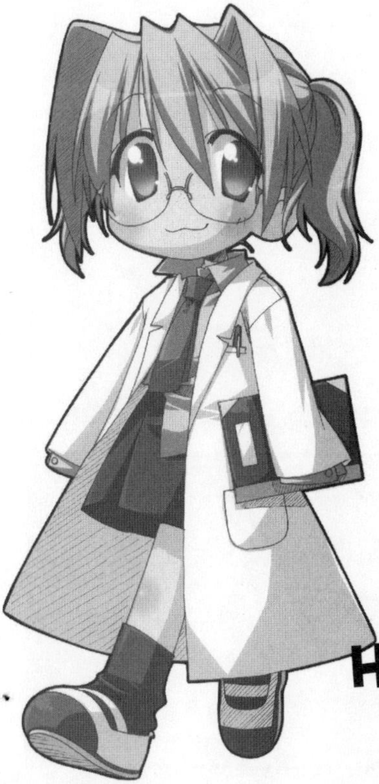

- Mini-size
- Old-man personality
- High-handed

HIKARU SAKURABA

Lucky☆Star

episode 139
hit batsman

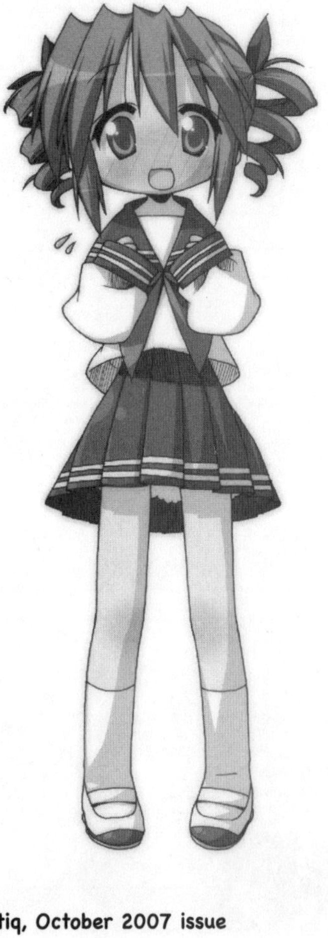

●Comptiq, October 2007 issue

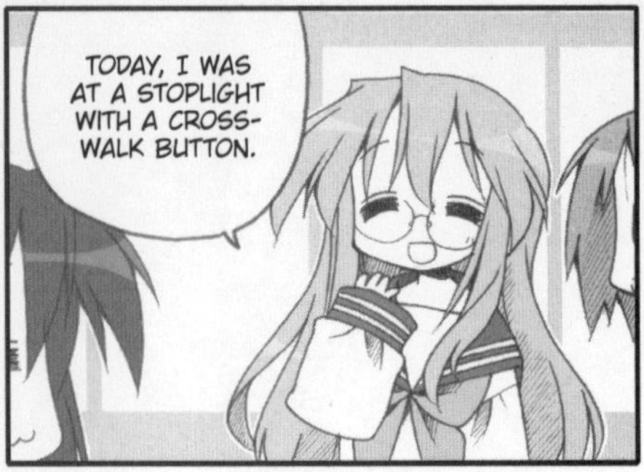
TODAY, I WAS AT A STOPLIGHT WITH A CROSS-WALK BUTTON.

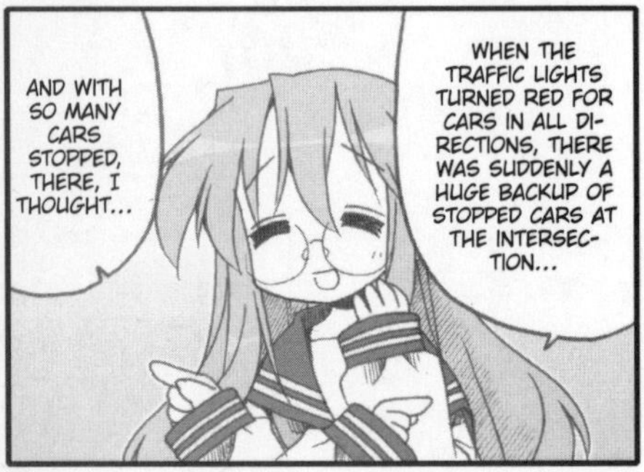
WHEN THE TRAFFIC LIGHTS TURNED RED FOR CARS IN ALL DI-RECTIONS, THERE WAS SUDDENLY A HUGE BACKUP OF STOPPED CARS AT THE INTERSEC-TION...
AND WITH SO MANY CARS STOPPED, THERE, I THOUGHT...

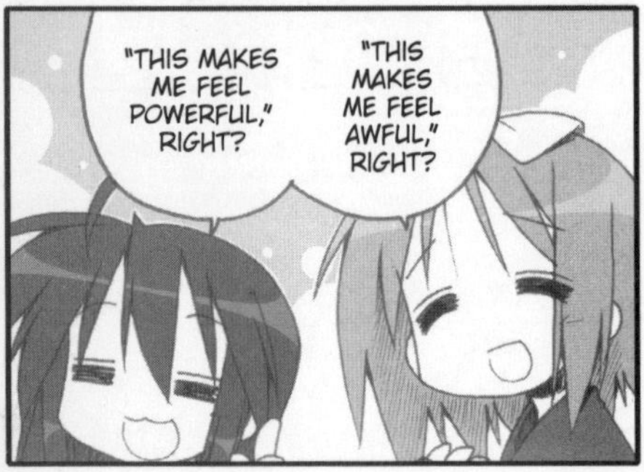
"THIS MAKES ME FEEL AWFUL," RIGHT?
"THIS MAKES ME FEEL POWERFUL," RIGHT?

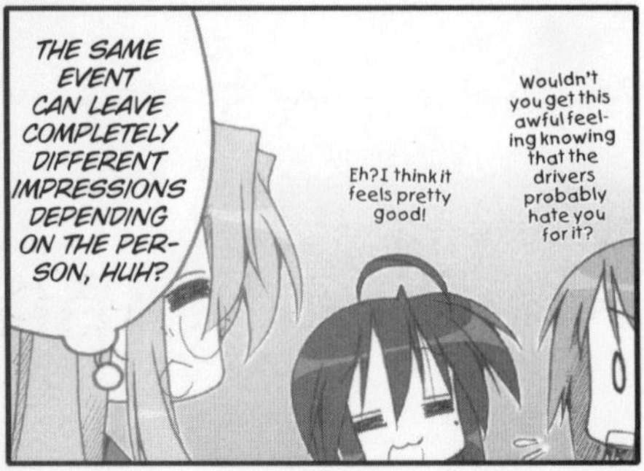
Wouldn't you get this awful feel-ing knowing that the drivers probably hate you for it?
Eh? I think it feels pretty good!
THE SAME EVENT CAN LEAVE COMPLETELY DIFFERENT IMPRESSIONS DEPENDING ON THE PER-SON, HUH?

smiling you

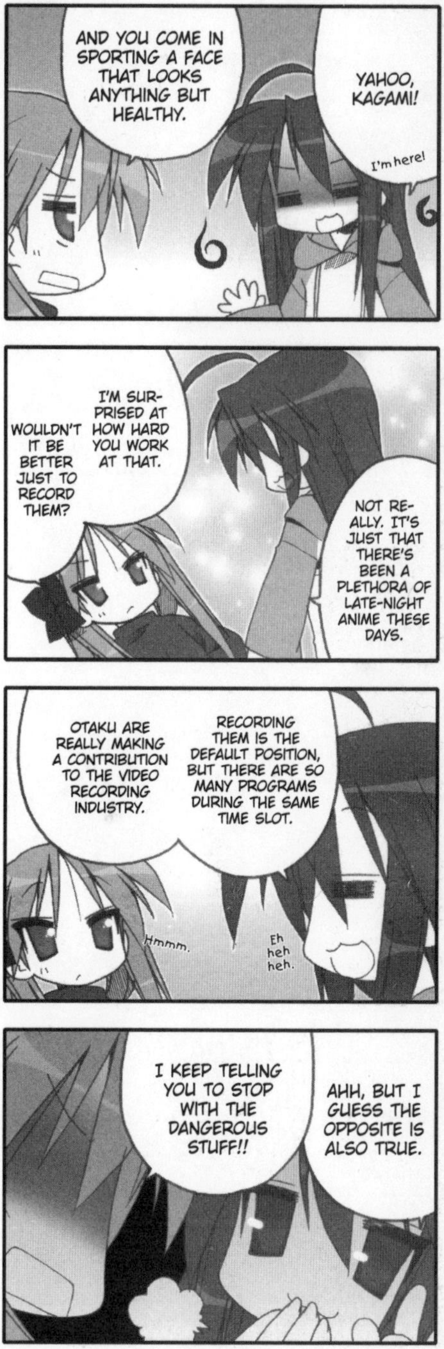
YAHOO, KAGAMI!
I'm here!
AND YOU COME IN SPORTING A FACE THAT LOOKS ANYTHING BUT HEALTHY.
I'M SUR-PRISED AT HOW HARD YOU WORK AT THAT.
NOT RE-ALLY. IT'S JUST THAT THERE'S BEEN A PLETHORA OF LATE-NIGHT ANIME THESE DAYS.
WOULDN'T IT BE BETTER JUST TO RECORD THEM?
RECORDING THEM IS THE DEFAULT POSITION, BUT THERE ARE SO MANY PROGRAMS DURING THE SAME TIME SLOT.
OTAKU ARE REALLY MAKING A CONTRIBUTION TO THE VIDEO RECORDING INDUSTRY.
Eh heh heh.
Hmmm.
AHH, BUT I GUESS THE OPPOSITE IS ALSO TRUE.
I KEEP TELLING YOU TO STOP WITH THE DANGEROUS STUFF!!

strong girl

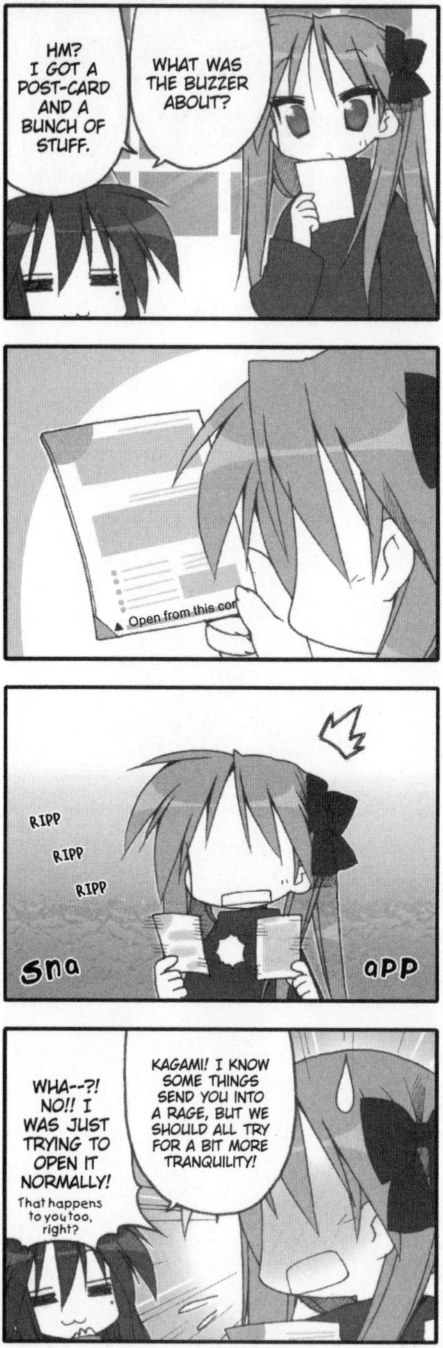
WHAT WAS THE BUZZER ABOUT?
HM? I GOT A POST-CARD AND A BUNCH OF STUFF.
Open from this cor
RIPP
RIPP
RIPP
sna
app
KAGAMI! I KNOW SOME THINGS SEND YOU INTO A RAGE, BUT WE SHOULD ALL TRY FOR A BIT MORE TRANQUILITY!
WHA--?! NO!! I WAS JUST TRYING TO OPEN IT NORMALLY!
That happens to you too, right?

reality sneaks up on you

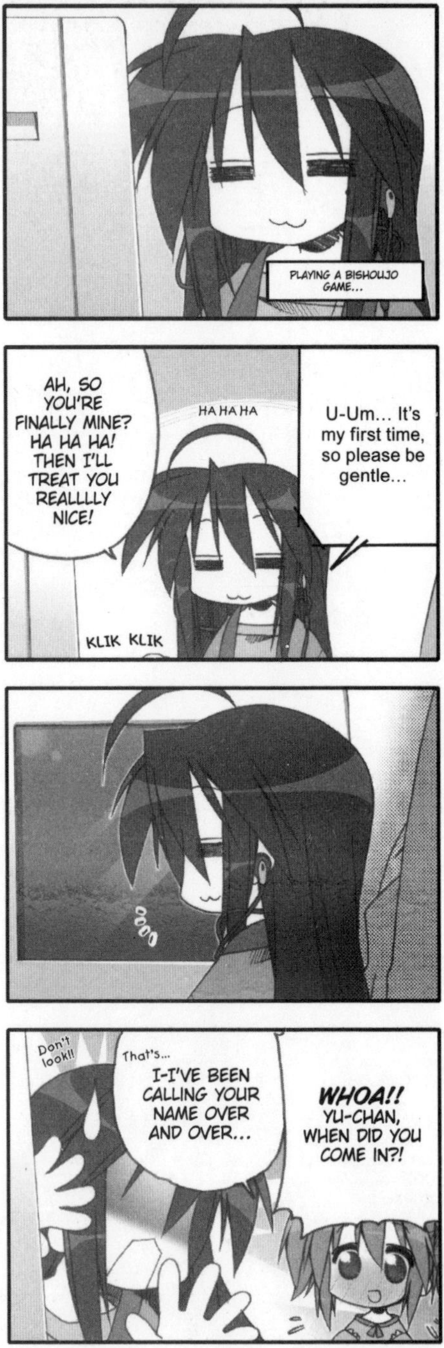
PLAYING A BISHOUJO GAME...
U-Um... It's my first time, so please be gentle...
HA HA HA
AH, SO YOU'RE FINALLY MINE? HA HA HA! THEN I'LL TREAT YOU REALLLLY NICE!
KLIK KLIK
WHOA!! YU-CHAN, WHEN DID YOU COME IN?!
That's...
I-I'VE BEEN CALLING YOUR NAME OVER AND OVER...
Don't look!!

a word of doubt

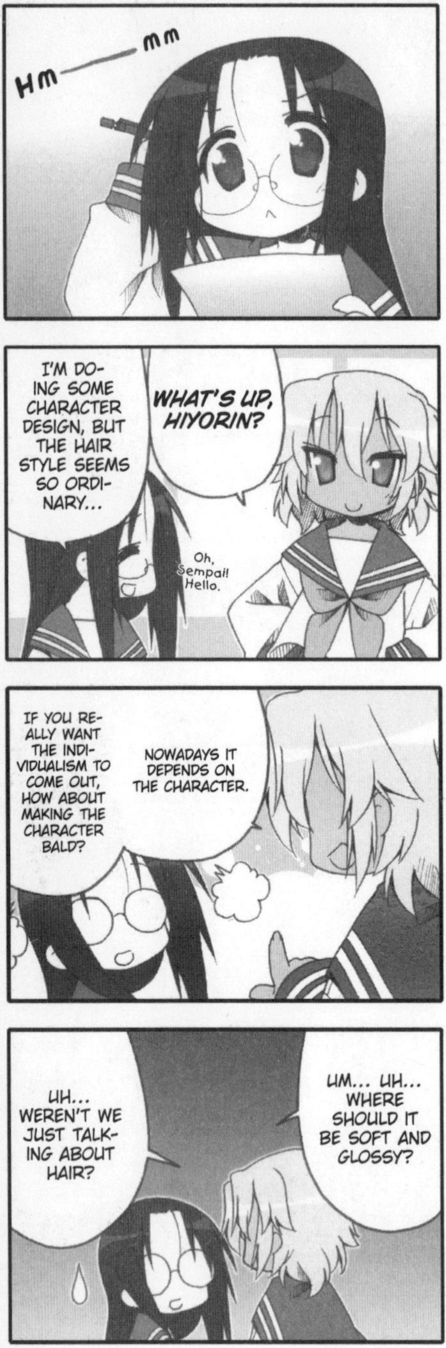
HM——MM
WHAT'S UP, HIYORIN?
I'M DO-ING SOME CHARACTER DESIGN, BUT THE HAIR STYLE SEEMS SO ORDI-NARY...
Oh, Sempai! Hello.
NOWADAYS IT DEPENDS ON THE CHARACTER.
IF YOU RE-ALLY WANT THE INDI-VIDUALISM TO COME OUT, HOW ABOUT MAKING THE CHARACTER BALD?
UM... UH... WHERE SHOULD IT BE SOFT AND GLOSSY?
UH... WEREN'T WE JUST TALK-ING ABOUT HAIR?

(SCHOOL'S) NICE OLDER SISTER

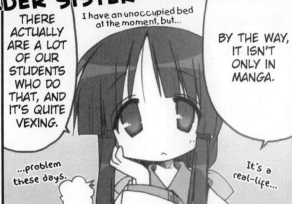

BY THE WAY, IT ISN'T ONLY IN MANGA.
It's a real-life...
...problem these days.
THERE ACTUALLY ARE A LOT OF OUR STUDENTS WHO DO THAT, AND IT'S QUITE VEXING.
I have an unoccupied bed at the moment, but...

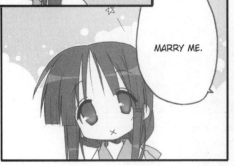

MARRY ME.

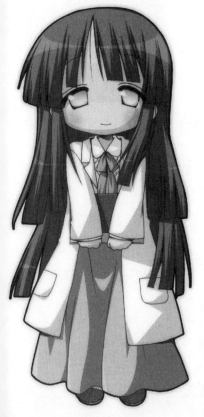

- Health Office Nurse
- Placid
- Protector

FUYUKI AMAHARA

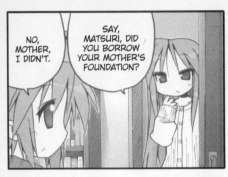

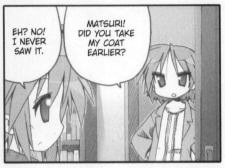

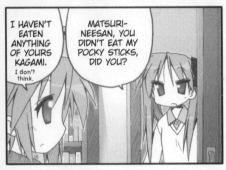

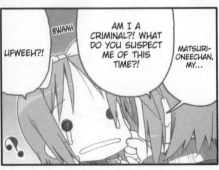

Lucky☆Star

episode 140
agreement and enthusiasm

● Comptiq, October 2007 issue

the face that comes to mind

SAY, MATSURI, DID YOU BORROW YOUR MOTHER'S FOUNDATION?
NO, MOTHER, I DIDN'T.
MATSURI! DID YOU TAKE MY COAT EARLIER?
EH? NO! I NEVER SAW IT.
MATSURI-NEESAN, YOU DIDN'T EAT MY POCKY STICKS, DID YOU?
I HAVEN'T EATEN ANYTHING OF YOURS KAGAMI.
I don't think.
MATSURI-ONEECHAN, MY...
AM I A CRIMINAL?! WHAT DO YOU SUSPECT ME OF THIS TIME?!
BWAAH
UFWEEH?!

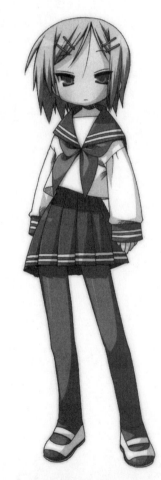

creativity

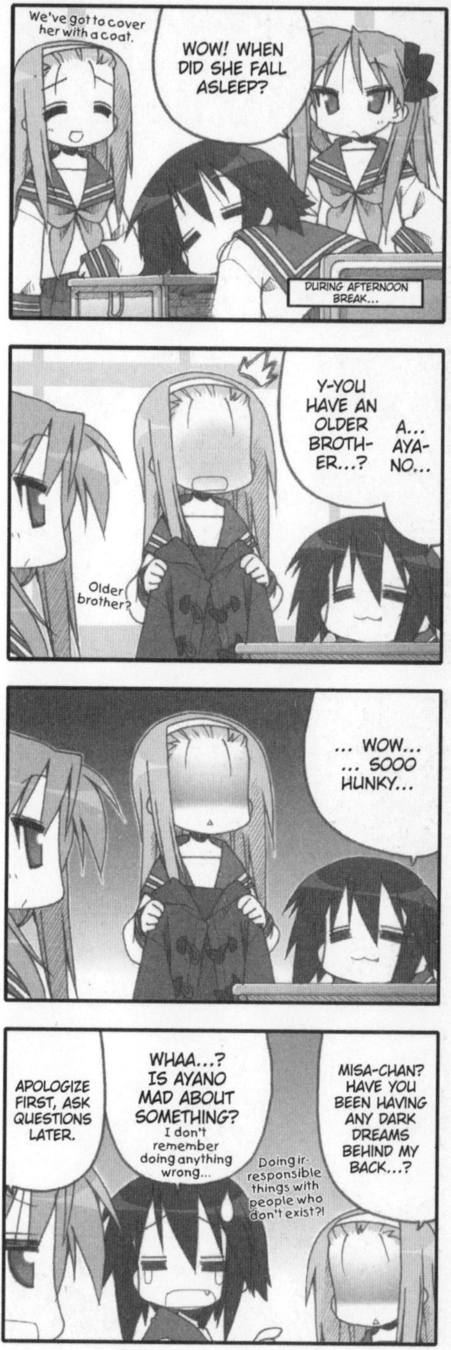
WOW! WHEN DID SHE FALL ASLEEP?
We've got to cover her with a coat.
DURING AFTERNOON BREAK...
A... AYA-NO...
Y-YOU HAVE AN OLDER BROTHER...?
Older brother?
... WOW... ... SOOO HUNKY...
MISA-CHAN? HAVE YOU BEEN HAVING ANY DARK DREAMS BEHIND MY BACK...?
Doing irresponsible things with people who don't exist?!
WHAA...? IS AYANO MAD ABOUT SOMETHING?
I don't remember doing anything wrong...
APOLOGIZE FIRST, ASK QUESTIONS LATER.

charge ahead

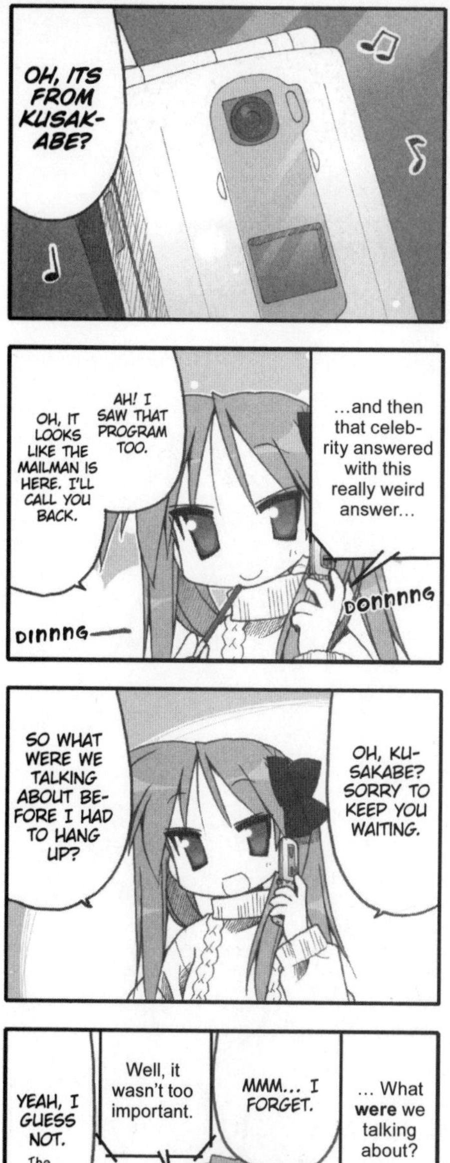
OH, ITS FROM KUSAKABE?
...and then that celebrity answered with this really weird answer...
AH! I SAW THAT PROGRAM TOO.
OH, IT LOOKS LIKE THE MAILMAN IS HERE. I'LL CALL YOU BACK.
DONNNNG
DINNNG——
OH, KUSAKABE? SORRY TO KEEP YOU WAITING.
SO WHAT WERE WE TALKING ABOUT BEFORE I HAD TO HANG UP?
... What were we talking about?
MMM... I FORGET.
Well, it wasn't too important.
YEAH, I GUESS NOT.
The same stuff as always.
Okay... Um... So...

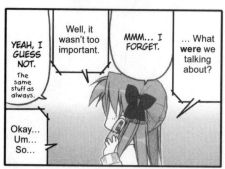

entertainer

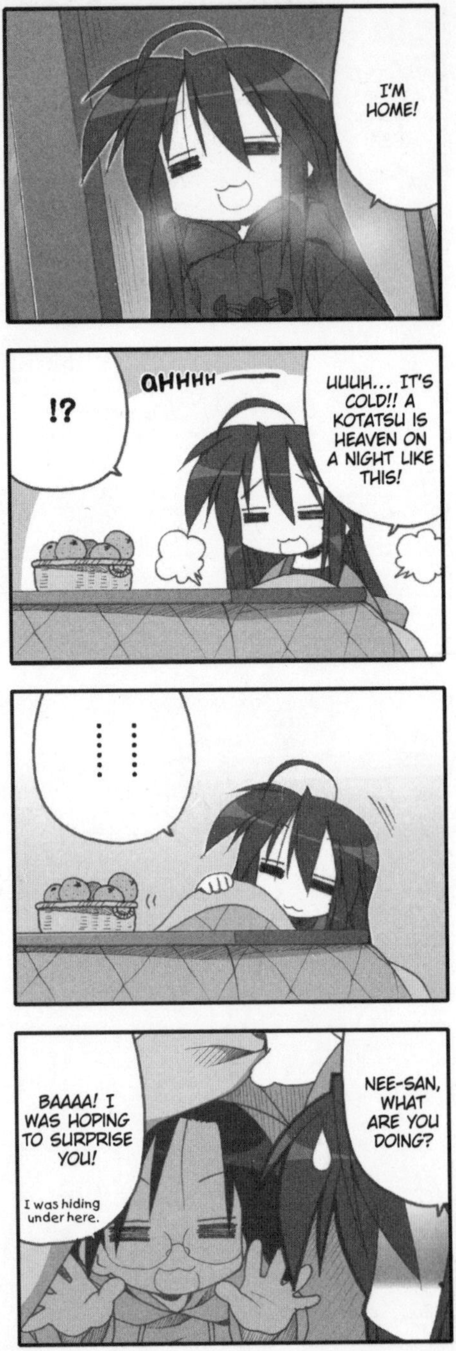
I'M HOME!
UUUH... IT'S COLD!! A KOTATSU IS HEAVEN ON A NIGHT LIKE THIS!
aHHHH—
!?
....
NEE-SAN, WHAT ARE YOU DOING?
BAAAA! I WAS HOPING TO SURPRISE YOU!
I was hiding under here.

a soul for practical jokes

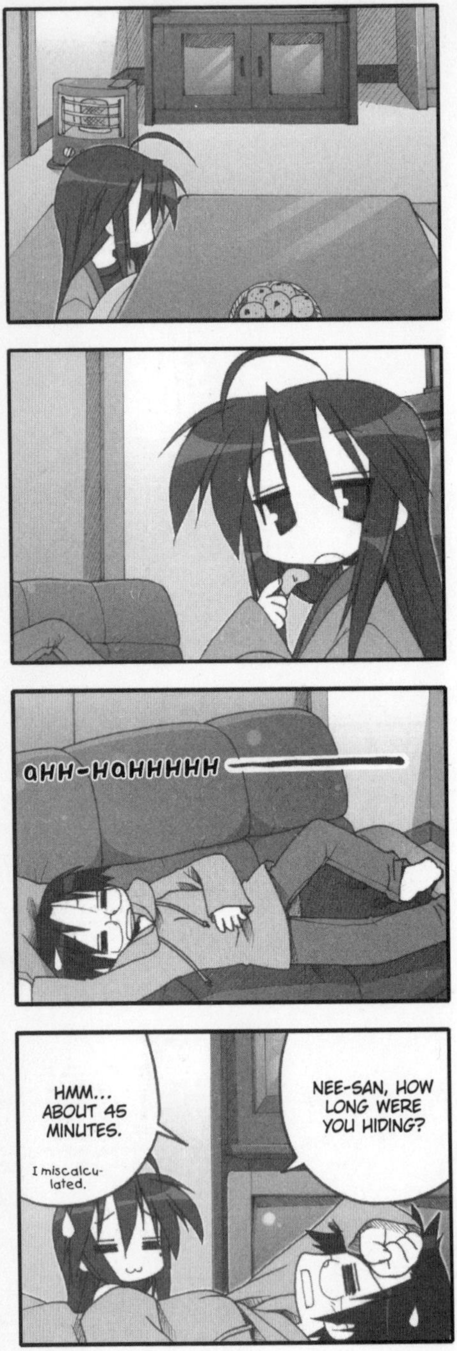
aHH-HaHHHHHH——
NEE-SAN, HOW LONG WERE YOU HIDING?
HMM... ABOUT 45 MINUTES.
I miscalcu-lated.

A LITTLE DEVIL WITH THE HEART OF AN ANGEL

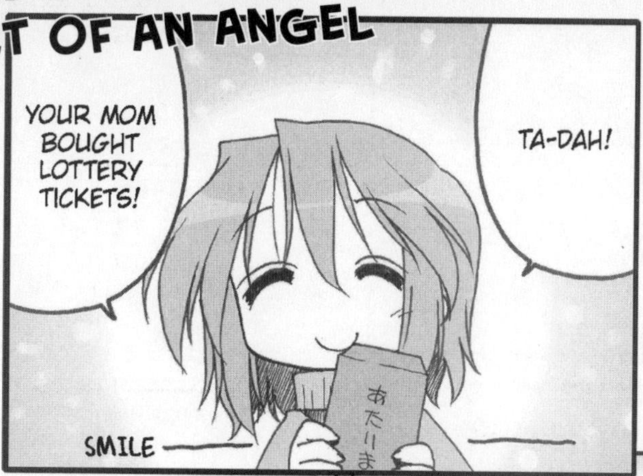
TA-DAH!
YOUR MOM BOUGHT LOTTERY TICKETS!
あたりま
SMILE

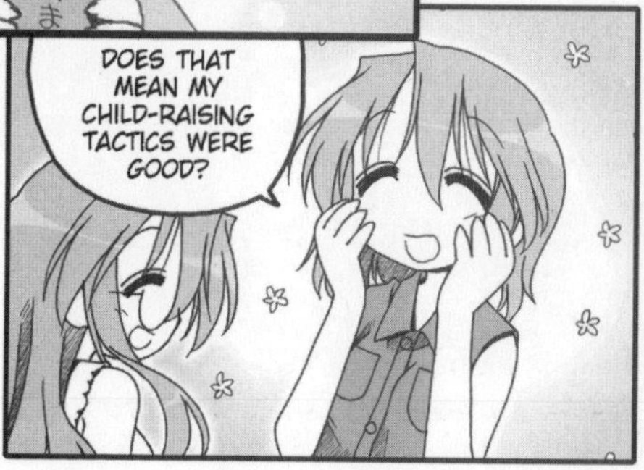
DOES THAT MEAN MY CHILD-RAISING TACTICS WERE GOOD?

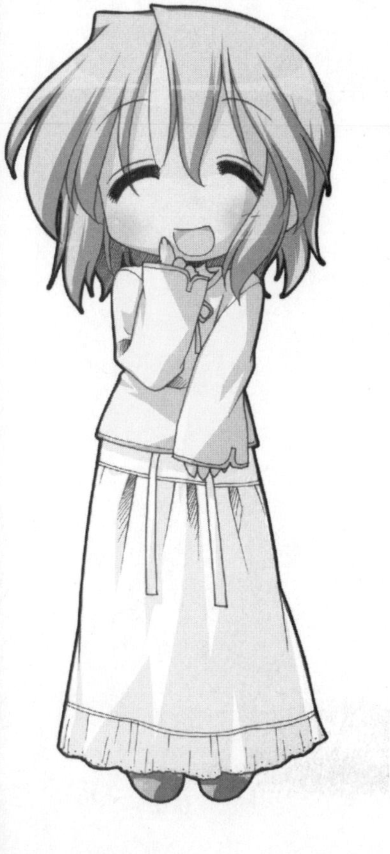

- Selfish
- Bigspender
- Fashionable

YUKARI TAKARA

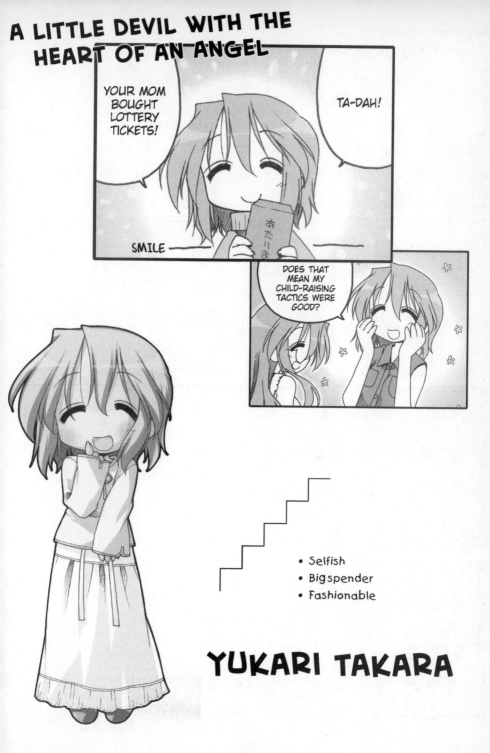

Lucky☆Star

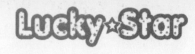

episode 141
cushy cushy

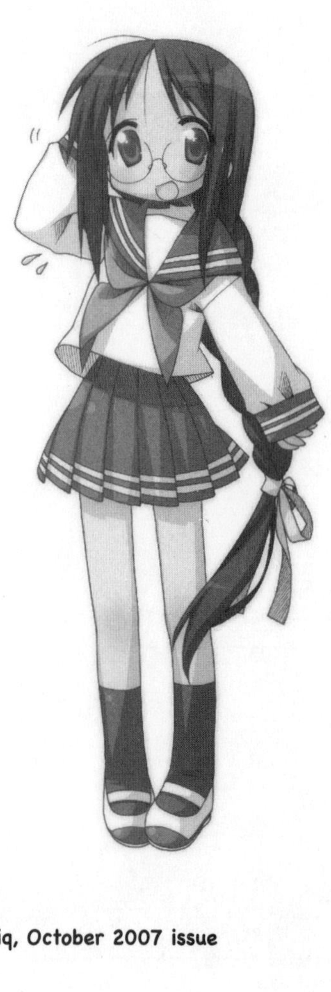

●Comptiq, October 2007 issue

both me and my partner

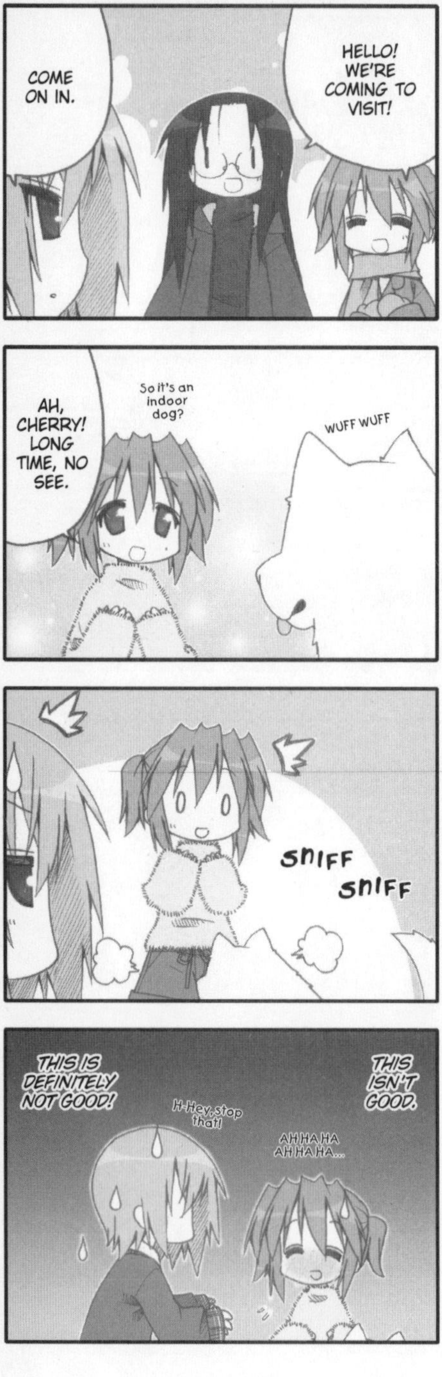

HELLO! WE'RE COMING TO VISIT!
COME ON IN.
WUFF WUFF
So it's an indoor dog?
AH, CHERRY! LONG TIME, NO SEE.
SNIFF
SNIFF
THIS ISN'T GOOD.
AH HA HA AH HA HA...
H-Hey, stop that!
THIS IS DEFINITELY NOT GOOD!

played with

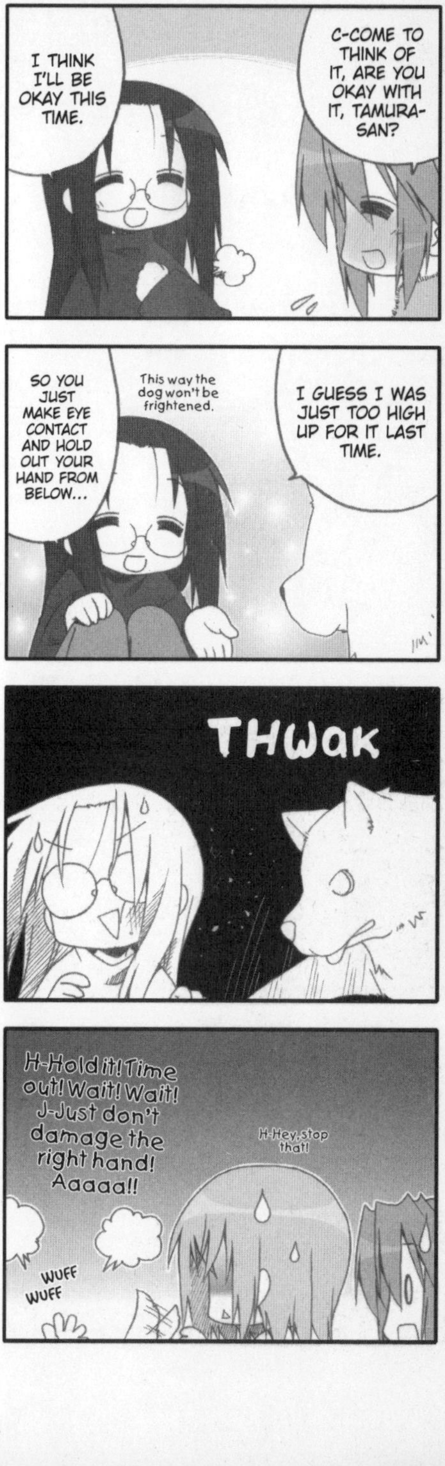
C-COME TO THINK OF IT, ARE YOU OKAY WITH IT, TAMURA-SAN?
I THINK I'LL BE OKAY THIS TIME.
I GUESS I WAS JUST TOO HIGH UP FOR IT LAST TIME.
This way the dog won't be frightened.
SO YOU JUST MAKE EYE CONTACT AND HOLD OUT YOUR HAND FROM BELOW...
THWak
H-Hold it! Time out! Wait! Wait! J-Just don't damage the right hand! Aaaaa!!
H-Hey, stop that!
WUFF WUFF

toyed with

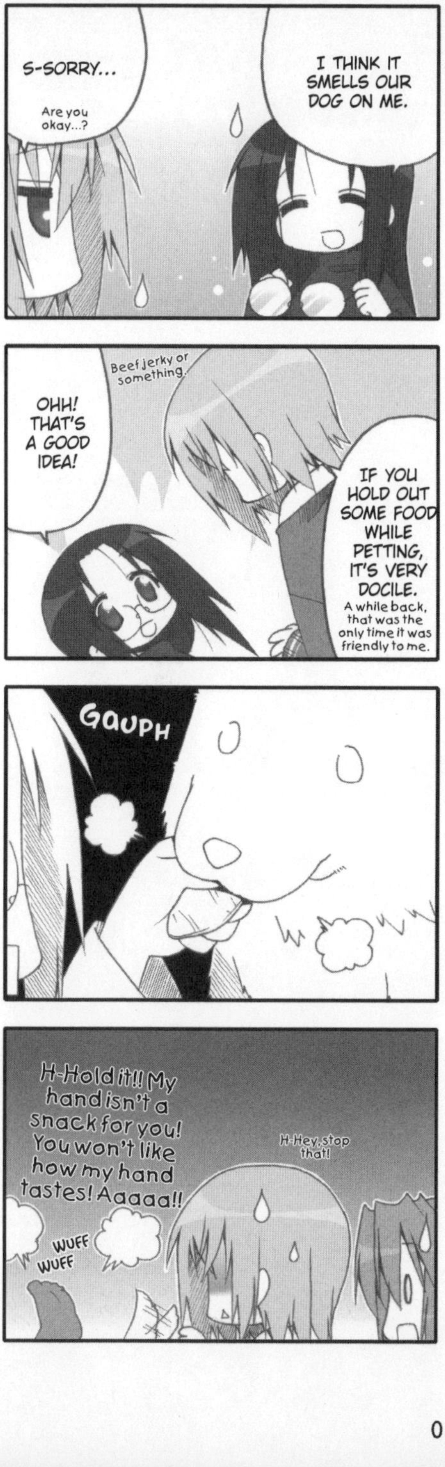
I THINK IT SMELLS OUR DOG ON ME.
S-SORRY...
Are you okay...?
IF YOU HOLD OUT SOME FOOD WHILE PETTING, IT'S VERY DOCILE.
A while back, that was the only time it was friendly to me.
Beef jerky or something...
OHH! THAT'S A GOOD IDEA!
GAUPH
H-Hold it!! My hand isn't a snack for you! You won't like how my hand tastes! Aaaaa!!
H-Hey, stop that!
WUFF WUFF

the feeling boiling up

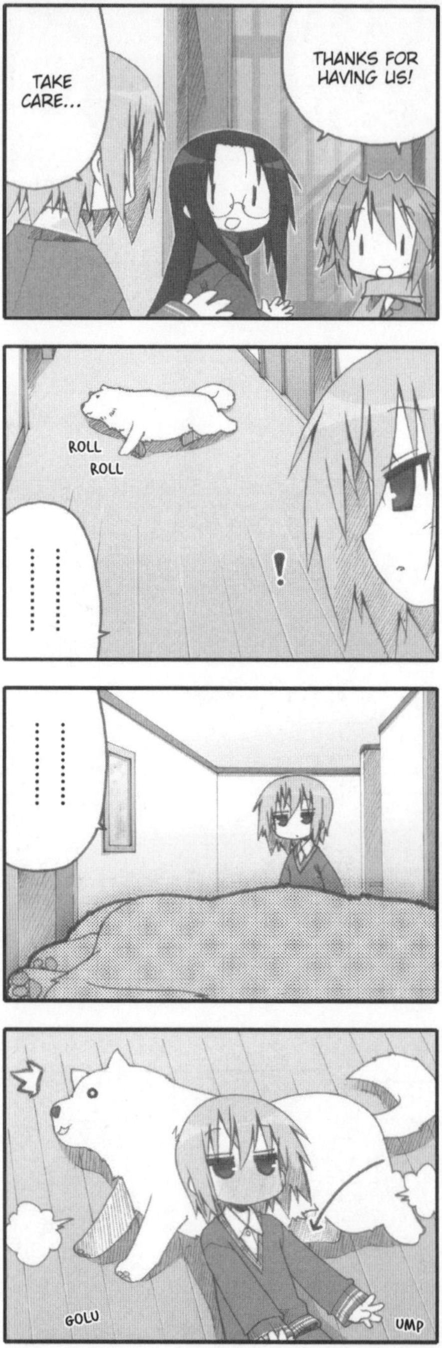
THANKS FOR HAVING US!
TAKE CARE...
ROLL
ROLL
!
......
......
UMP
GOLU

sighting

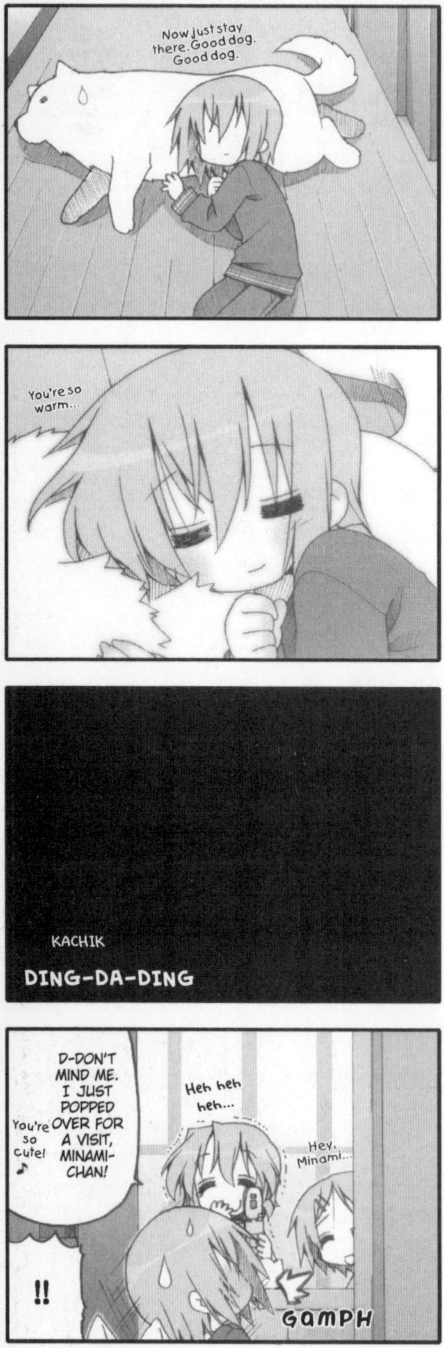
Now just stay there. Good dog. Good dog.
You're so warm...
KACHIK
DING-DA-DING
Hey, Minami...
Heh heh heh...
GAMPH
D-DON'T MIND ME. I JUST POPPED OVER FOR A VISIT, MINAMI-CHAN!
You're so cute! ♪
!!

THE DAUGHTER IS A CHIP OFF THE FATHER'S BLOCK

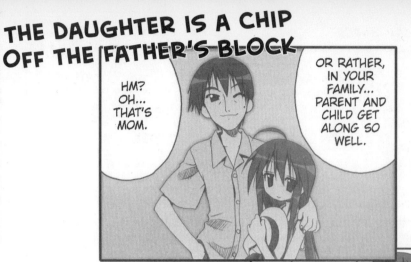

OR RATHER, IN YOUR FAMILY... PARENT AND CHILD GET ALONG SO WELL.
HM? OH... THAT'S MOM.

I ABSOLUTELY FORBID IT!!!
I will accept no "boyfriend" from you!!
DAD, DON'T YOU SEE THE HYPOCRISY IN WHAT YOU'RE SAYING?

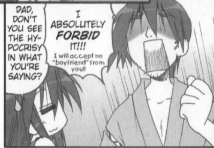

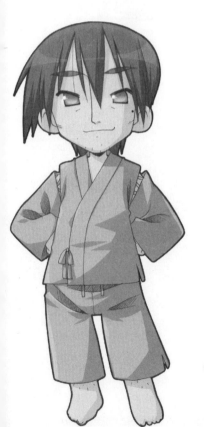

- A married otaku
- Workman's clothes
- Five-o'clock shadow

SOUJIROU IZUMI

Lucky☆Star

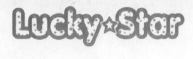

episode 142
dark ages

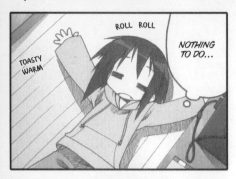

● Comp Ace, Vol. 013 May 2007 issue

requirements before one acts

NOTHING TO DO...
ROLL ROLL
TOASTY WARM
I'M SICK OF MY GAMES, AND I'VE READ ALL MY MANGA.
UMPH
NO GUESTS AND NOBODY'S CALLING ON THE PHONE. WHAT'LL I DO?
This is soooo boring!
HUH?
OH, NO...!!
!?
I HAD SOME AD-DITIONAL HOME-WORK! I'D FORGOTTEN ALL ABOUT IT!
I wonder if I can finish it?
RNGG
DARN IT... JUST WHEN I FINALLY FIGURED OUT SOME-THING TO DO...
And the phone too?
RINNNNG
DINNG DONNG
Is any-body home?

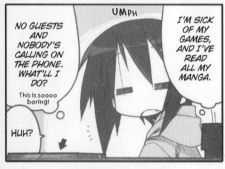

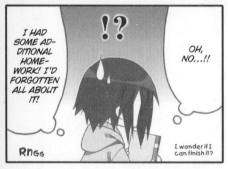

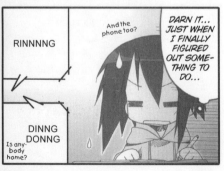

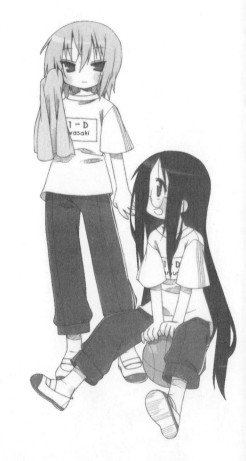

the studied history

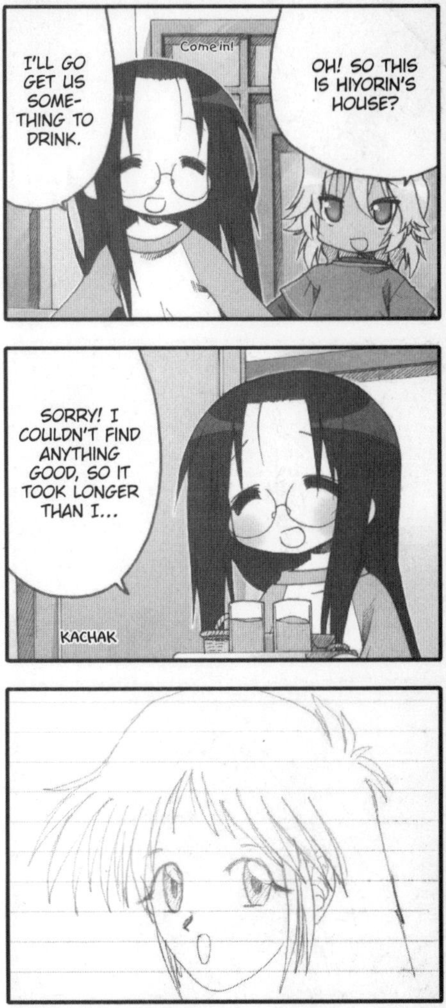
OH! SO THIS IS HIYORIN'S HOUSE?
Come in!
I'LL GO GET US SOME-THING TO DRINK.
SORRY! I COULDN'T FIND ANYTHING GOOD, SO IT TOOK LONGER THAN I...
KACHAK
HEH HEH...
SO HIYORIN WENT THROUGH THIS PHASE TOO...
Maybe I should take up draw-ing...
S-SOMEBODY PLEASE KILL ME...
KILL ME NOW! QUICK AND PAINFULLY!
HEHN HEHN
AAAAAAA
Why are you going through my things?

code

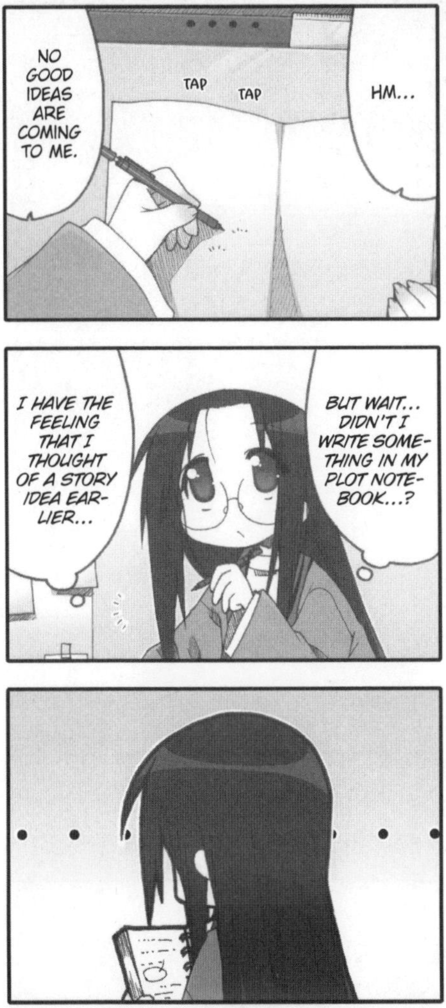
HM...
TAP
TAP
NO GOOD IDEAS ARE COMING TO ME.
BUT WAIT... DIDN'T I WRITE SOME-THING IN MY PLOT NOTE-BOOK...?
I HAVE THE FEELING THAT I THOUGHT OF A STORY IDEA EAR-LIER...
WHEN I GET AN IDEA, I SHOULDN'T JUST RUSH TO WRITE DOWN THE MAIN POINTS AS FAST AS I CAN... I SHOULD WRITE IT IN DETAIL.
BECAUSE NOW I HAVE NO IDEA WHAT I WAS WRITING ABOUT!!

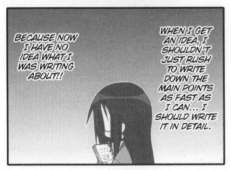

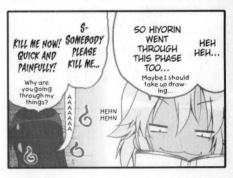

japanese reading

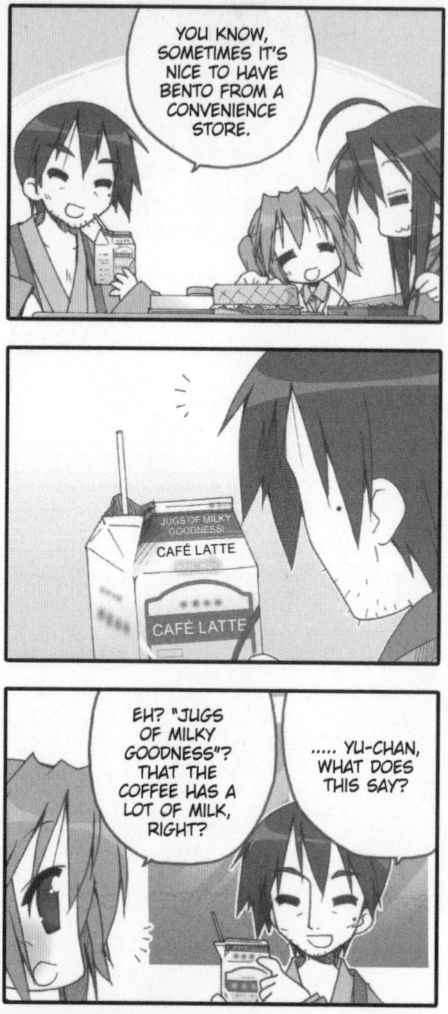
YOU KNOW, SOMETIMES IT'S NICE TO HAVE BENTO FROM A CONVENIENCE STORE.
JUGS OF MILKY GOODNESS!
CAFÉ LATTE
CAFÉ LATTE
..... YU-CHAN, WHAT DOES THIS SAY?
EH? "JUGS OF MILKY GOODNESS"? THAT THE COFFEE HAS A LOT OF MILK, RIGHT?
YEAH... YEAH... THAT'S WHAT IT MEANS, HUH?
YOUR DAD IS GETTING WORSE IN HIS OLD AGE.
I interpreted it differently just by default.
NO MATTER HOW IT'S READ, THE FACT THAT I ASKED YU-CHAN MEANS I'M CLOSE TO THE END!!
That can be considered sexual harassment, you know!

an autumn festival

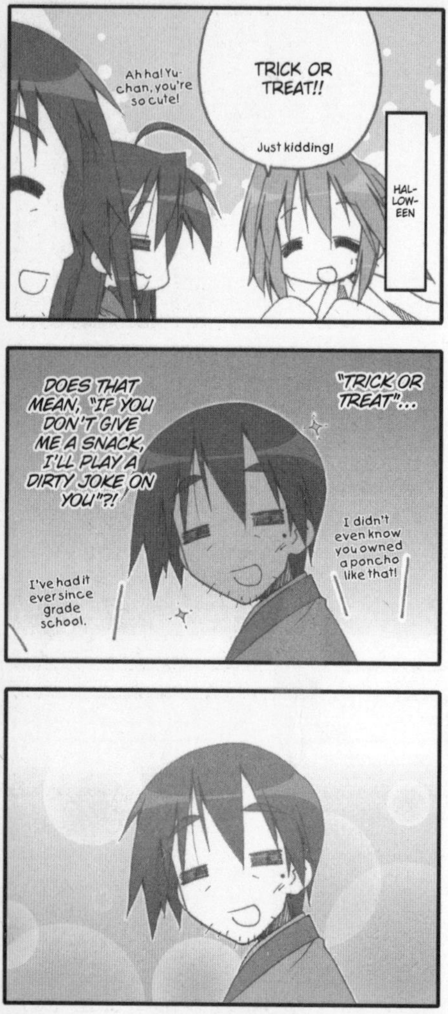
HAL-LOW-EEN
TRICK OR TREAT!!
Just kidding!
Ah ha! Yu-chan, you're so cute!
"TRICK OR TREAT"...
DOES THAT MEAN, "IF YOU DON'T GIVE ME A SNACK, I'LL PLAY A DIRTY JOKE ON YOU"?!
I didn't even know you owned a poncho like that!
I've had it ever since grade school.
I WANT YU-CHAN TO PLAY DIRTY JOKES ON ME! OR ACTUALLY, I WANT TO BE THE ONE TO PLAY...!!
DAD, YOU LOOK REALLLLLY TIRED.
Is it because you're close to deadline time?

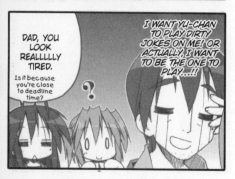

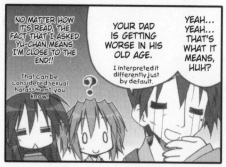

EVERYBODY'S SUPER-IDOL

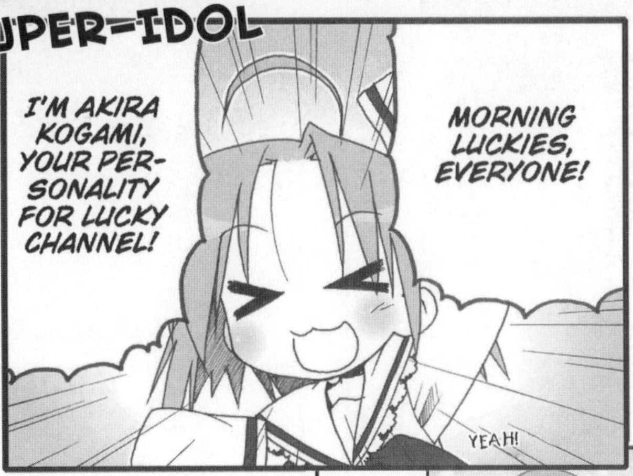
MORNING LUCKIES, EVERYONE!
I'M AKIRA KOGAMI, YOUR PER-SONALITY FOR LUCKY CHANNEL!
YEAH!

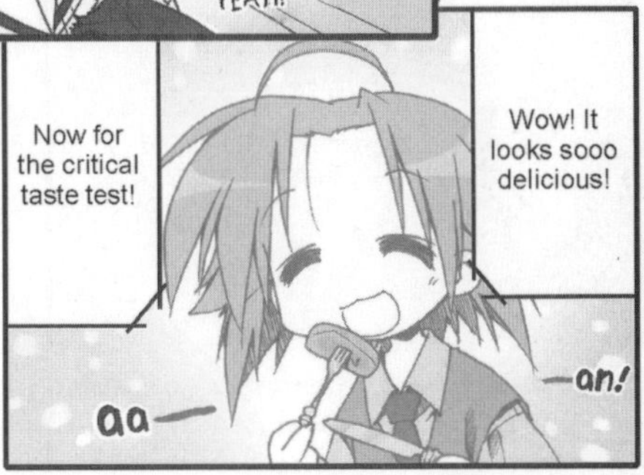
Wow! It looks sooo delicious!
Now for the critical taste test!
—an!
aa—

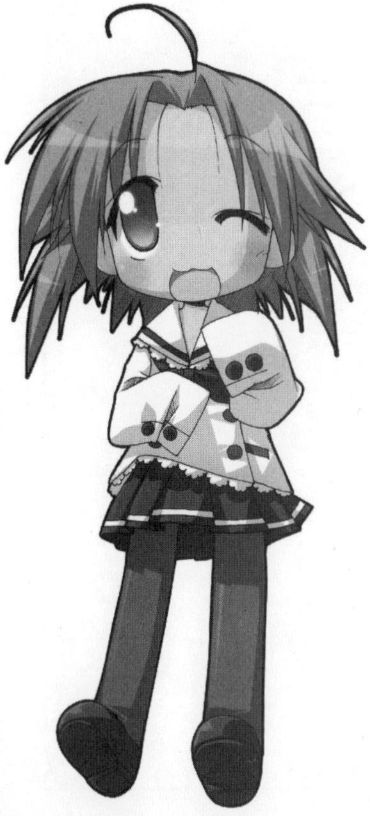

- 14 years old
- Idol
- Evil...

AKIRA KOGAMI

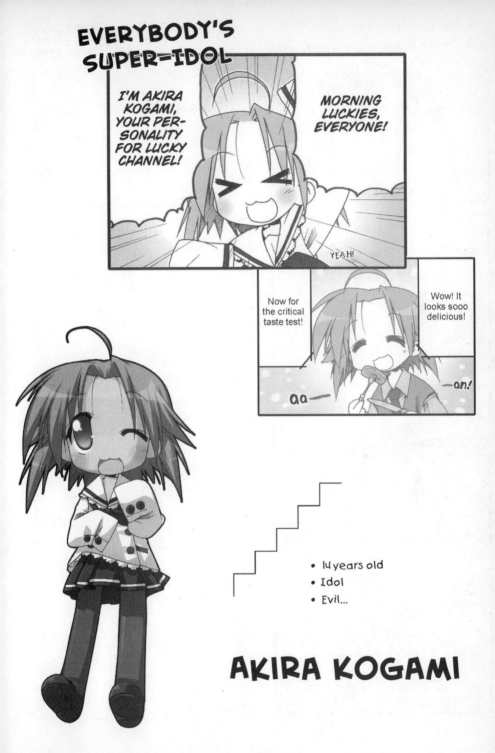

Lucky☆Star

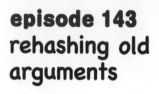

episode 143
rehashing old arguments

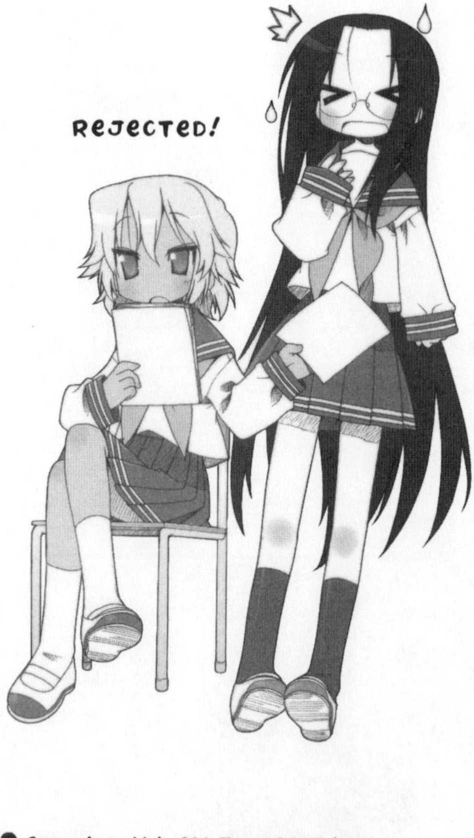

REJECTED!

● Comp Ace, Vol. 014 June 2007 issue

a decision after two years

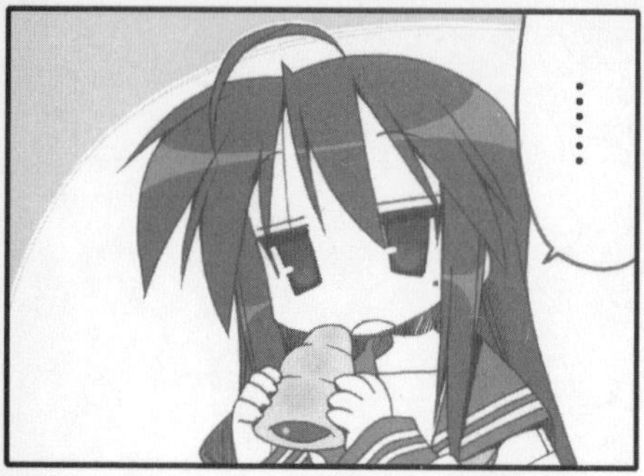

......

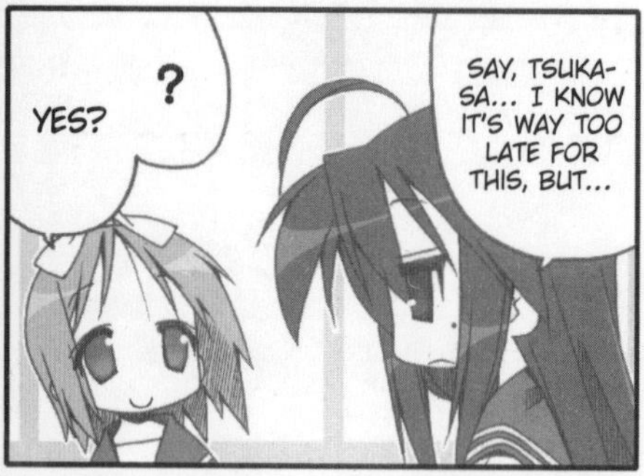

SAY, TSUKA-SA... I KNOW IT'S WAY TOO LATE FOR THIS, BUT...
?
YES?

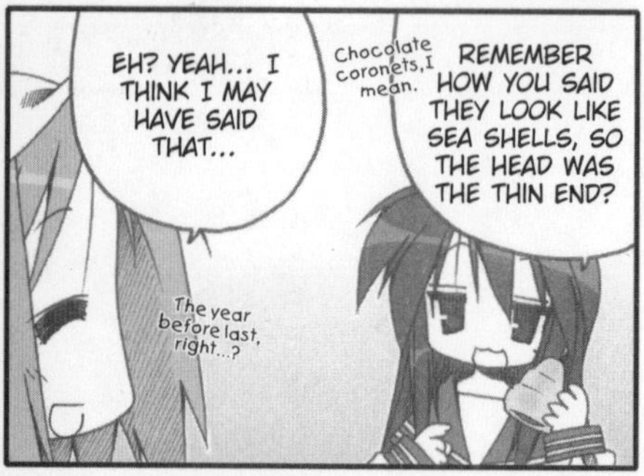

REMEMBER HOW YOU SAID THEY LOOK LIKE SEA SHELLS, SO THE HEAD WAS THE THIN END?
Chocolate coronets, I mean.
EH? YEAH... I THINK I MAY HAVE SAID THAT...
The year before last, right...?

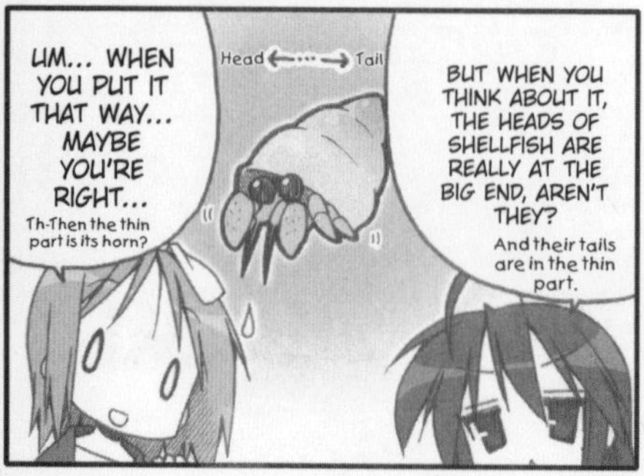

BUT WHEN YOU THINK ABOUT IT, THE HEADS OF SHELLFISH ARE REALLY AT THE BIG END, AREN'T THEY?
And their tails are in the thin part.
Head ←···→ Tail
UM... WHEN YOU PUT IT THAT WAY... MAYBE YOU'RE RIGHT...
Th-Then the thin part is its horn?

the new enemy

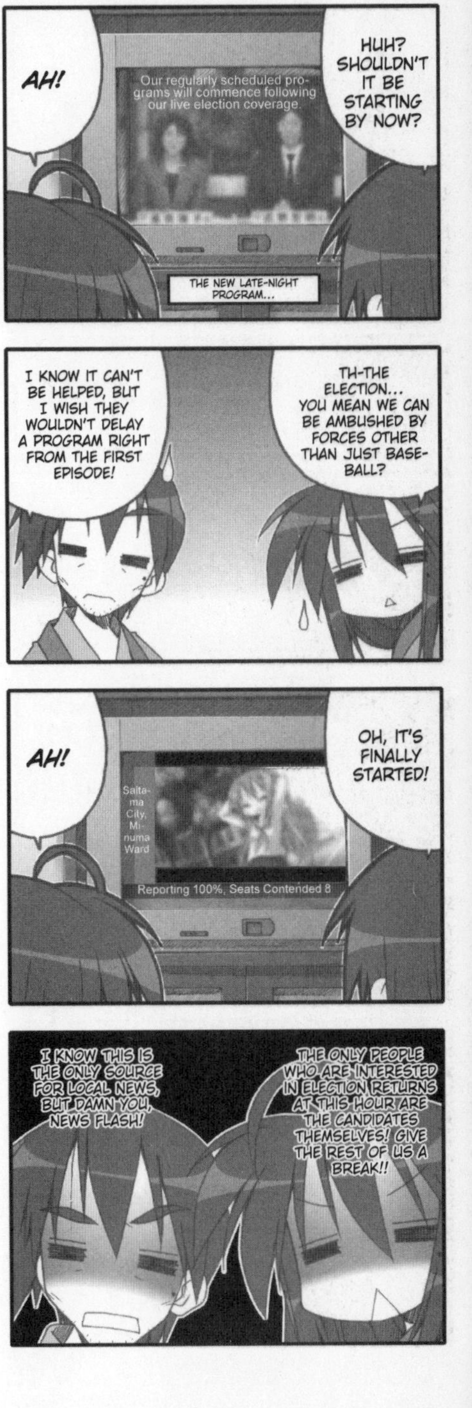
HUH? SHOULDN'T IT BE STARTING BY NOW?
AH!
Our regularly scheduled programs will commence following our live election coverage.
THE NEW LATE-NIGHT PROGRAM...
TH-THE ELECTION... YOU MEAN WE CAN BE AMBUSHED BY FORCES OTHER THAN JUST BASEBALL?
I KNOW IT CAN'T BE HELPED, BUT I WISH THEY WOULDN'T DELAY A PROGRAM RIGHT FROM THE FIRST EPISODE!
OH, IT'S FINALLY STARTED!
AH!
Saitama City, Minuma Ward
Reporting 100%, Seats Contended 8
THE ONLY PEOPLE WHO ARE INTERESTED IN ELECTION RETURNS AT THIS HOUR ARE THE CANDIDATES THEMSELVES! GIVE THE REST OF US A BREAK!!
I KNOW THIS IS THE ONLY SOURCE FOR LOCAL NEWS, BUT DAMN YOU, NEWS FLASH!

impulse

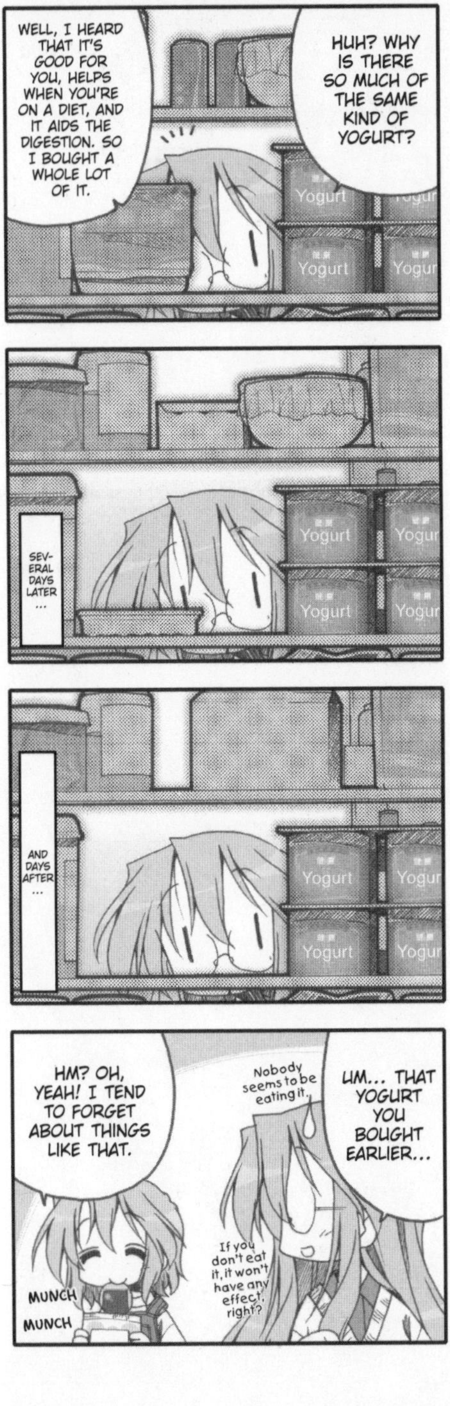
HUH? WHY IS THERE SO MUCH OF THE SAME KIND OF YOGURT?
WELL, I HEARD THAT IT'S GOOD FOR YOU, HELPS WHEN YOU'RE ON A DIET, AND IT AIDS THE DIGESTION. SO I BOUGHT A WHOLE LOT OF IT.
Yogurt
SEVERAL DAYS LATER ...
Yogurt
AND DAYS AFTER ...
Yogurt
UM... THAT YOGURT YOU BOUGHT EARLIER...
Nobody seems to be eating it.
HM? OH, YEAH! I TEND TO FORGET ABOUT THINGS LIKE THAT.
If you don't eat it, it won't have any effect, right?
MUNCH MUNCH

all or nothing

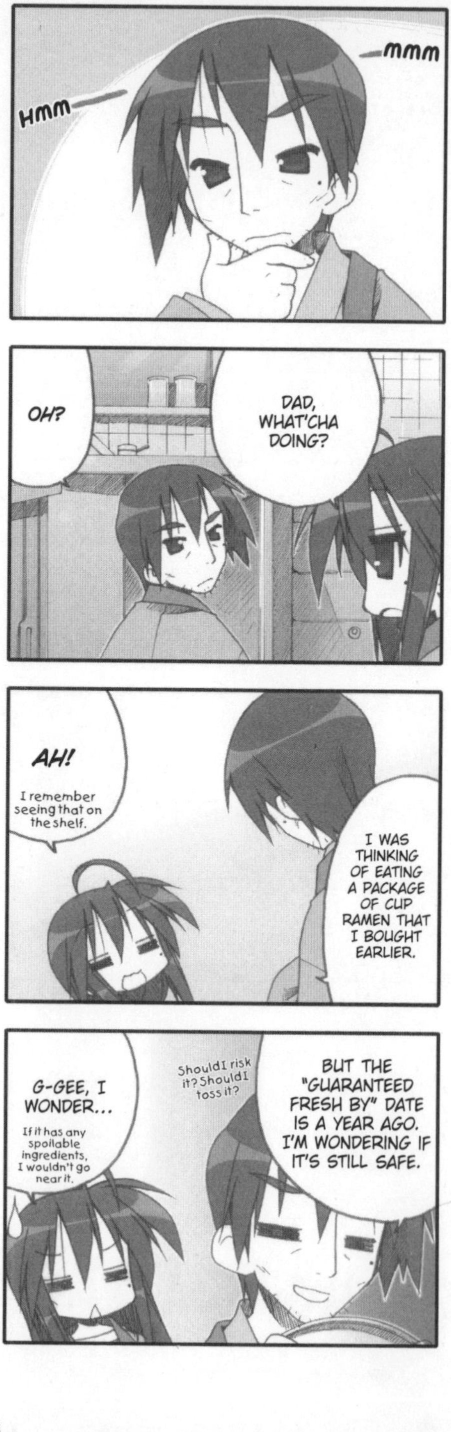

Hmm——
—mmm
DAD, WHAT'CHA DOING?
OH?
I WAS THINKING OF EATING A PACKAGE OF CUP RAMEN THAT I BOUGHT EARLIER.
AH!
I remember seeing that on the shelf.
BUT THE "GUARANTEED FRESH BY" DATE IS A YEAR AGO. I'M WONDERING IF IT'S STILL SAFE.
Should I risk it? Should I toss it?
G-GEE, I WONDER...
If it has any spoilable ingredients, I wouldn't go near it.

pitiful

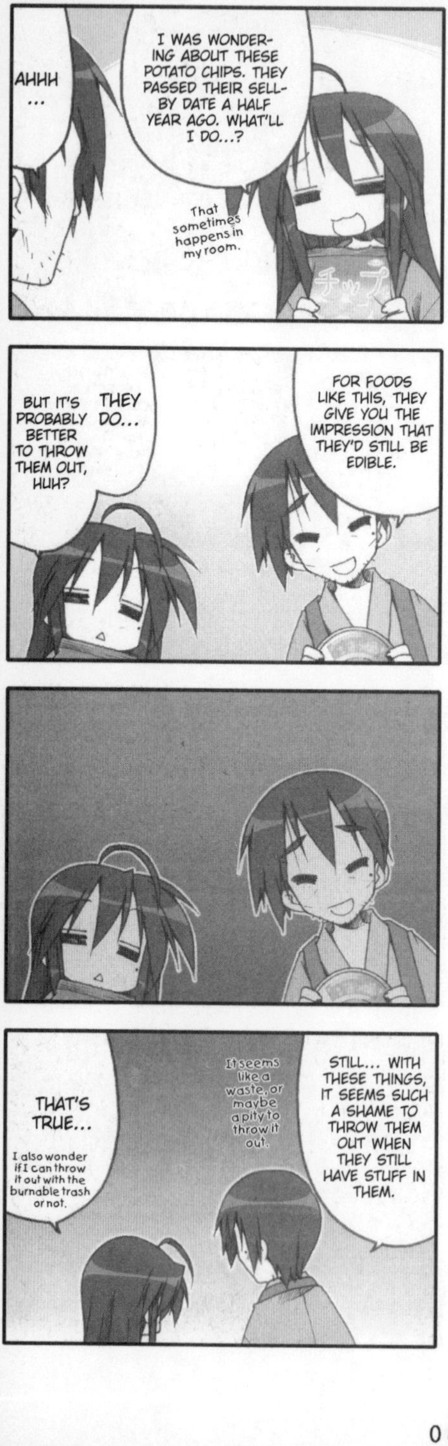

I WAS WONDERING ABOUT THESE POTATO CHIPS. THEY PASSED THEIR SELL-BY DATE A HALF YEAR AGO. WHAT'LL I DO...?
That sometimes happens in my room.
チップ
AHHH ...
FOR FOODS LIKE THIS, THEY GIVE YOU THE IMPRESSION THAT THEY'D STILL BE EDIBLE.
THEY DO...
BUT IT'S PROBABLY BETTER TO THROW THEM OUT, HUH?
STILL... WITH THESE THINGS, IT SEEMS SUCH A SHAME TO THROW THEM OUT WHEN THEY STILL HAVE STUFF IN THEM.
It seems like a waste, or maybe a pity to throw it out.
THAT'S TRUE...
I also wonder if I can throw it out with the burnable trash or not.

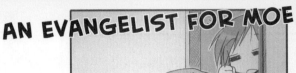

AN EVANGELIST FOR MOE

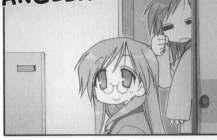

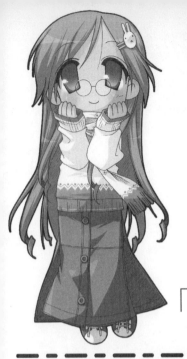

- Working girl
- Loves moe characters
- Loves doujinshi

HINATA MIYAKAWA

HARD WORKER WHO THINKS OF HER SISTER

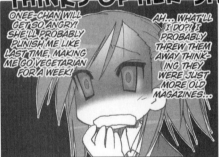

AH... WHAT'LL I DO?! I PROBABLY THREW THEM AWAY THINK-ING THEY WERE JUST MORE OLD MAGAZINES...
ONEE-CHAN WILL GET SO ANGRY! SHE'LL PROBABLY PUNISH ME LIKE LAST TIME, MAKING ME GO VEGETARIAN FOR A WEEK!

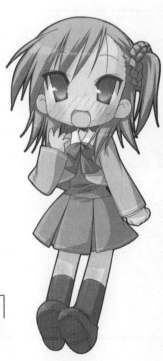

- Grade-schoolstudent
- Impoverished
- Loves to eat meat

HIKAGE MIYAKAWA

Lucky☆Star

episode 144
illogical

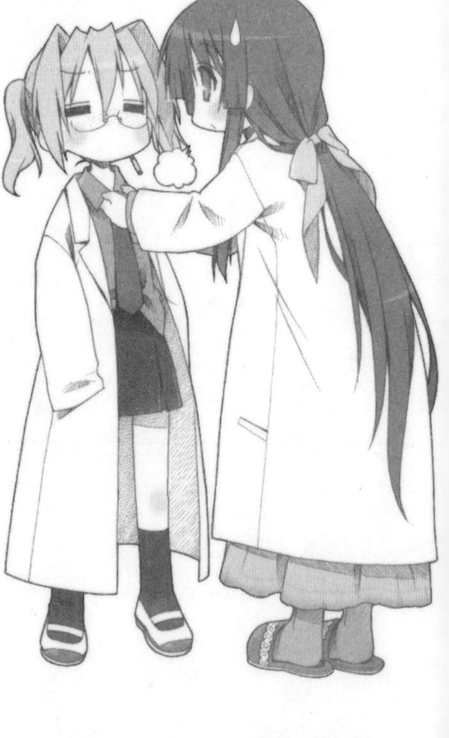

● Comp Ace, Vol. 015, July 2007 issue

really, it isn't like that

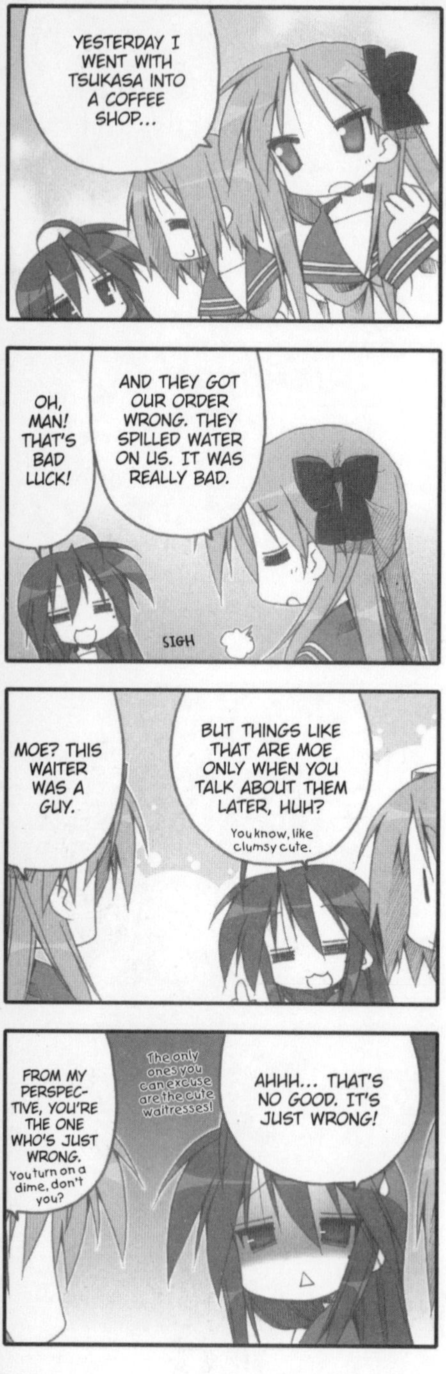
YESTERDAY I WENT WITH TSUKASA INTO A COFFEE SHOP...
AND THEY GOT OUR ORDER WRONG. THEY SPILLED WATER ON US. IT WAS REALLY BAD.
OH, MAN! THAT'S BAD LUCK!
SIGH
BUT THINGS LIKE THAT ARE MOE ONLY WHEN YOU TALK ABOUT THEM LATER, HUH?
You know, like clumsy cute.
MOE? THIS WAITER WAS A GUY.
AHHH... THAT'S NO GOOD. IT'S JUST WRONG!
The only ones you can excuse are the cute waitresses!
FROM MY PERSPECTIVE, YOU'RE THE ONE WHO'S JUST WRONG.
You turn on a dime, don't you?

impression

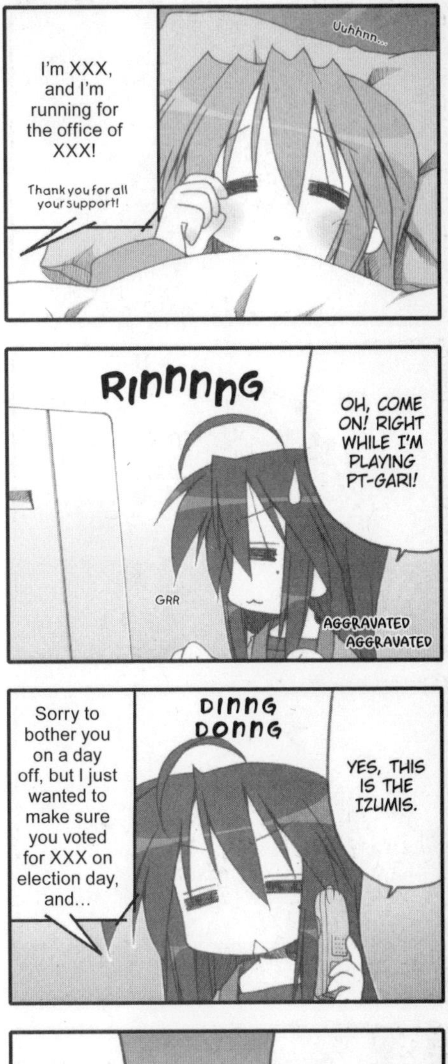
Uuhhnn...
I'm XXX, and I'm running for the office of XXX!
Thank you for all your support!
RINNNNG
OH, COME ON! RIGHT WHILE I'M PLAYING PT-GARI!
GRR
AGGRAVATED AGGRAVATED
DINNG DONNG
YES, THIS IS THE IZUMIS.
Sorry to bother you on a day off, but I just wanted to make sure you voted for XXX on election day, and...
IT SEEMS KIND OF LIKE OVERABUN-DANCE OF POLITICAL ADVERTISEMENTS ON OUR DAY OFF MAKES ME LESS ANXIOUS TO VOTE AT ALL.
Not that I'm of vot-ing age, though...
Don't you ever think of it that way?
T-TRUE... THEY JUST WANT YOU TO REMEMBER THEIR NAMES NO MATTER WHAT YOU REMEMBER IT FOR.

one additional rule

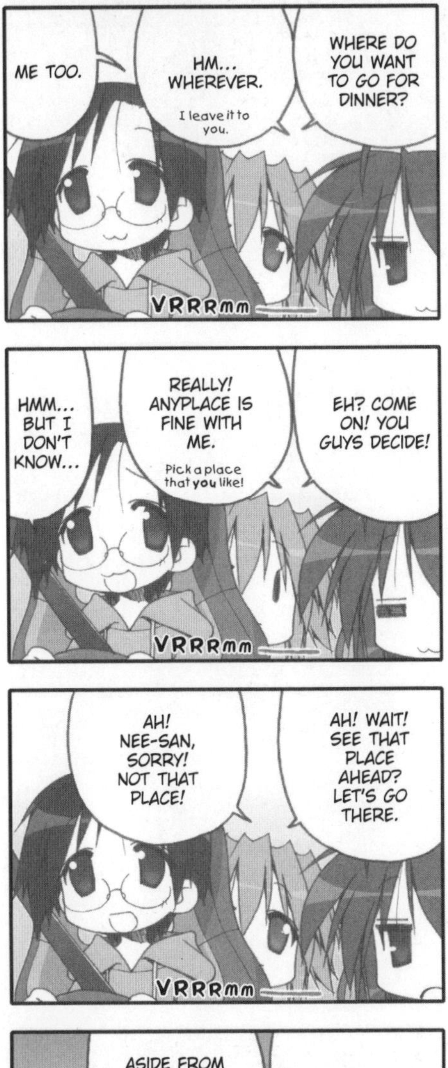
WHERE DO YOU WANT TO GO FOR DINNER?
HM... WHEREVER.
I leave it to you.
ME TOO.
VRRRmm
EH? COME ON! YOU GUYS DECIDE!
REALLY! ANYPLACE IS FINE WITH ME.
Pick a place that you like!
HMM... BUT I DON'T KNOW...
VRRRmm
AH! WAIT! SEE THAT PLACE AHEAD? LET'S GO THERE.
AH! NEE-SAN, SORRY! NOT THAT PLACE!
VRRRmm
....
OKAY, THEN. WHERE?
ASIDE FROM THAT PLACE BACK THERE, ANYPLACE IS FINE.
VRRRmm

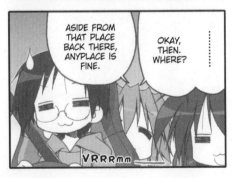

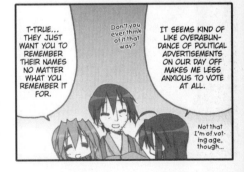

wait! waiiit!

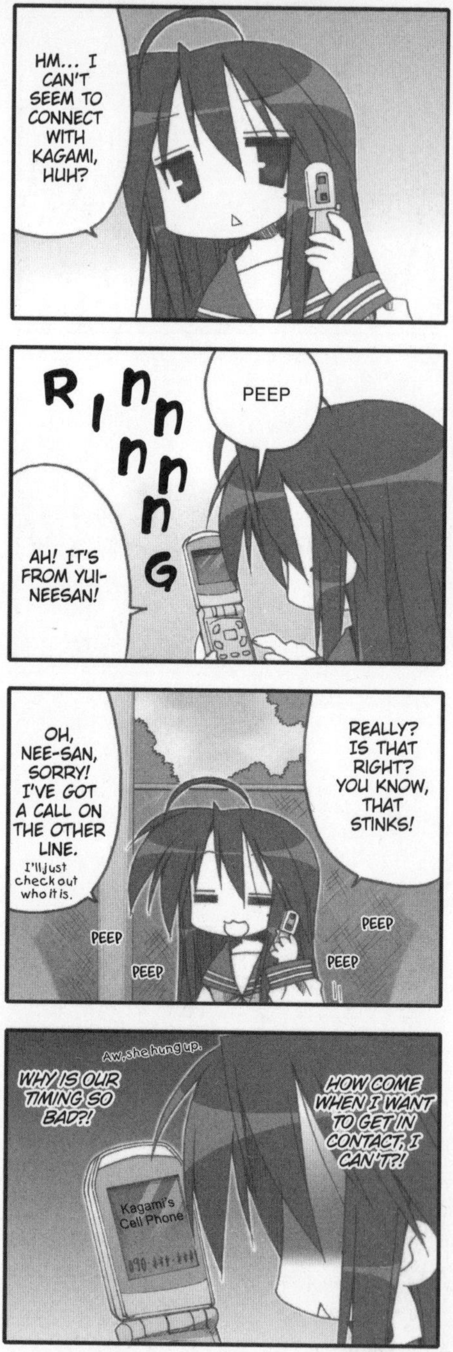
HM... I CAN'T SEEM TO CONNECT WITH KAGAMI, HUH?
PEEP
RInnnnnG
AH! IT'S FROM YUI-NEESAN!
REALLY? IS THAT RIGHT? YOU KNOW, THAT STINKS!
PEEP
PEEP
OH, NEE-SAN, SORRY! I'VE GOT A CALL ON THE OTHER LINE.
I'll just check out who it is.
PEEP
PEEP
HOW COME WHEN I WANT TO GET IN CONTACT, I CAN'T?!
Aw, she hung up.
WHY IS OUR TIMING SO BAD?!
Kagami's Cell Phone

just try connecting

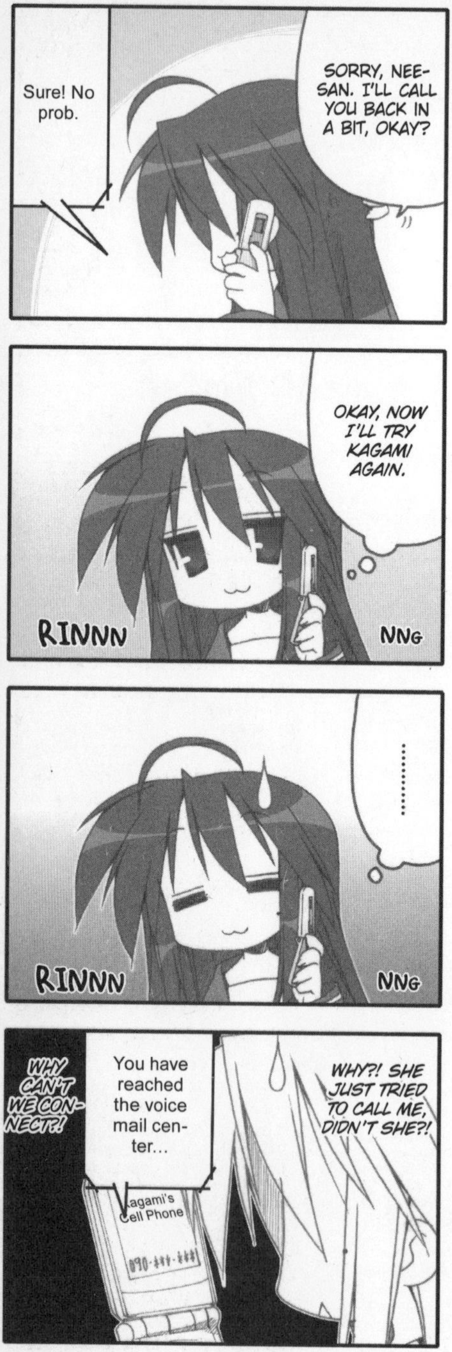
SORRY, NEE-SAN. I'LL CALL YOU BACK IN A BIT, OKAY?
Sure! No prob.
OKAY, NOW I'LL TRY KAGAMI AGAIN.
NNG
RINNN
....
NNG
RINNN
WHY?! SHE JUST TRIED TO CALL ME, DIDN'T SHE?!
You have reached the voice mail center...
Kagami's Cell Phone
WHY CAN'T WE CONNECT?!

Lucky☆Star

episode 145
baby adults

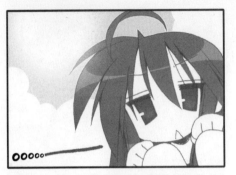

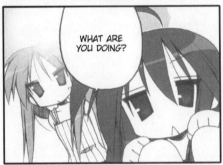

● Comp Ace, August 2007 issue

a little thing

OOOOo
WHAT ARE YOU DOING?
RIBBT
RIBBT
NOTHING. I WAS JUST LOOKING AT THE TAD-POLES, AND IT SUDDENLY STRUCK ME.
WHERE WERE THEY IN WINTER OR BEFORE THEY FILLED THIS PADDY WITH WATER?
It's like they suddenly come out the minute they put water in the paddy.
JEEE——EEET
JEEE——EEET
AHHH...
Yeah, I guess.

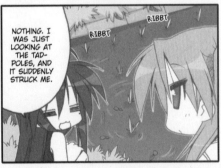

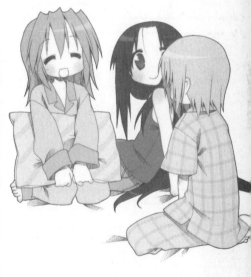

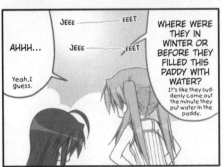

lost magic

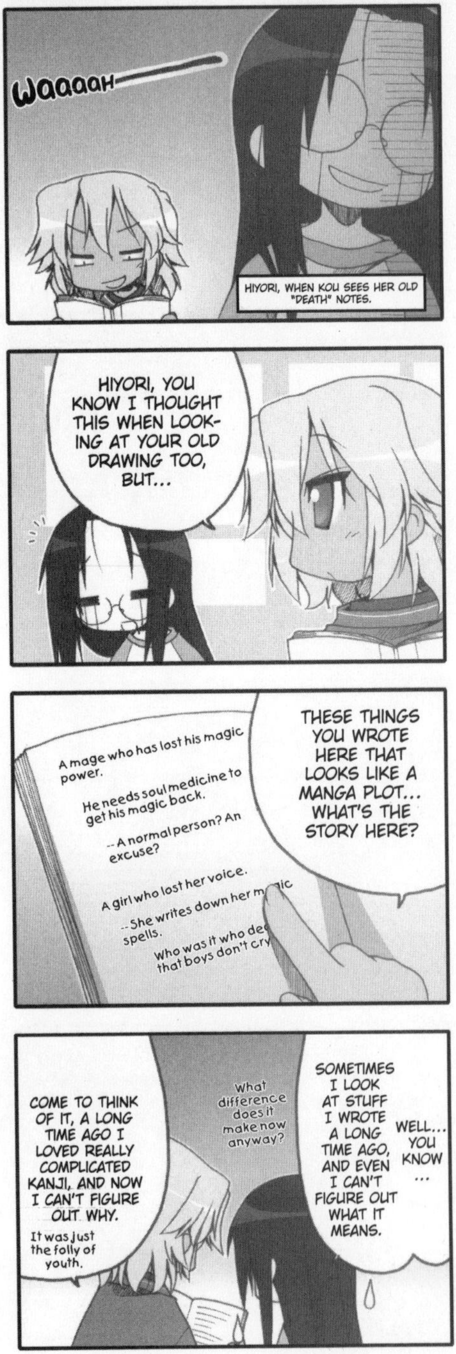
Waaaah
HIYORI, WHEN KOU SEES HER OLD "DEATH" NOTES.
HIYORI, YOU KNOW I THOUGHT THIS WHEN LOOKING AT YOUR OLD DRAWING TOO, BUT...
THESE THINGS YOU WROTE HERE THAT LOOKS LIKE A MANGA PLOT... WHAT'S THE STORY HERE?
A mage who has lost his magic power.
He needs soul medicine to get his magic back.
-- A normal person? An excuse?
A girl who lost her voice.
-- She writes down her m gic spells.
Who was it who dec that boys don't cry
SOMETIMES I LOOK AT STUFF I WROTE A LONG TIME AGO, AND EVEN I CAN'T FIGURE OUT WHAT IT MEANS.
WELL... YOU KNOW ...
What difference does it make now anyway?
COME TO THINK OF IT, A LONG TIME AGO I LOVED REALLY COMPLICATED KANJI, AND NOW I CAN'T FIGURE OUT WHY.
It was just the folly of youth.

not a mistake

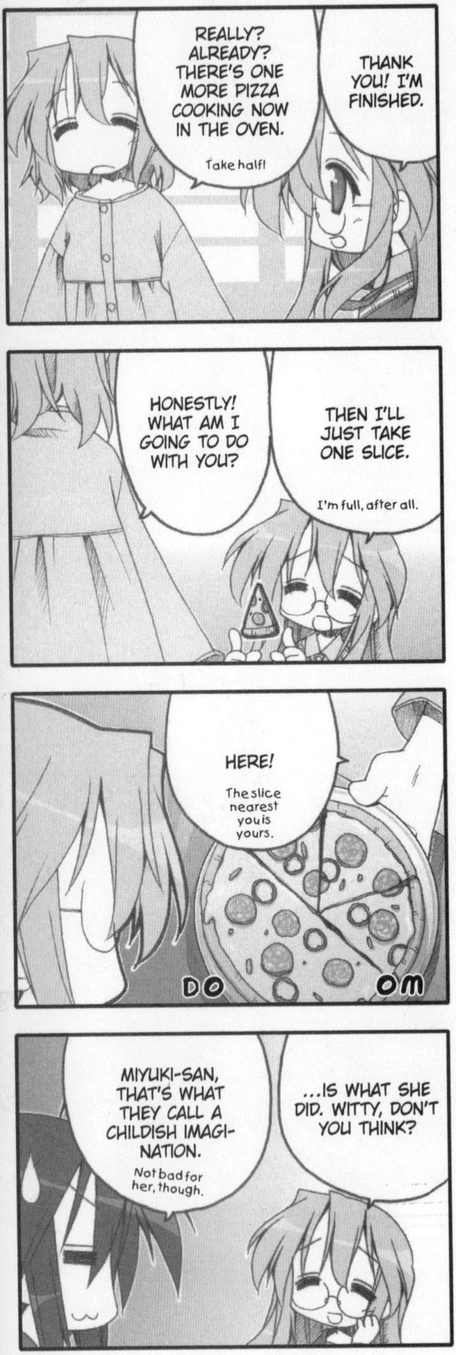
THANK YOU! I'M FINISHED.
REALLY? ALREADY? THERE'S ONE MORE PIZZA COOKING NOW IN THE OVEN.
Take half!
THEN I'LL JUST TAKE ONE SLICE.
I'm full, after all.
HONESTLY! WHAT AM I GOING TO DO WITH YOU?
HERE!
The slice nearest you is yours.
DO
OM
...IS WHAT SHE DID. WITTY, DON'T YOU THINK?
MIYUKI-SAN, THAT'S WHAT THEY CALL A CHILDISH IMAGINATION.
Not bad for her, though.

delete

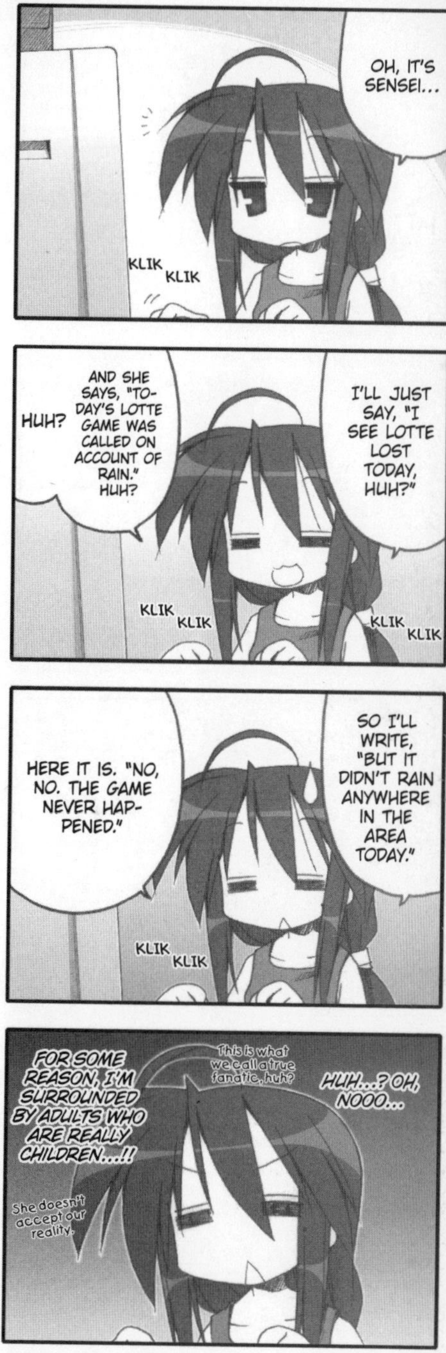
OH, IT'S SENSEI...
KLIK KLIK
I'LL JUST SAY, "I SEE LOTTE LOST TODAY, HUH?"
AND SHE SAYS, "TO-DAY'S LOTTE GAME WAS CALLED ON ACCOUNT OF RAIN." HUH?
HUH?
KLIK KLIK
KLIK KLIK
SO I'LL WRITE, "BUT IT DIDN'T RAIN ANYWHERE IN THE AREA TODAY."
HERE IT IS. "NO, NO. THE GAME NEVER HAP-PENED."
KLIK KLIK
HUH...? OH, NOOO...
This is what we call a true fanatic, huh?
FOR SOME REASON, I'M SURROUNDED BY ADULTS WHO ARE REALLY CHILDREN...!!
She doesn't accept our reality.

home alone

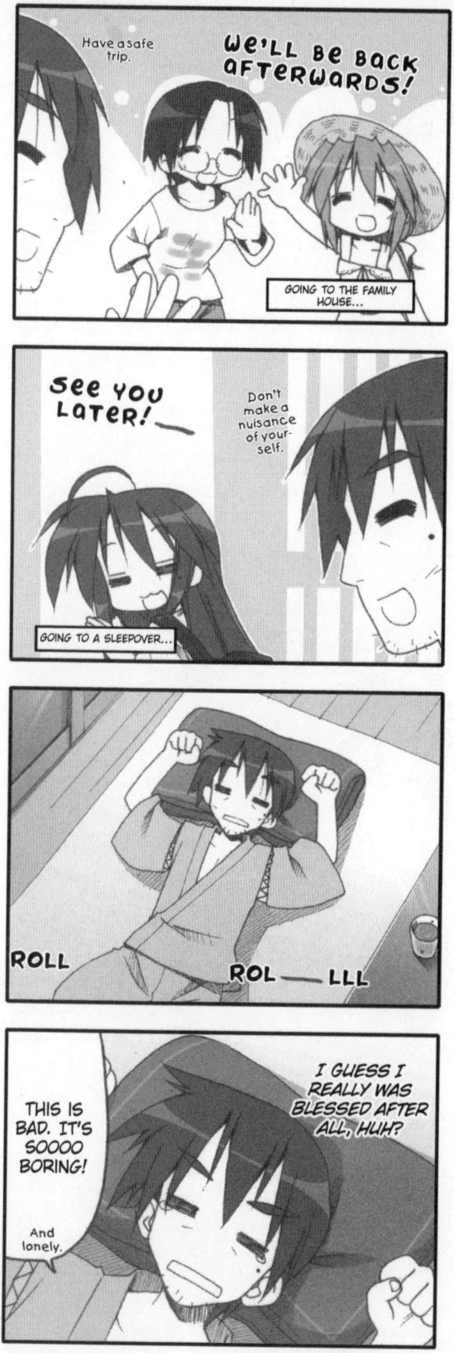
WE'LL BE BACK AFTERWARDS!
Have a safe trip.
GOING TO THE FAMILY HOUSE...
Don't make a nuisance of your-self.
SEE YOU LATER!
GOING TO A SLEEPOVER...
ROLL
ROL—LLL
I GUESS I REALLY WAS BLESSED AFTER ALL, HUH?
THIS IS BAD. IT'S SOOOO BORING!
And lonely.

episode 146
image goes first

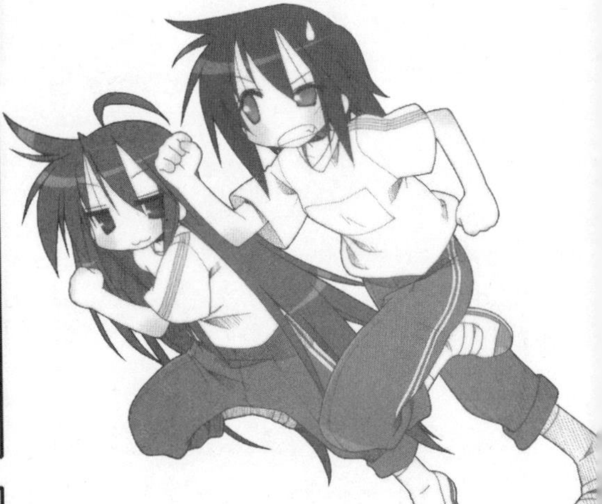

● Comp Ace, September 2007 issue

impact

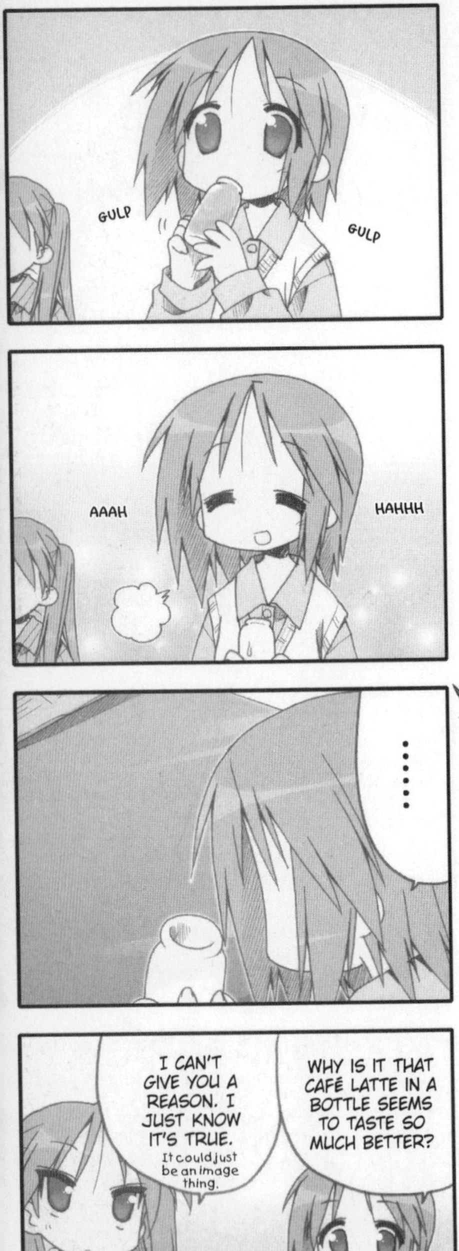
GULP
GULP
AAAH
HAHHH
......
WHY IS IT THAT CAFÉ LATTE IN A BOTTLE SEEMS TO TASTE SO MUCH BETTER?
I CAN'T GIVE YOU A REASON. I JUST KNOW IT'S TRUE.
It could just be an image thing.
HMM

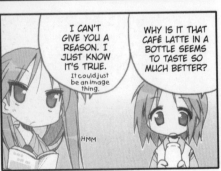

left behind

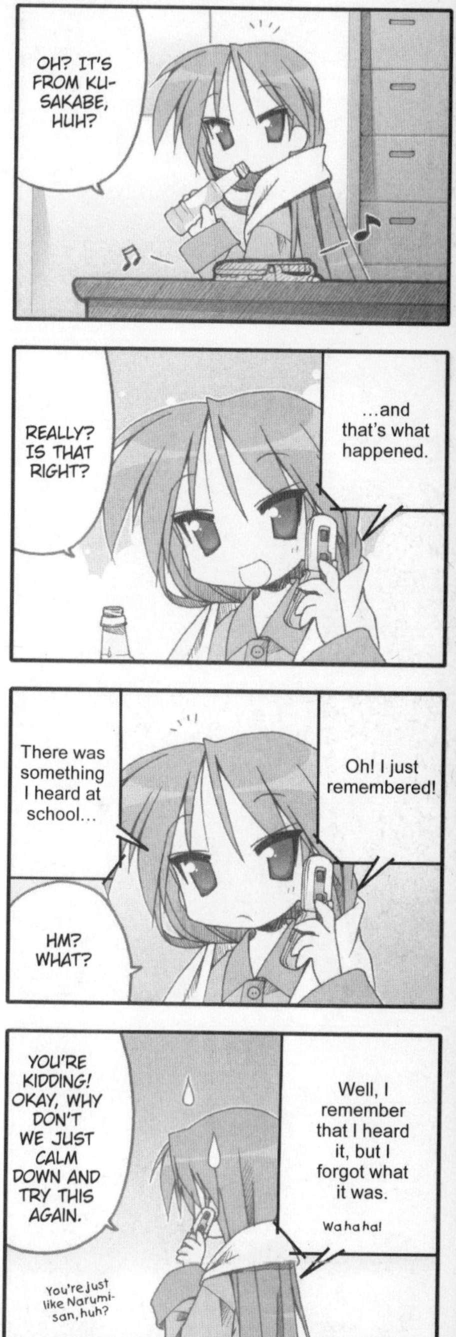

OH? IT'S FROM KU-SAKABE, HUH?
...and that's what happened.
REALLY? IS THAT RIGHT?
Oh! I just remembered!
There was something I heard at school...
HM? WHAT?
Well, I remember that I heard it, but I forgot what it was.
Wahaha!
YOU'RE KIDDING! OKAY, WHY DON'T WE JUST CALM DOWN AND TRY THIS AGAIN.
You're just like Narumi-san, huh?

bite back

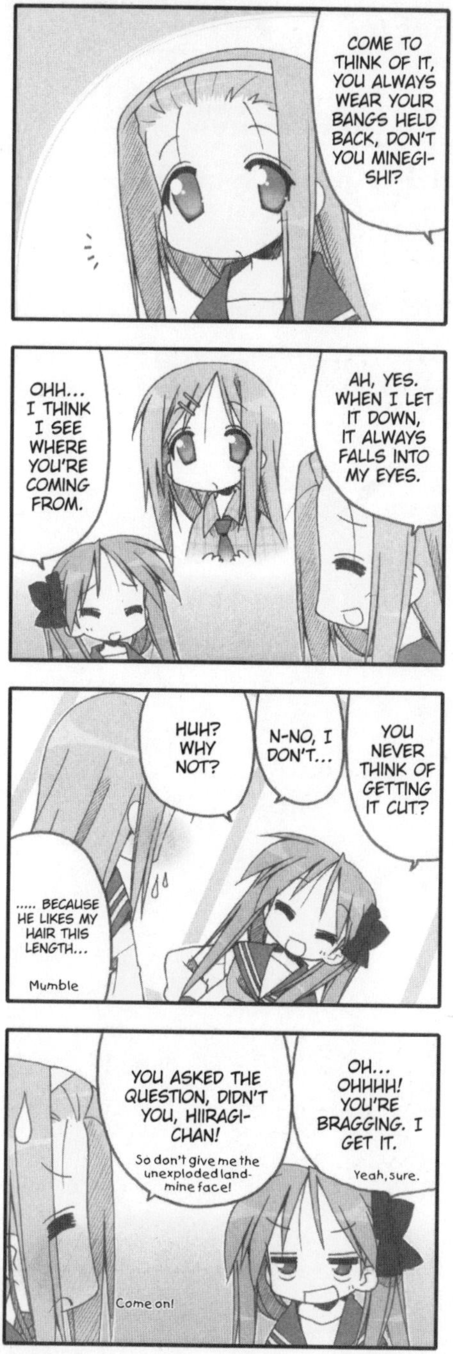

COME TO THINK OF IT, YOU ALWAYS WEAR YOUR BANGS HELD BACK, DON'T YOU MINEGI-SHI?
AH, YES. WHEN I LET IT DOWN, IT ALWAYS FALLS INTO MY EYES.
OHH... I THINK I SEE WHERE YOU'RE COMING FROM.
YOU NEVER THINK OF GETTING IT CUT?
N-NO, I DON'T...
HUH? WHY NOT?
..... BECAUSE HE LIKES MY HAIR THIS LENGTH...
Mumble
OH... OHHHH! YOU'RE BRAGGING. I GET IT.
Yeah, sure.
YOU ASKED THE QUESTION, DIDN'T YOU, HIIRAGI-CHAN!
So don't give me the unexploded land-mine face!
Come on!

name

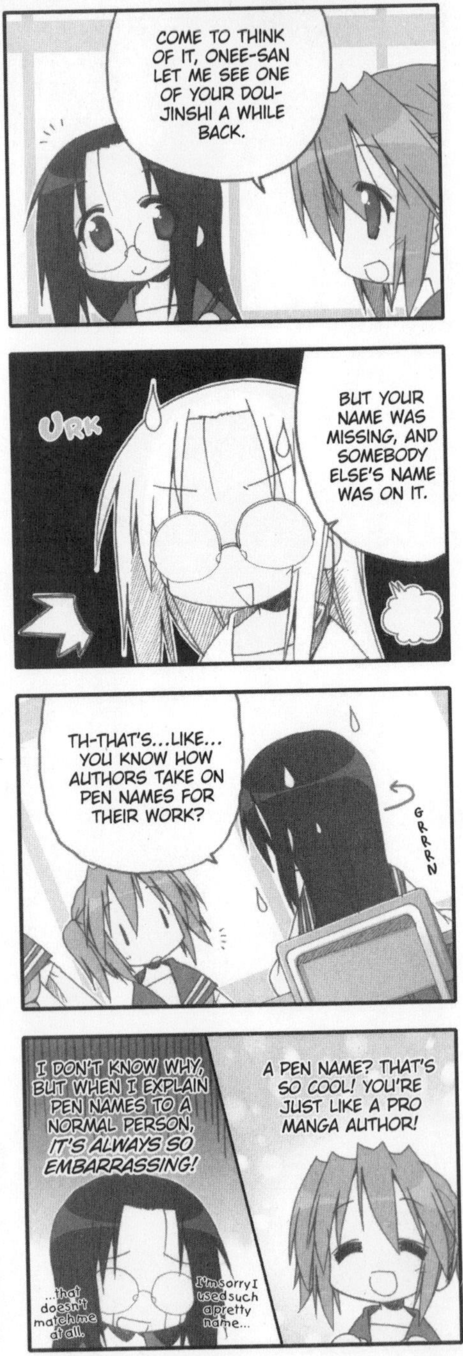

COME TO THINK OF IT, ONEE-SAN LET ME SEE ONE OF YOUR DOU-JINSHI A WHILE BACK.
BUT YOUR NAME WAS MISSING, AND SOMEBODY ELSE'S NAME WAS ON IT.
URK
TH-THAT'S...LIKE... YOU KNOW HOW AUTHORS TAKE ON PEN NAMES FOR THEIR WORK?
GRRRN
A PEN NAME? THAT'S SO COOL! YOU'RE JUST LIKE A PRO MANGA AUTHOR!
I DON'T KNOW WHY, BUT WHEN I EXPLAIN PEN NAMES TO A NORMAL PERSON, IT'S ALWAYS SO EMBARRASSING!
I'm sorry I used such a pretty name...
...that doesn't match me at all.

suspicion

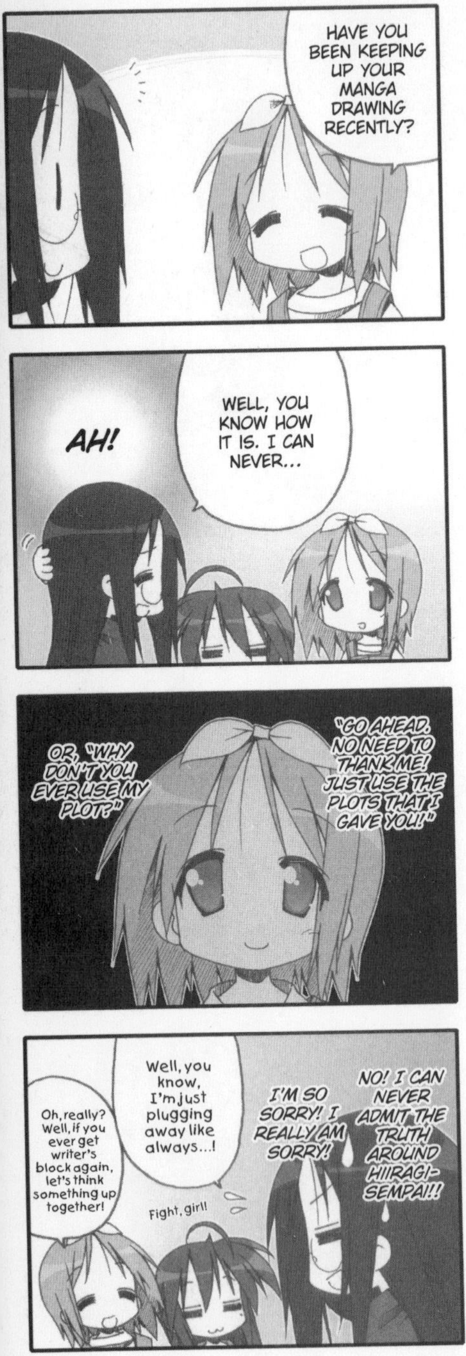

HAVE YOU BEEN KEEPING UP YOUR MANGA DRAWING RECENTLY?
WELL, YOU KNOW HOW IT IS. I CAN NEVER...
AH!
"GO AHEAD. NO NEED TO THANK ME! JUST USE THE PLOTS THAT I GAVE YOU!"
OR, "WHY DON'T YOU EVER USE MY PLOT?"
NO! I CAN NEVER ADMIT THE TRUTH AROUND HIIRAGI-SEMPAI!!
I'M SO SORRY! I REALLY AM SORRY!
Well, you know, I'm just plugging away like always...!
Oh, really? Well, if you ever get writer's block again, let's think something up together!
Fight, girl!

Lucky☆Star

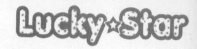

episode 147
a time of decline

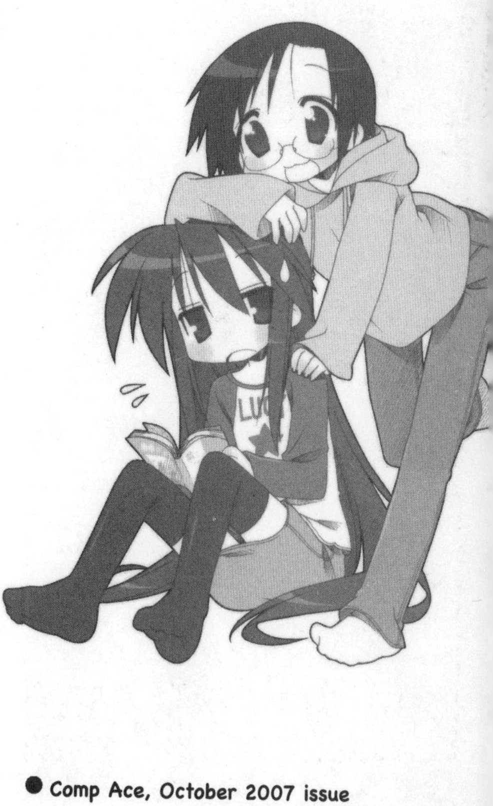

● Comp Ace, October 2007 issue

politics and education too

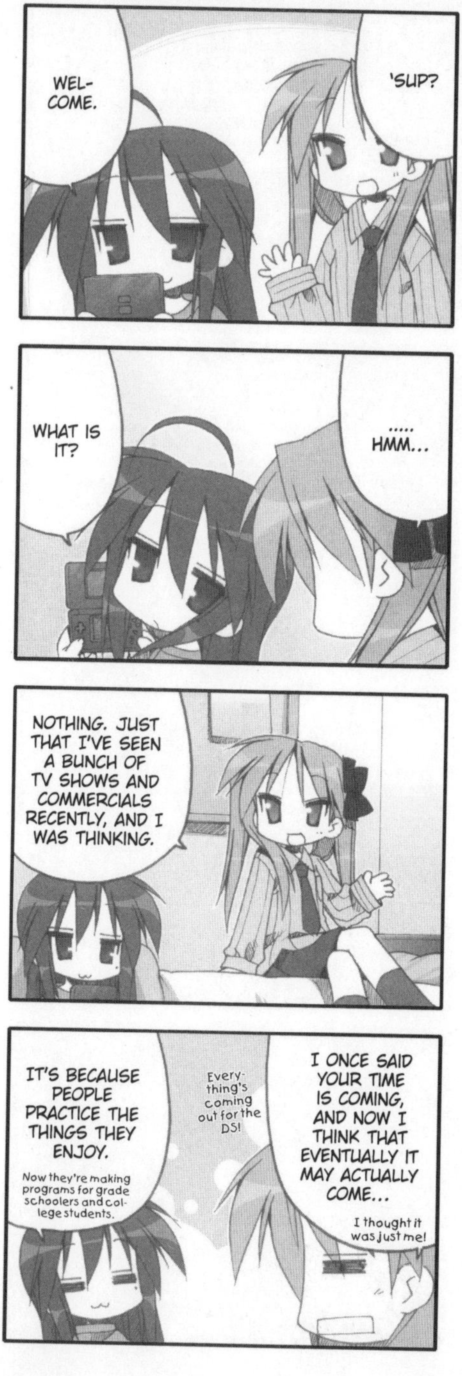
'SUP?
WEL-COME.
..... HMM...
WHAT IS IT?
NOTHING. JUST THAT I'VE SEEN A BUNCH OF TV SHOWS AND COMMERCIALS RECENTLY, AND I WAS THINKING.
I ONCE SAID YOUR TIME IS COMING, AND NOW I THINK THAT EVENTUALLY IT MAY ACTUALLY COME...
I thought it was just me!
Every-thing's coming out for the DS!
IT'S BECAUSE PEOPLE PRACTICE THE THINGS THEY ENJOY.
Now they're making programs for grade schoolers and col-lege students.

a woman in defeat

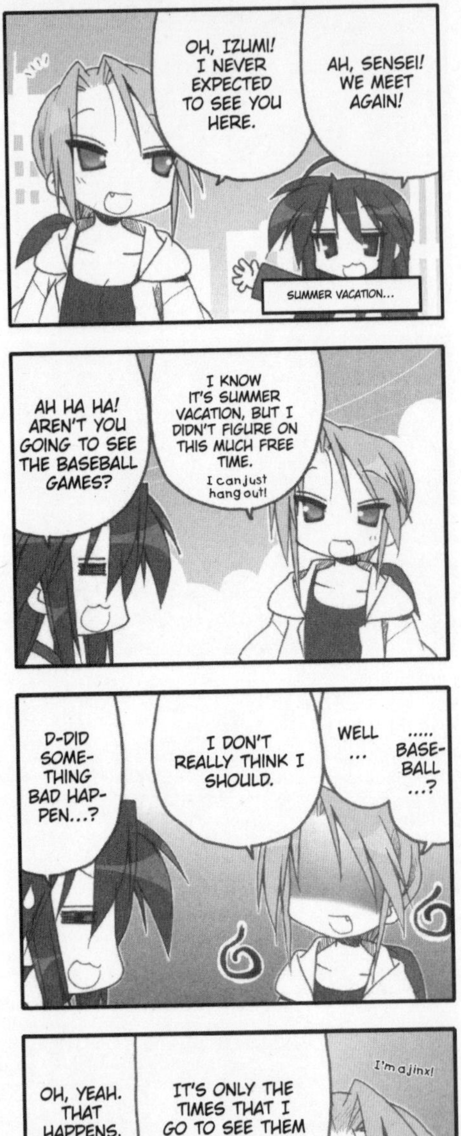
AH, SENSEI! WE MEET AGAIN!
OH, IZUMI! I NEVER EXPECTED TO SEE YOU HERE.
SUMMER VACATION...
I KNOW IT'S SUMMER VACATION, BUT I DIDN'T FIGURE ON THIS MUCH FREE TIME.
I can just hang out!
AH HA HA! AREN'T YOU GOING TO SEE THE BASEBALL GAMES?
.....BASE-BALL...?
WELL...
I DON'T REALLY THINK I SHOULD.
D-DID SOME-THING BAD HAP-PEN...?
I'm a jinx!
IT'S ONLY THE TIMES THAT I GO TO SEE THEM PLAY THAT THEY LOSE!
So I don't go!
OH, YEAH. THAT HAPPENS, DOESN'T IT?
B-By coinci-dence.

interjection

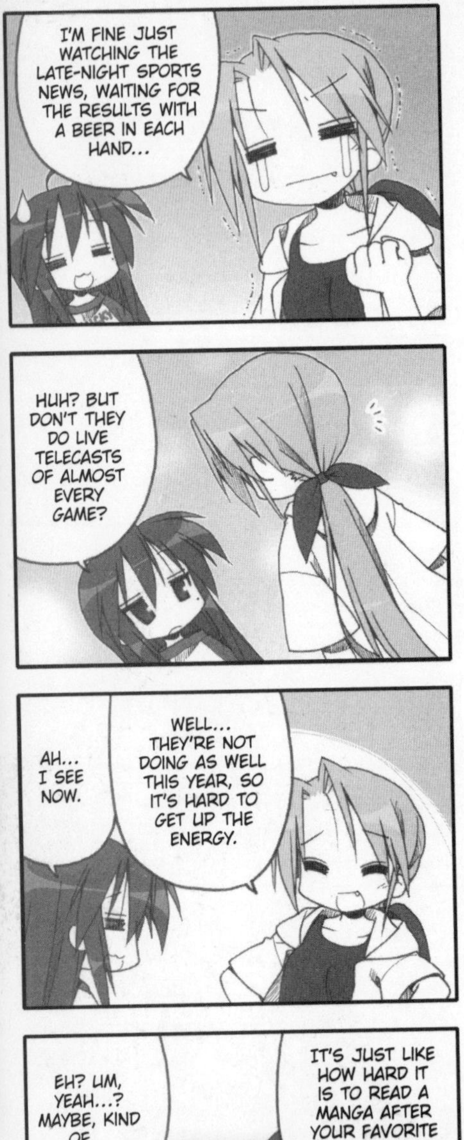
I'M FINE JUST WATCHING THE LATE-NIGHT SPORTS NEWS, WAITING FOR THE RESULTS WITH A BEER IN EACH HAND...
HUH? BUT DON'T THEY DO LIVE TELECASTS OF ALMOST EVERY GAME?
WELL... THEY'RE NOT DOING AS WELL THIS YEAR, SO IT'S HARD TO GET UP THE ENERGY.
AH... I SEE NOW.
IT'S JUST LIKE HOW HARD IT IS TO READ A MANGA AFTER YOUR FAVORITE SUPPORTING CHARACTER IS KILLED OFF.
EH? UM, YEAH...? MAYBE, KIND OF...

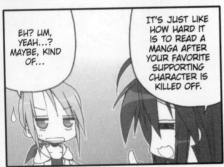

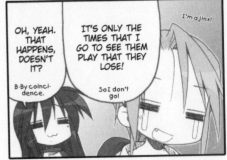

euphoria

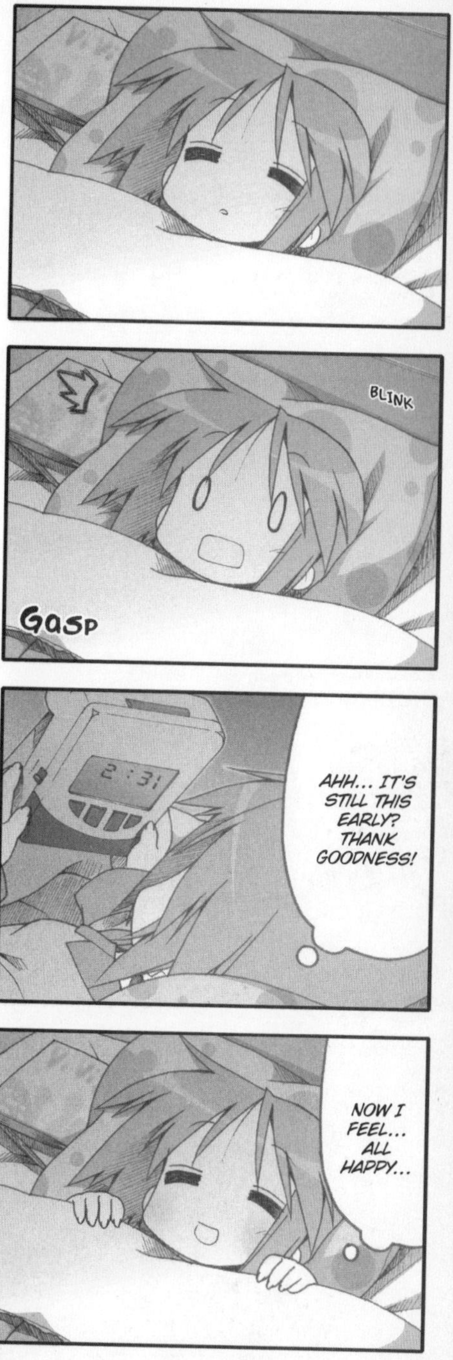
BLINK
Gasp
AHH... IT'S STILL THIS EARLY? THANK GOODNESS!
NOW I FEEL... ALL HAPPY...

despair

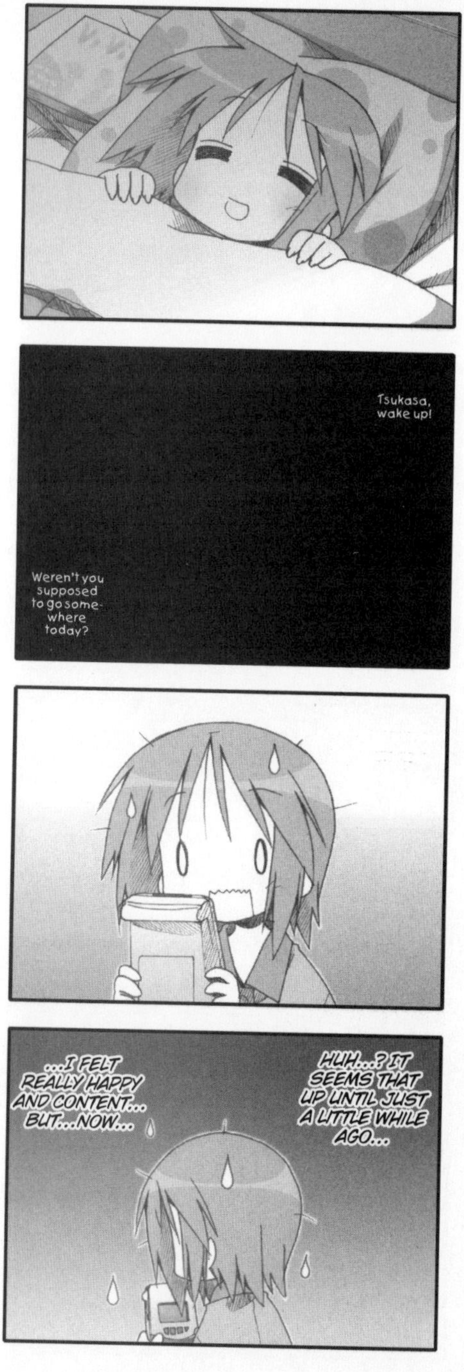
Tsukasa, wake up!
Weren't you supposed to go some-where today?
HUH...? IT SEEMS THAT UP UNTIL JUST A LITTLE WHILE AGO...
...I FELT REALLY HAPPY AND CONTENT... BUT...NOW...

episode 148
doing business

Kadokawa Hot Line
Kadokawa Shouten New Releases News
You Can Use

Unfortunately these catalogs are not released to the general public.

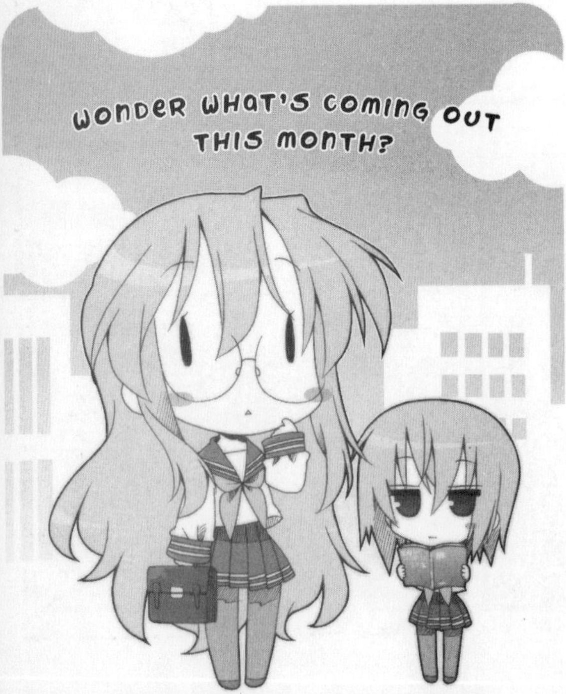
WONDER WHAT'S COMING OUT THIS MONTH?

※ KADOKAWA HOT LINE IS NOT SOLD OR OTHERWISE RELEASED TO THE GENERAL PUBLIC.

NO. 1 THE BIG STAGE
To celebrate the first installment for Kadokawa Hot Line, we present a Lucky ☆ Star advertisement.
(2005, January issue)

NO. 2 SPECIAL CONNECTION
And introduction to the Movie Version of Chakushin Ari 2.
(2005, February issue)

NO. 3 NO, IT ISN'T OVERBLOWN
An introduction to Volume 10 of the Keroro Gunsou (Sgt. Frog) manga and the TV anime.
(2005, March issue)

No. 1 the big stage

HEY EVERYBODY! THEY SAY WE'RE GOING TO BE ON THE COVER OF A MAGAZINE!
Over here! Over here!
HUH?!
IT'S A CATALOG OF BOOKS FROM KADOKAWA CALLED THE KADOKAWA HOT LINE!
WE'RE OUT OF OUR LEAGUE WITH THIS! SO COME OVER HERE AND DON'T GET IN THE WAY!
That isn't a magazine!
UMM...
SO WHAT YOU'RE SAYING IS...
What are you getting so worked up for?
...THAT I SHOULD GO GET INTO A GOWN OR SOMETHING?
FYI: I don't have a gown.
NO! I'M SAYING WE SHOULD STAND ASIDE AND MAKE WAY FOR THOSE PEOPLE WHO ARE ACTUALLY FAMOUS!
We don't rate!

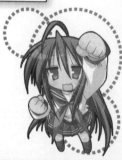

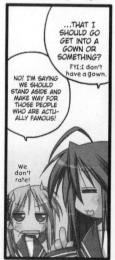

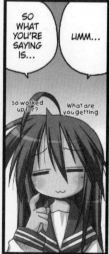

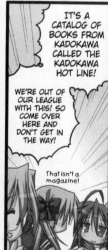

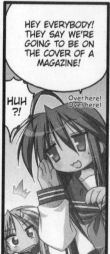

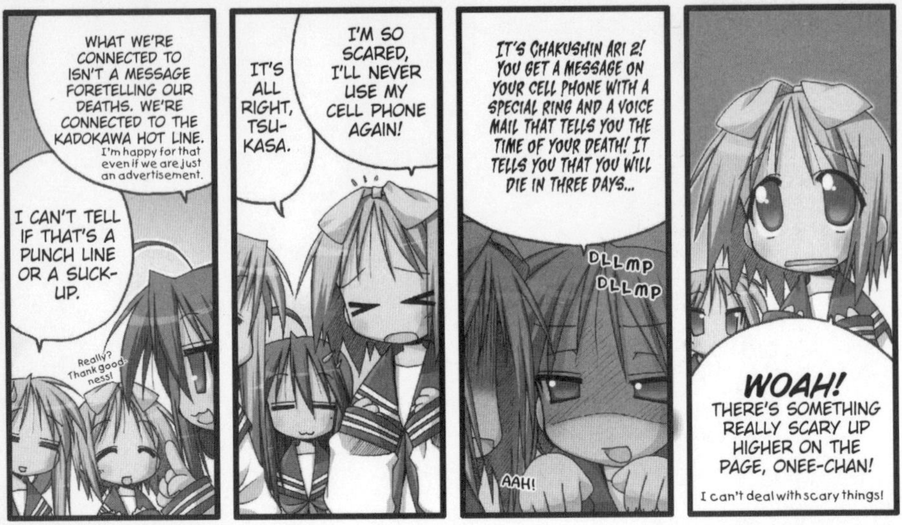
WOAH!
THERE'S SOMETHING REALLY SCARY UP HIGHER ON THE PAGE, ONEE-CHAN!
I can't deal with scary things!
IT'S CHAKUSHIN ARI 2! YOU GET A MESSAGE ON YOUR CELL PHONE WITH A SPECIAL RING AND A VOICE MAIL THAT TELLS YOU THE TIME OF YOUR DEATH! IT TELLS YOU THAT YOU WILL DIE IN THREE DAYS...
DLLMP DLLMP
AAH!
I'M SO SCARED, I'LL NEVER USE MY CELL PHONE AGAIN!
IT'S ALL RIGHT, TSU-KASA.
WHAT WE'RE CONNECTED TO ISN'T A MESSAGE FORETELLING OUR DEATHS. WE'RE CONNECTED TO THE KADOKAWA HOT LINE.
I'm happy for that even if we are just an advertisement.
I CAN'T TELL IF THAT'S A PUNCH LINE OR A SUCK-UP.
Really? Thank good-ness!

No. 2 special connection

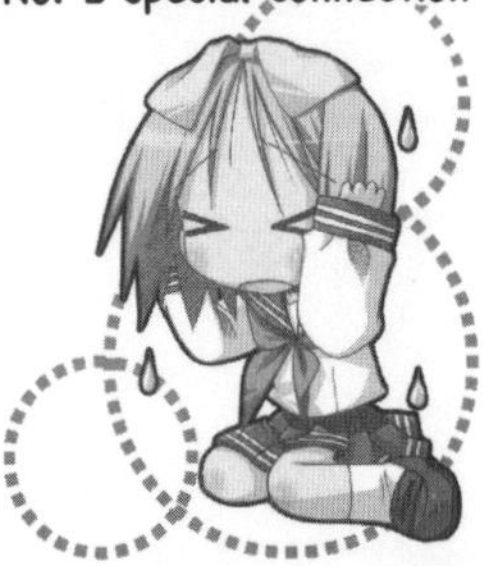

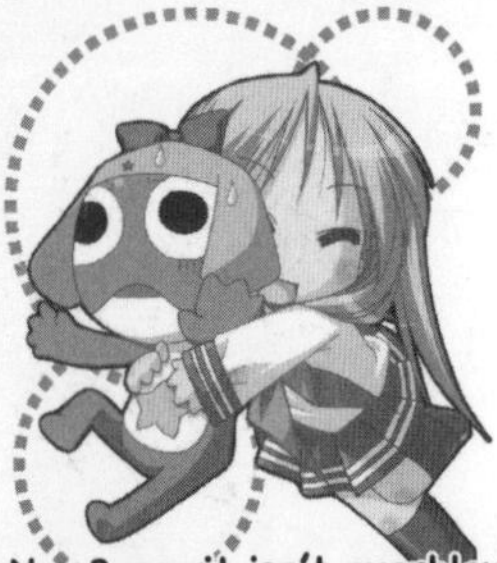

No. 3 no, it isn't overblown

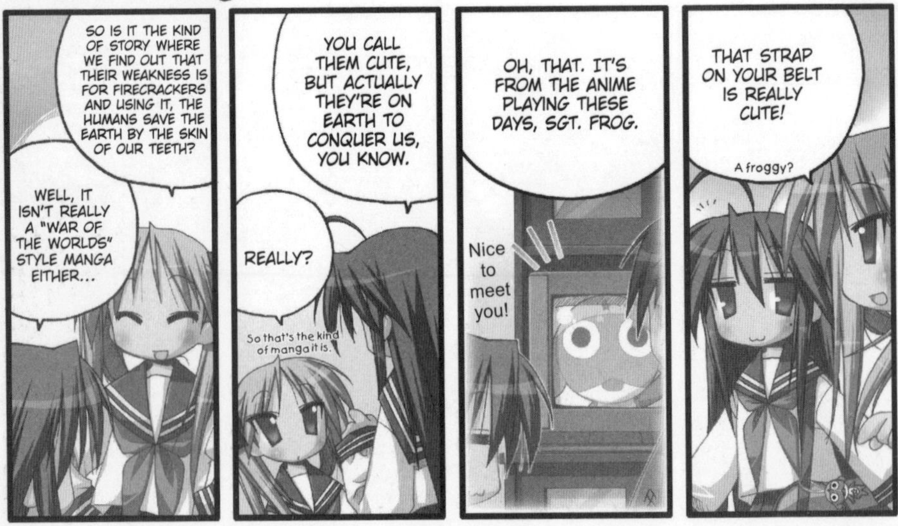
THAT STRAP ON YOUR BELT IS REALLY CUTE!
A froggy?
OH, THAT. IT'S FROM THE ANIME PLAYING THESE DAYS, SGT. FROG.
Nice to meet you!
YOU CALL THEM CUTE, BUT ACTUALLY THEY'RE ON EARTH TO CONQUER US, YOU KNOW.
REALLY?
So that's the kind of manga it is.
SO IS IT THE KIND OF STORY WHERE WE FIND OUT THAT THEIR WEAKNESS IS FOR FIRECRACKERS AND USING IT, THE HUMANS SAVE THE EARTH BY THE SKIN OF OUR TEETH?
WELL, IT ISN'T REALLY A "WAR OF THE WORLDS" STYLE MANGA EITHER...

NO. 4 FAR AND WIDE
An introduction to the two-volume novel, The Da Vinci Code.
(2005, April issue)

NO. 5 SEPARATION
An introduction to Sengoku Jieitai 1549 ("Warring-States Self Defense Force 1549").
(2005, May issue)

NO. 6 COUNTER ATTACK
An introduction to Kadokawa Bunko's campaign, Discovery: The Hundred Books of Summer.
(2005, June issue)

No. 4 far and wide

MIYUKI-SAN! WHAT ARE YOU READING?
DA VINCI CODE, A SUSPENSE NOVEL BEST-SELLER WHERE WESTERN CULTURE AND HISTORY PROVIDE CLUES TO A MYSTERY.
They say it'll soon be made into a movie too.
MIYUKI-SAN, I'M AMAZED AT HOW YOU CAN READ THOSE WHOPPING-BIG BOOKS!
Heavy too!
BUT IT'S A LOT EASIER TO READ THAN IT LOOKS.
HOW ABOUT YOU TRY IT TOO, IZUMI-SAN?
NAW... IT SOUNDS INTERESTING THE WAY YOU TALK ABOUT IT, BUT...
ZLIMM
SINCE IT'S GOING TO BE MADE INTO A MOVIE, DON'T YOU THINK THE MOVIE WILL BE EASIER, CHEAPER AND BETTER?
No... Um... Books have their own good points, don't you think?

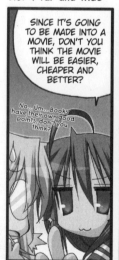

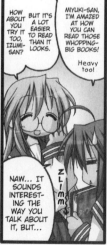

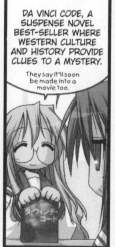

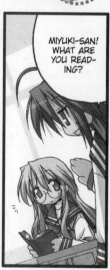

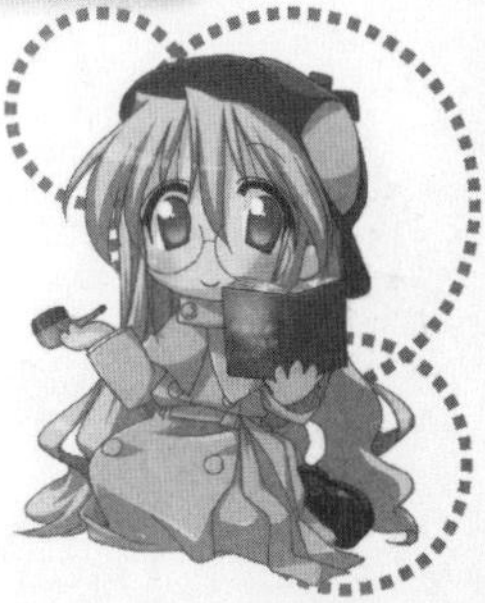

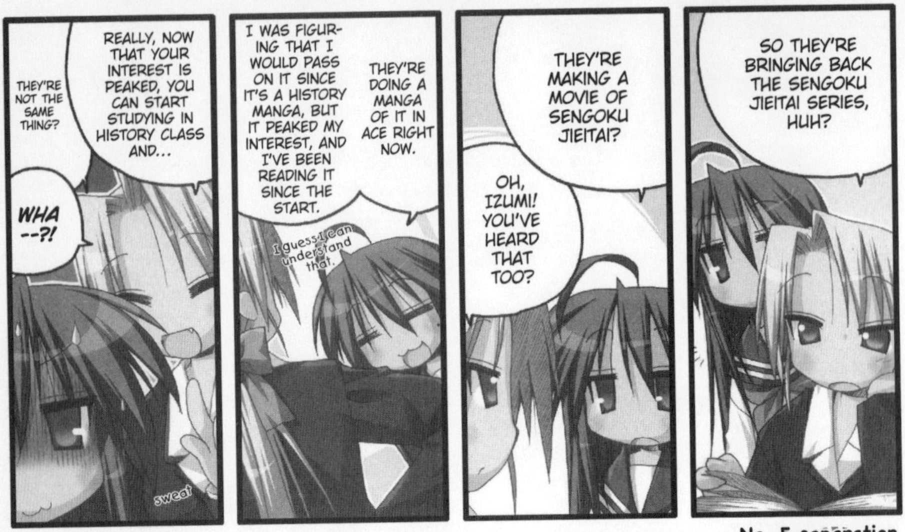
SO THEY'RE BRINGING BACK THE SENGOKU JIEITAI SERIES, HUH?
THEY'RE MAKING A MOVIE OF SENGOKU JIEITAI?
OH, IZUMI! YOU'VE HEARD THAT TOO?
THEY'RE DOING A MANGA OF IT IN ACE RIGHT NOW.
I WAS FIGURING THAT I WOULD PASS ON IT SINCE IT'S A HISTORY MANGA, BUT IT PEAKED MY INTEREST, AND I'VE BEEN READING IT SINCE THE START.
I guess I can understand that.
REALLY, NOW THAT YOUR INTEREST IS PEAKED, YOU CAN START STUDYING IN HISTORY CLASS AND...
THEY'RE NOT THE SAME THING?
WHA--?!
sweat

No. 5 separation

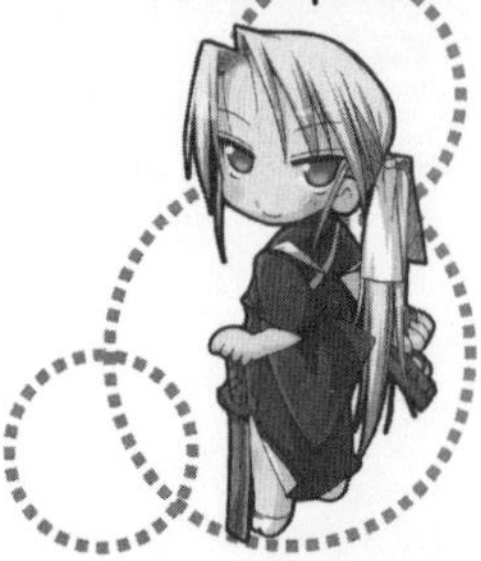

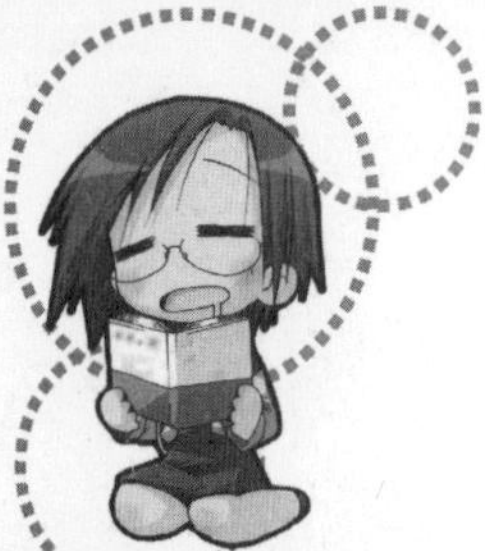

No. 6 counter attack

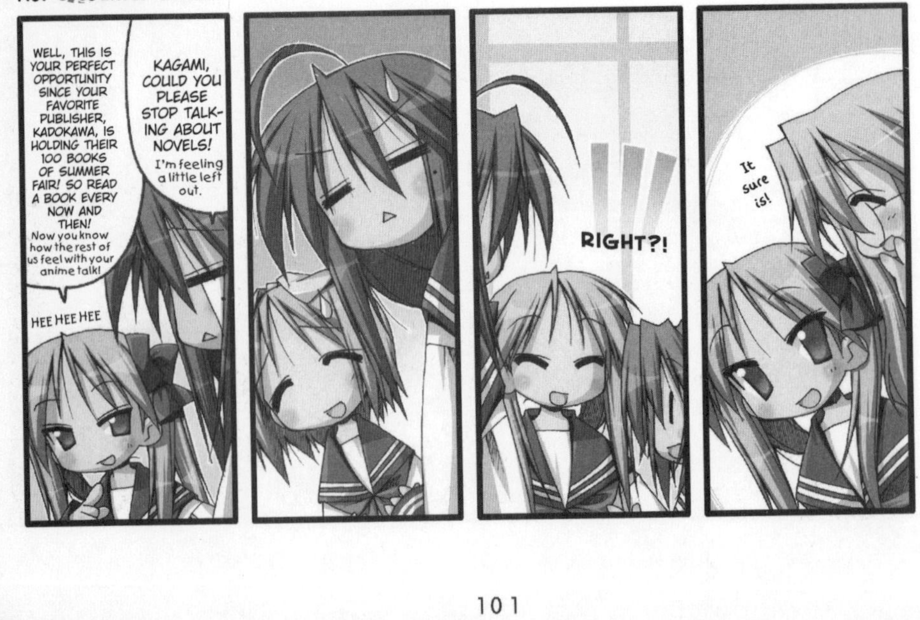
It sure is!
RIGHT?!
KAGAMI, COULD YOU PLEASE STOP TALKING ABOUT NOVELS! I'm feeling a little left out.
WELL, THIS IS YOUR PERFECT OPPORTUNITY SINCE YOUR FAVORITE PUBLISHER, KADOKAWA, IS HOLDING THEIR 100 BOOKS OF SUMMER FAIR! SO READ A BOOK EVERY NOW AND THEN! Now you know how the rest of us feel with your anime talk!
HEE HEE HEE

NO. 7 OUR BEST REGARDS
An introduction to the Comp Festa and Lucky ☆ Star Vol. 2.
(2005, July issue)

NO. 8 GOOD POINTS
An advertisement for Lucky ☆ Star .
(2005, August issue)

NO. 9 AS ALWAYS, YOU'RE...
Sgt. Frog is being made into a movie! Konata gives her desires with regard to the film.
(2005, September issue)

No. 7 our best regards

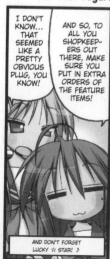

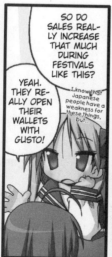

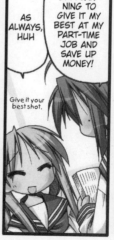

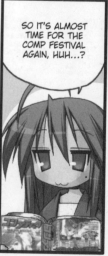

SO IT'S ALMOST TIME FOR THE COMP FESTIVAL AGAIN, HUH...?
I'M PLAN-NING TO GIVE IT MY BEST AT MY PART-TIME JOB AND SAVE UP MONEY!
AS ALWAYS, HUH
Give it your best shot.
SO DO SALES REAL-LY INCREASE THAT MUCH DURING FESTIVALS LIKE THIS?
YEAH. THEY RE-ALLY OPEN THEIR WALLETS WITH GUSTO!
I know that Japanese people have a weakness for these things, but...
AND SO, TO ALL YOU SHOPKEEP-ERS OUT THERE, MAKE SURE YOU PUT IN EXTRA ORDERS OF THE FEATURE ITEMS!
I DON'T KNOW... THAT SEEMED LIKE A PRETTY OBVIOUS PLUG, YOU KNOW!
AND DON'T FORGET LUCKY ☆ STAR! ♪

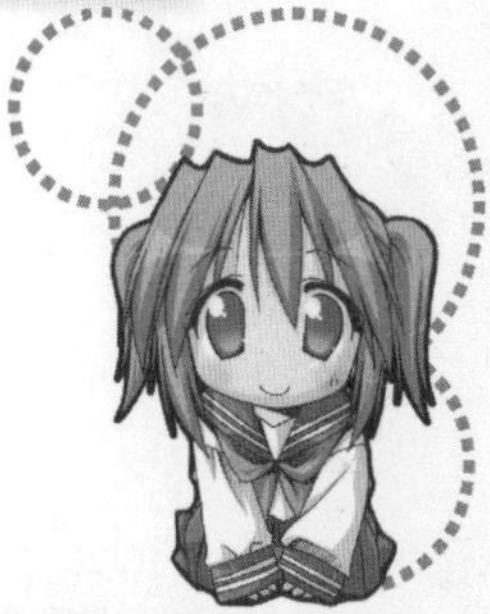

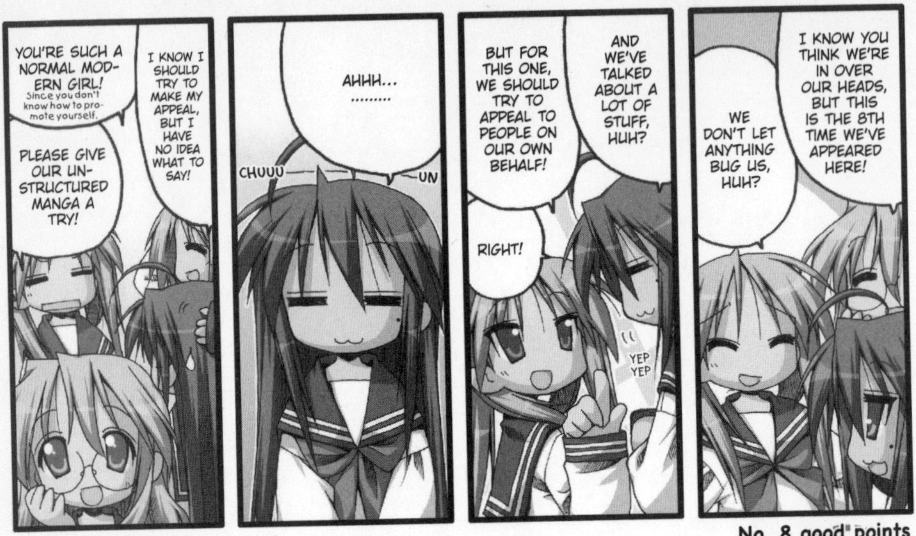
I KNOW YOU THINK WE'RE IN OVER OUR HEADS, BUT THIS IS THE 8TH TIME WE'VE APPEARED HERE!
WE DON'T LET ANYTHING BUG US, HUH?
AND WE'VE TALKED ABOUT A LOT OF STUFF, HUH?
BUT FOR THIS ONE, WE SHOULD TRY TO APPEAL TO PEOPLE ON OUR OWN BEHALF!
RIGHT!
YEP YEP
AHHH… ………
CHUUU— —UN
I KNOW I SHOULD TRY TO MAKE MY APPEAL, BUT I HAVE NO IDEA WHAT TO SAY!
YOU'RE SUCH A NORMAL MODERN GIRL! Since you don't know how to promote yourself.
PLEASE GIVE OUR UNSTRUCTURED MANGA A TRY!

No. 8 good points

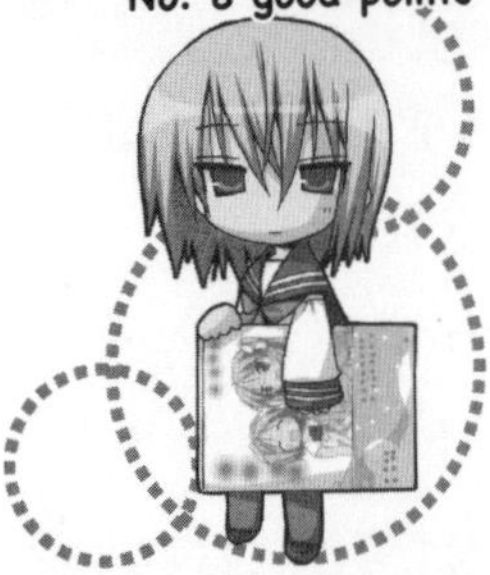

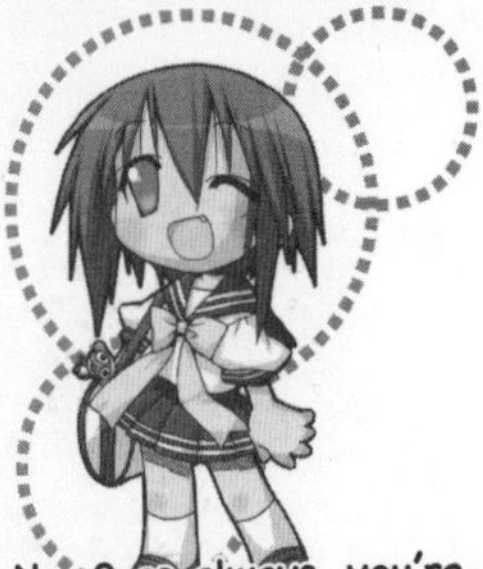

No. 9 as always, you're...

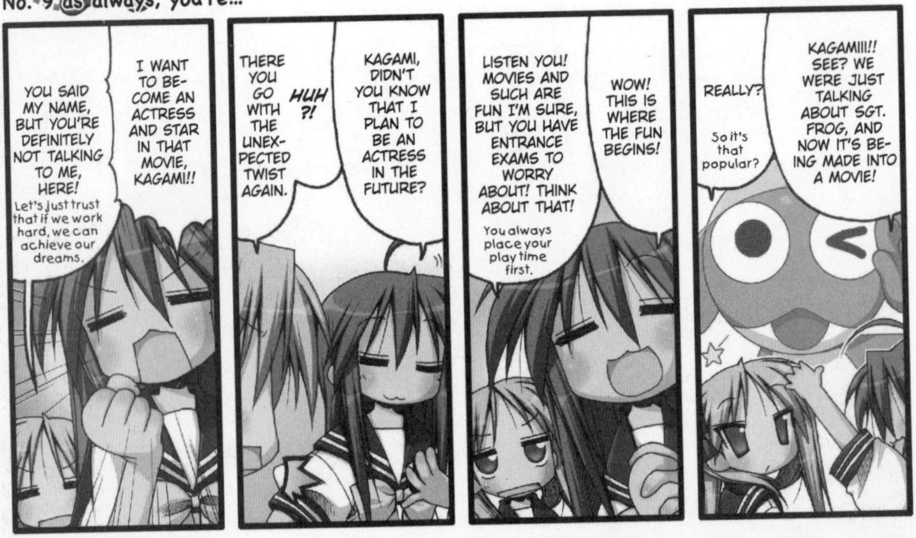
KAGAMIII!! SEE? WE WERE JUST TALKING ABOUT SGT. FROG, AND NOW IT'S BEING MADE INTO A MOVIE!
REALLY?
So it's that popular?
WOW! THIS IS WHERE THE FUN BEGINS!
LISTEN YOU! MOVIES AND SUCH ARE FUN I'M SURE, BUT YOU HAVE ENTRANCE EXAMS TO WORRY ABOUT! THINK ABOUT THAT!
You always place your play time first.
KAGAMI, DIDN'T YOU KNOW THAT I PLAN TO BE AN ACTRESS IN THE FUTURE?
HUH ?!
THERE YOU GO WITH THE UNEXPECTED TWIST AGAIN.
I WANT TO BECOME AN ACTRESS AND STAR IN THAT MOVIE, KAGAMI!!
YOU SAID MY NAME, BUT YOU'RE DEFINITELY NOT TALKING TO ME, HERE!
Let's just trust that if we work hard, we can achieve our dreams.

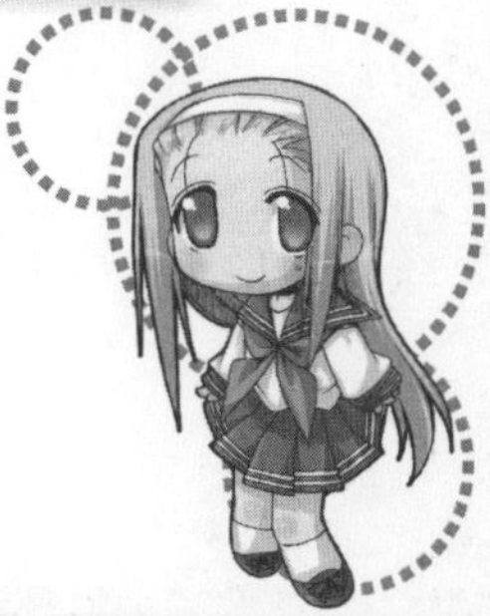

NO. 10 HERE'S TO YOUR HEALTH
An introduction to Chibi Vampire being made into an anime, and even more of Konata's desires.
(2005, October issue)

NO. 11 LOTS OF FUN THINGS
Introductions to Welcome to the NHK 4 and its Negative Campaign 4.
(2005, November issue)

NO. 12 STRAIGHT
An introduction to the Lucky ☆ Star comics and game adaptation.
(2005, December issue)

No. 10 here's to your health

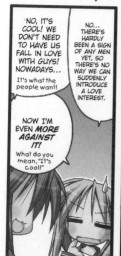

REALLY? CHIBI VAMPIRE IS BEING TURNED INTO AN ANIME? HEY GOOD THING, HUH?
You really liked it, didn't you?
THAT'S TRUE... I MUST SAY THAT IT MAKES ME HAPPY WHEN SOMETHING I LIKE GETS TURNED INTO AN ANIME.
BUT ISN'T THAT ONLY NATURAL?!
AND NOW WE SHOULD STOP SIMPLY BEING ENVIOUS OF OTHERS, AND TAKE MEASURES TO GET OURSELVES AN ANIME VERSION AS WELL!
WHEN YOU SAY "MEASURES..."
THE WAY I READ IT, ONE FACTOR... LOVE INTEREST!
IT'S THE MANGA THAT HAVE THE CHARACTERS WOUND UP IN LOVE COMPLICATIONS THAT MAKE THEM EVEN CUTER THAN THEY WERE BEFORE!
There's an unexpected aspect to it...
...and on the other hand, it goes best when it can be predicted.
NO... THERE'S HARDLY BEEN A SIGN OF ANY MEN YET, SO THERE'S NO WAY WE CAN SUDDENLY INTRODUCE A LOVE INTEREST.
NO, IT'S COOL! WE DON'T NEED TO HAVE US FALL IN LOVE WITH GUYS! NOWADAYS...
It's what the people want!
NOW I'M EVEN MORE AGAINST IT!
What do you mean, "It's cool!"

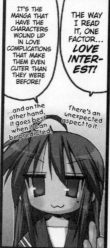

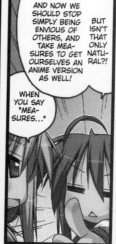

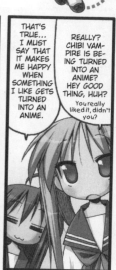

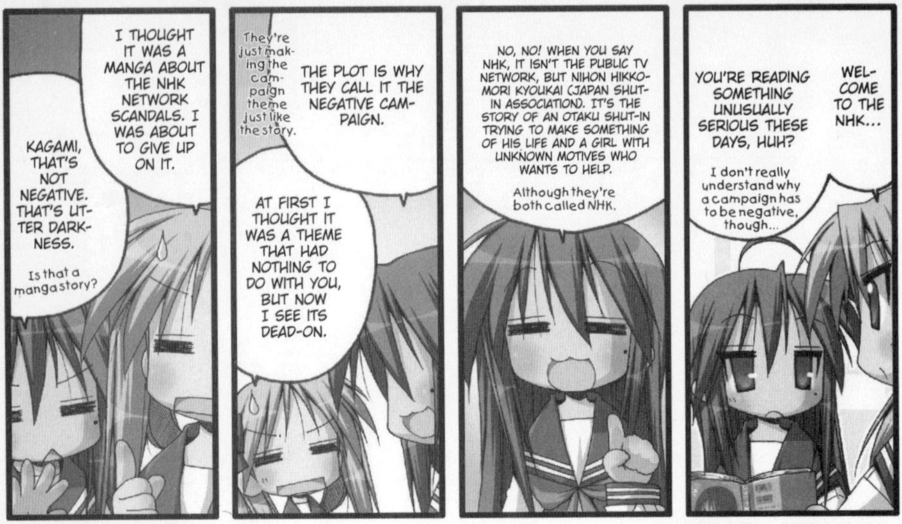
WEL-COME TO THE NHK...
YOU'RE READING SOMETHING UNUSUALLY SERIOUS THESE DAYS, HUH?
I don't really understand why a campaign has to be negative, though...
NO, NO! WHEN YOU SAY NHK, IT ISN'T THE PUBLIC TV NETWORK, BUT NIHON HIKKO-MORI KYOUKAI (JAPAN SHUT-IN ASSOCIATION). IT'S THE STORY OF AN OTAKU SHUT-IN TRYING TO MAKE SOMETHING OF HIS LIFE AND A GIRL WITH UNKNOWN MOTIVES WHO WANTS TO HELP.
Although they're both called NHK.
THE PLOT IS WHY THEY CALL IT THE NEGATIVE CAM-PAIGN.
They're just mak-ing the cam-paign theme just like the story.
AT FIRST I THOUGHT IT WAS A THEME THAT HAD NOTHING TO DO WITH YOU, BUT NOW I SEE ITS DEAD-ON.
I THOUGHT IT WAS A MANGA ABOUT THE NHK NETWORK SCANDALS. I WAS ABOUT TO GIVE UP ON IT.
KAGAMI, THAT'S NOT NEGATIVE. THAT'S UT-TER DARK-NESS.
Is that a manga story?

No. 11 lots of fun things

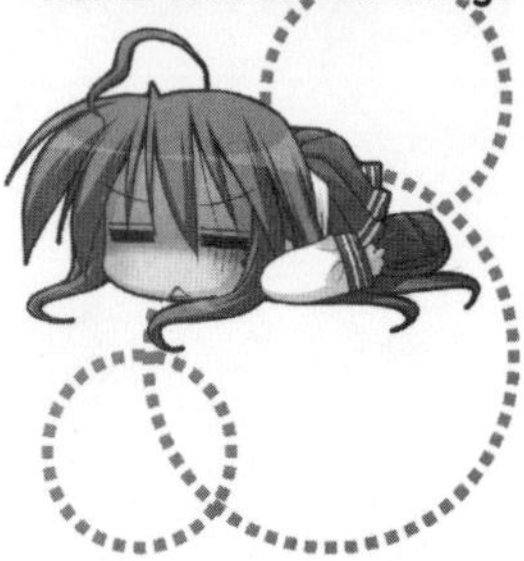

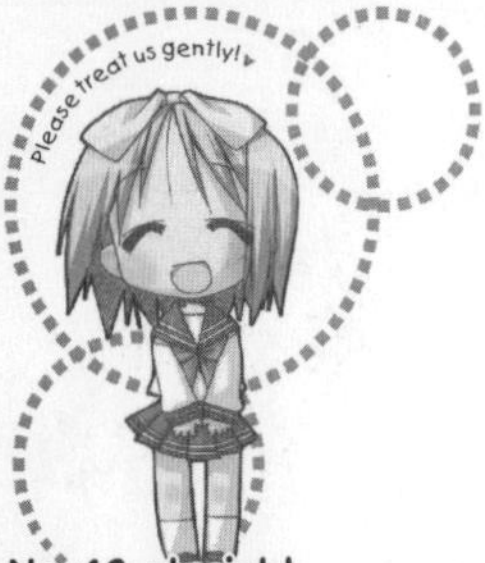
Please treat us gently!

No. 12 straight

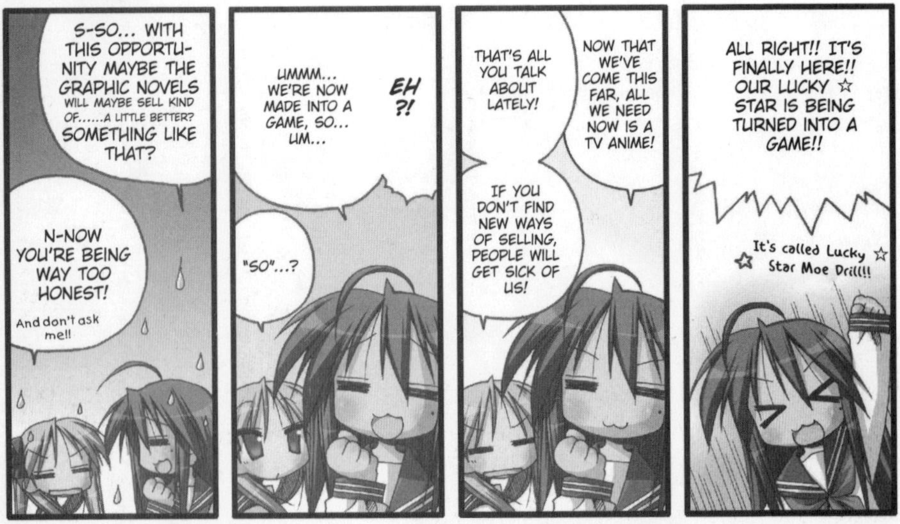
ALL RIGHT!! IT'S FINALLY HERE!! OUR LUCKY ☆ STAR IS BEING TURNED INTO A GAME!!
It's called Lucky ☆ Star Moe Drill!!!
NOW THAT WE'VE COME THIS FAR, ALL WE NEED NOW IS A TV ANIME!
THAT'S ALL YOU TALK ABOUT LATELY!
IF YOU DON'T FIND NEW WAYS OF SELLING, PEOPLE WILL GET SICK OF US!
EH ?!
UMMM... WE'RE NOW MADE INTO A GAME, SO... UM...
"SO"...?
S-SO... WITH THIS OPPORTU-NITY MAYBE THE GRAPHIC NOVELS WILL MAYBE SELL KIND OF......A LITTLE BETTER? SOMETHING LIKE THAT?
N-NOW YOU'RE BEING WAY TOO HONEST!
And don't ask me!!

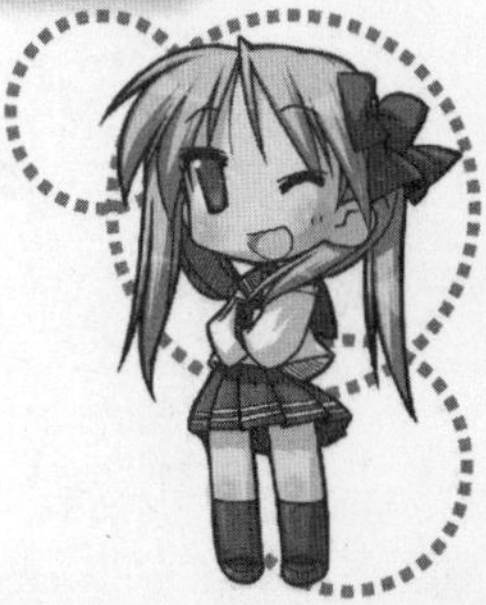

NO. 13 BAD AT ADVERTISING
An introduction to the Lucky ☆ Star manga, game and drama CD. (2006, January issue)

NO. 14 SUCKING UP
A special Valentine's Day message from the Lucky ☆ Star cast with love. (2006, February issue)

NO. 15 THANKS TO ALL OF YOU
Is the introduction to the Movie Version of Sgt. Frog a secret message about the progress of the anime version?
(2006, March issue)

No. 13 bad at advertising

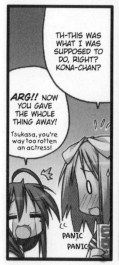

TO ALL OF YOU FINE BOOK-SHOP PEOPLE READING THE KA-DOKAWA HOT LINE ....
THANK YOU ALL FOR ORDER-ING FROM KADOKAWA SHOUTEN!
OUR RECOM-MENDED BOOK IS THIS. AN UNFOCUSSED 4-PANEL MANGA THAT WILL MAKE YOU CHUCKLE. LUCKY ☆ STAR!
UM... WAIT, I DON'T MEAN THIS BOOK...
AND NOW THERE IS A GAME AND A DRAMA CD...
IT'S GAINING POPULARITY IN AN UNFO-CUSSED KIND OF WAY, SO PLEASE CONTINUE YOUR SUP-PORT...?
GLANCE
TH-THIS WAS WHAT I WAS SUPPOSED TO DO, RIGHT? KONA-CHAN?
ARG!! NOW YOU GAVE THE WHOLE THING AWAY!
Tsukasa, you're way too rotten an actress!
PANIC
PANIC

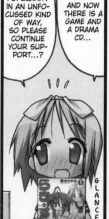

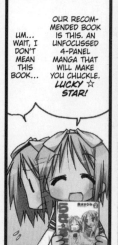

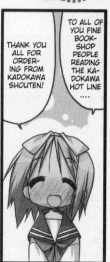

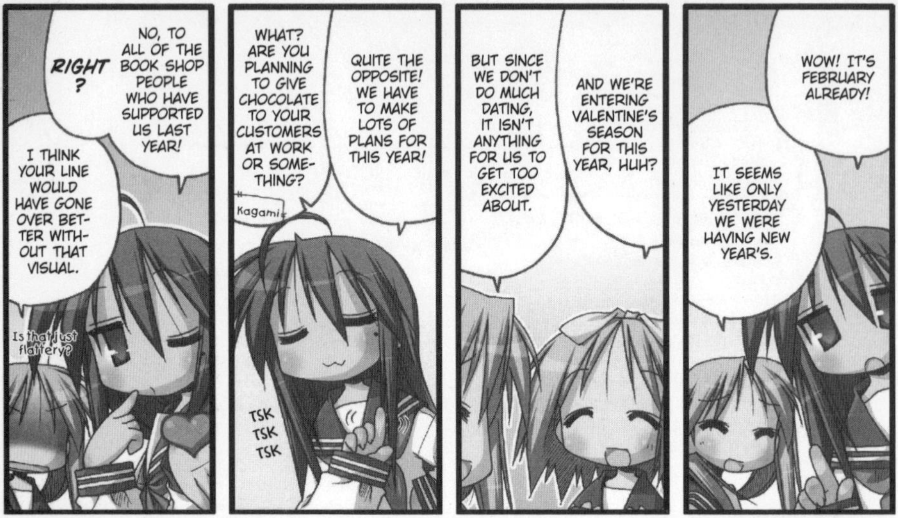
WOW! IT'S FEBRUARY ALREADY!
IT SEEMS LIKE ONLY YESTERDAY WE WERE HAVING NEW YEAR'S.
AND WE'RE ENTERING VALENTINE'S SEASON FOR THIS YEAR, HUH?
BUT SINCE WE DON'T DO MUCH DATING, IT ISN'T ANYTHING FOR US TO GET TOO EXCITED ABOUT.
QUITE THE OPPOSITE! WE HAVE TO MAKE LOTS OF PLANS FOR THIS YEAR!
WHAT? ARE YOU PLANNING TO GIVE CHOCOLATE TO YOUR CUSTOMERS AT WORK OR SOMETHING?
Kagami
TSK TSK TSK
NO, TO ALL OF THE BOOK SHOP PEOPLE WHO HAVE SUPPORTED US LAST YEAR!
RIGHT?
I THINK YOUR LINE WOULD HAVE GONE OVER BETTER WITHOUT THAT VISUAL.
Is that just flattery?

No. 14 sucking up

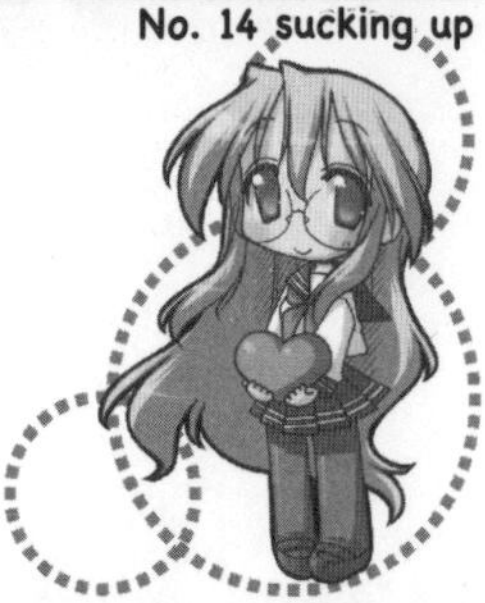

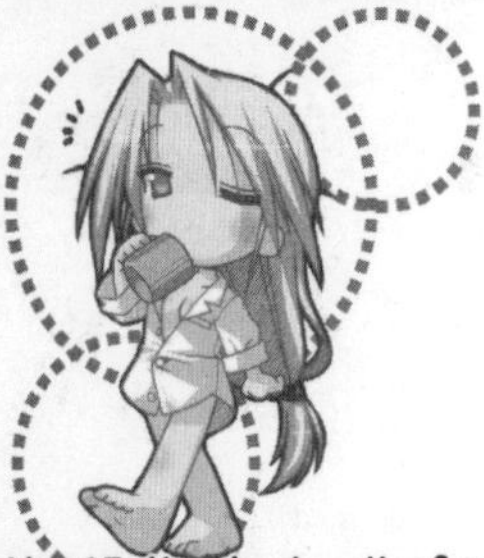

No. 15 thanks to all of you

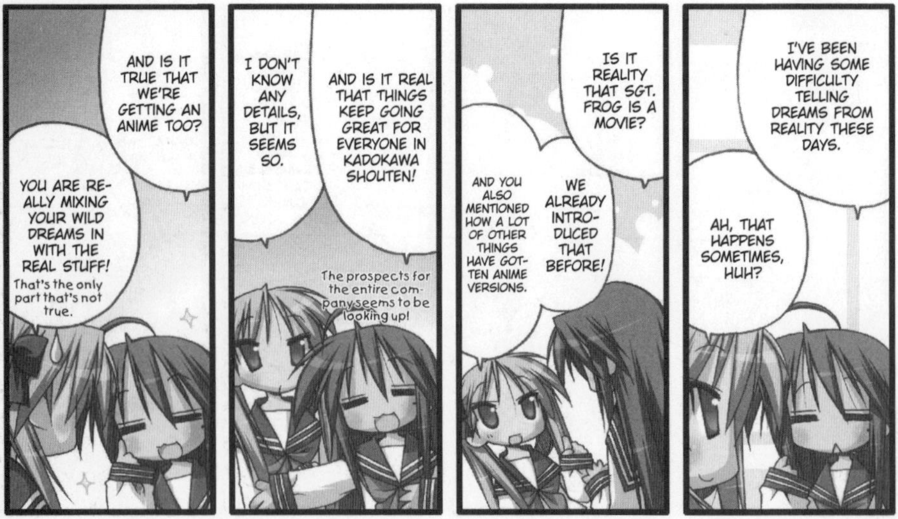
I'VE BEEN HAVING SOME DIFFICULTY TELLING DREAMS FROM REALITY THESE DAYS.
AH, THAT HAPPENS SOMETIMES, HUH?
IS IT REALITY THAT SGT. FROG IS A MOVIE?
WE ALREADY INTRODUCED THAT BEFORE!
AND YOU ALSO MENTIONED HOW A LOT OF OTHER THINGS HAVE GOTTEN ANIME VERSIONS.
AND IS IT REAL THAT THINGS KEEP GOING GREAT FOR EVERYONE IN KADOKAWA SHOUTEN!
I DON'T KNOW ANY DETAILS, BUT IT SEEMS SO.
The prospects for the entire company seems to be looking up!
AND IS IT TRUE THAT WE'RE GETTING AN ANIME TOO?
YOU ARE REALLY MIXING YOUR WILD DREAMS IN WITH THE REAL STUFF!
That's the only part that's not true.

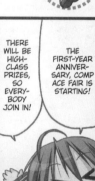

NO. 16 SORRY, I GUESS
An introduction to the 1st-year anniversary, Comp Ace Fair
(2006, April issue)

NO. 17 EVERYBODY'S HAPPY
An introduction to bunko version of the Da Vinci Code.
(2006, May issue)

NO. 18 TRUE STORY
An introduction to Welcome to the NHK, Vol. 5 and the Negative Campaign.
(2006, June issue)

No. 16 sorry, i guess

THE FIRST-YEAR ANNIVERSARY, COMP ACE FAIR IS STARTING!
THERE WILL BE HIGH-CLASS PRIZES, SO EVERYBODY JOIN IN!
THERE WILL ALSO BE THE VERY FIRST VOLUMES OF MANY OF THE COMP ACE MANGA ON SALE. PLEASE SUPPORT THEM.
AND SPEAKING OF GRAPHIC NOVELS, IT'S ABOUT TIME FOR OUR NEXT ONE TO COME OUT, RIGHT?
NO... IT LOOKS LIKE OURS WILL COME OUT SOMEWHERE AROUND SUMMER.
It's been a half year.
HEY! IT'S ONLY SPRING! IT'S WAY TOO EARLY TO BE OVERSLEEPING!
N-NO... THAT'S THE TRUTH...
Again!
Wake up to reality, Kagami!

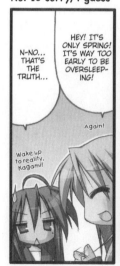

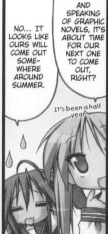

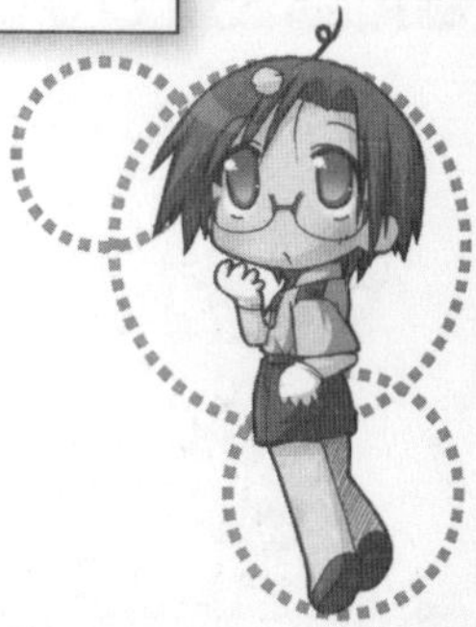

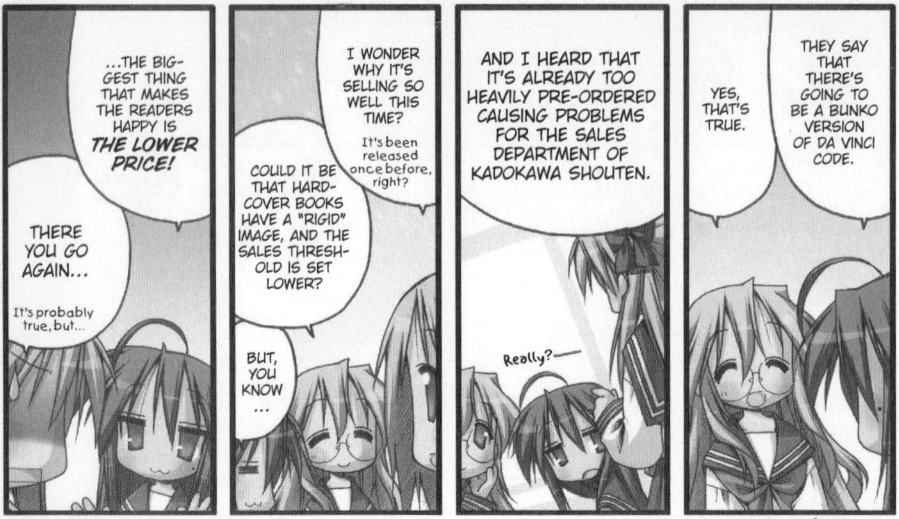
THEY SAY THAT THERE'S GOING TO BE A BUNKO VERSION OF DA VINCI CODE.
YES, THAT'S TRUE.
AND I HEARD THAT IT'S ALREADY TOO HEAVILY PRE-ORDERED CAUSING PROBLEMS FOR THE SALES DEPARTMENT OF KADOKAWA SHOUTEN.
Really?
I WONDER WHY IT'S SELLING SO WELL THIS TIME?
It's been released once before, right?
COULD IT BE THAT HARDCOVER BOOKS HAVE A "RIGID" IMAGE, AND THE SALES THRESHOLD IS SET LOWER?
BUT, YOU KNOW ...
...THE BIGGEST THING THAT MAKES THE READERS HAPPY IS **THE LOWER PRICE!**
THERE YOU GO AGAIN...
It's probably true, but...

No. 17 everybody's happy

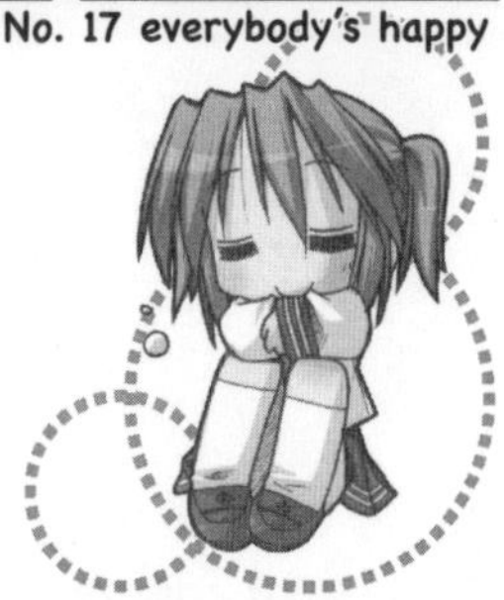

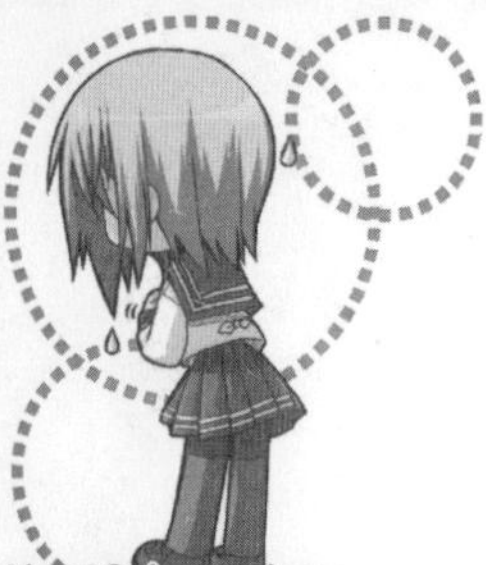

No. 18 true story

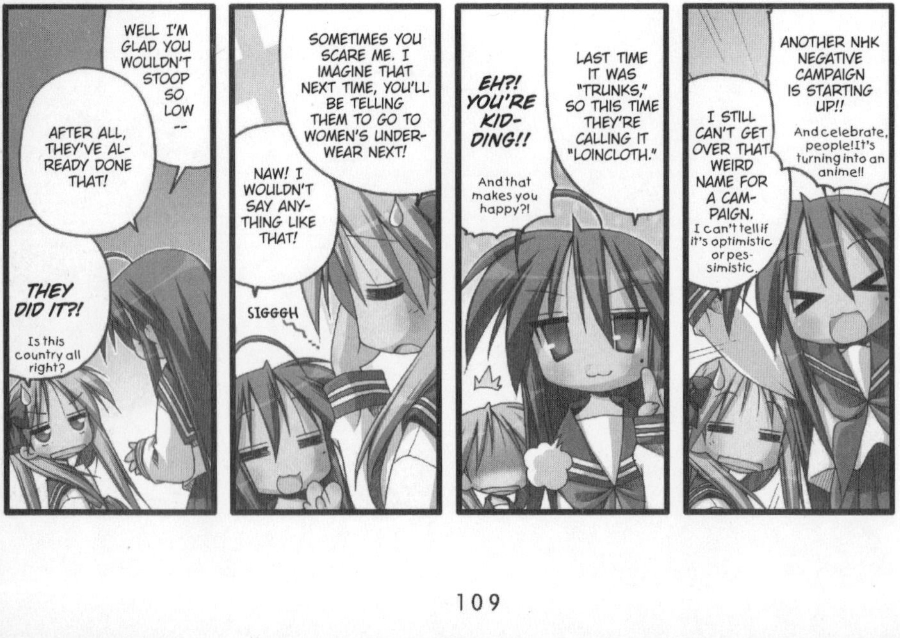
ANOTHER NHK NEGATIVE CAMPAIGN IS STARTING UP!!
And celebrate, people! It's turning into an anime!!
I STILL CAN'T GET OVER THAT WEIRD NAME FOR A CAMPAIGN.
I can't tell if it's optimistic or pessimistic.
LAST TIME IT WAS "TRUNKS," SO THIS TIME THEY'RE CALLING IT "LOINCLOTH."
EH?! YOU'RE KIDDING!!
And that makes you happy?!
SOMETIMES YOU SCARE ME. I IMAGINE THAT NEXT TIME, YOU'LL BE TELLING THEM TO GO TO WOMEN'S UNDERWEAR NEXT!
NAW! I WOULDN'T SAY ANYTHING LIKE THAT!
SIGGGH
WELL I'M GLAD YOU WOULDN'T STOOP SO LOW --
AFTER ALL, THEY'VE ALREADY DONE THAT!
THEY DID IT?!
Is this country all right?

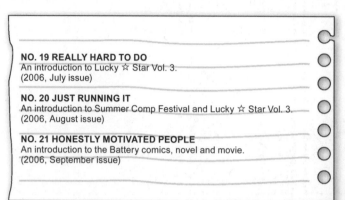

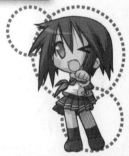

NO. 19 REALLY HARD TO DO
An introduction to Lucky ☆ Star Vol. 3.
(2006, July issue)

NO. 20 JUST RUNNING IT
An introduction to Summer Comp Festival and Lucky ☆ Star Vol. 3.
(2006, August issue)

NO. 21 HONESTLY MOTIVATED PEOPLE
An introduction to the Battery comics, novel and movie.
(2006, September issue)

No. 19 really hard to do

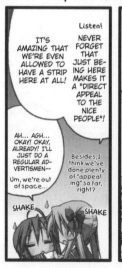

HELLO TO ALL OF YOU BOOKSTORE PEOPLE.
WE HOPE YOU ARE, BY NOW, FAMILIAR WITH US.
BOW
BOW
AND SOON, ON JUL 10TH, LUCKY ☆ STAR VOL. 3 WILL BE RELEASED!
WE WOULD LIKE TO ASK FOR YOUR KIND SUPPORT.
Yaay!!
ARE YOU SUPPOSED TO DO IT THAT STRAIGHTFORWARD?
WELL... WE'VE GOT THIS CHANCE HERE, AND I THOUGHT THAT IT'D BE NICE TO MAKE A DIRECT APPEAL TO THE NICE PEOPLE OUT THERE.
Listen! NEVER FORGET THAT JUST BEING HERE MAKES IT A "DIRECT APPEAL TO THE NICE PEOPLE"!
IT'S AMAZING THAT WE'RE EVEN ALLOWED TO HAVE A STRIP HERE AT ALL!
Besides, I think we've done plenty of "appealing" so far, right?
AH... AGH... OKAY! OKAY, ALREADY! I'LL JUST DO A REGULAR ADVERTISMEN--
Um, we're out of space...
SHAKE
SHAKE

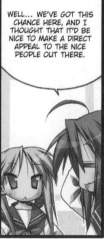

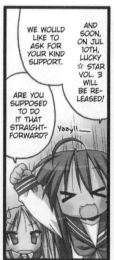

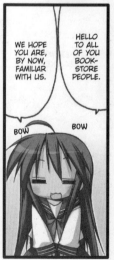

No. 20 just running the strip

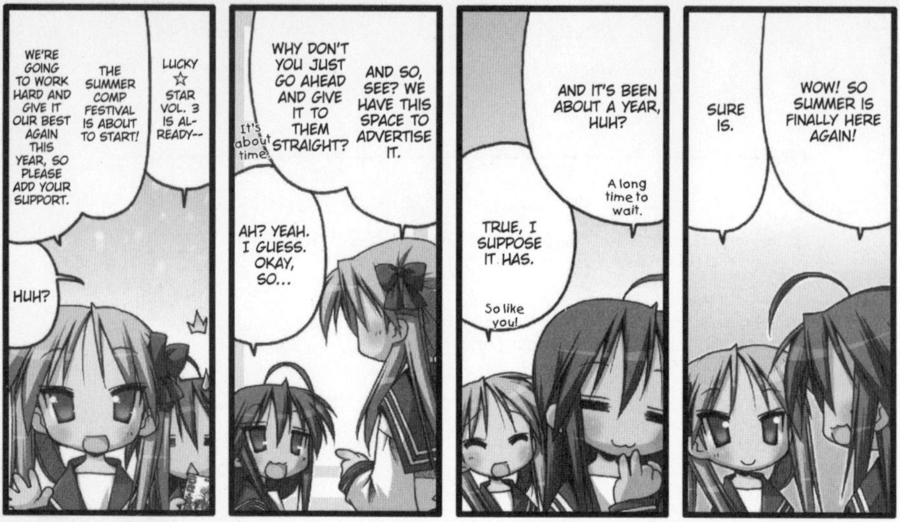
WOW! SO SUMMER IS FINALLY HERE AGAIN!
SURE IS.
AND IT'S BEEN ABOUT A YEAR, HUH?
A long time to wait.
TRUE, I SUPPOSE IT HAS.
So like you!
AND SO, SEE? WE HAVE THIS SPACE TO ADVERTISE IT.
WHY DON'T YOU JUST GO AHEAD AND GIVE IT TO THEM STRAIGHT?
It's about time.
AH? YEAH. I GUESS. OKAY, SO...
LUCKY ☆ STAR VOL. 3 IS AL-READY--
THE SUMMER COMP FESTIVAL IS ABOUT TO START!
WE'RE GOING TO WORK HARD AND GIVE IT OUR BEST AGAIN THIS YEAR, SO PLEASE ADD YOUR SUPPORT.
HUH?

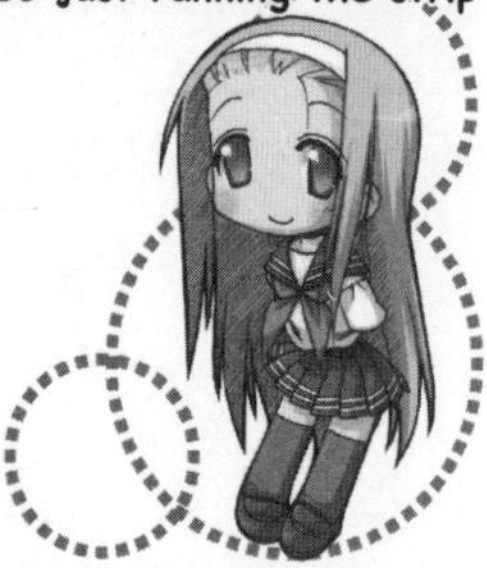

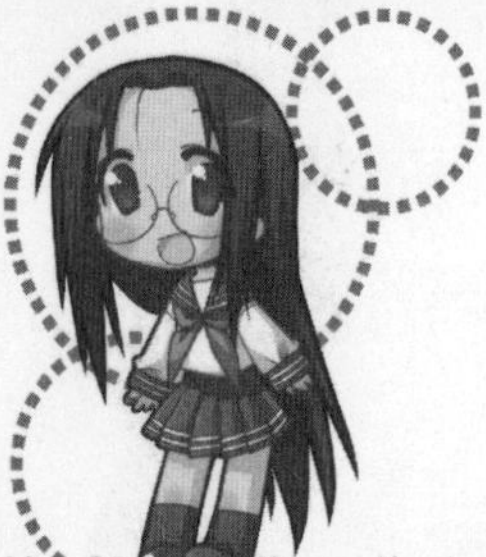

No. 21 honestly motivated people

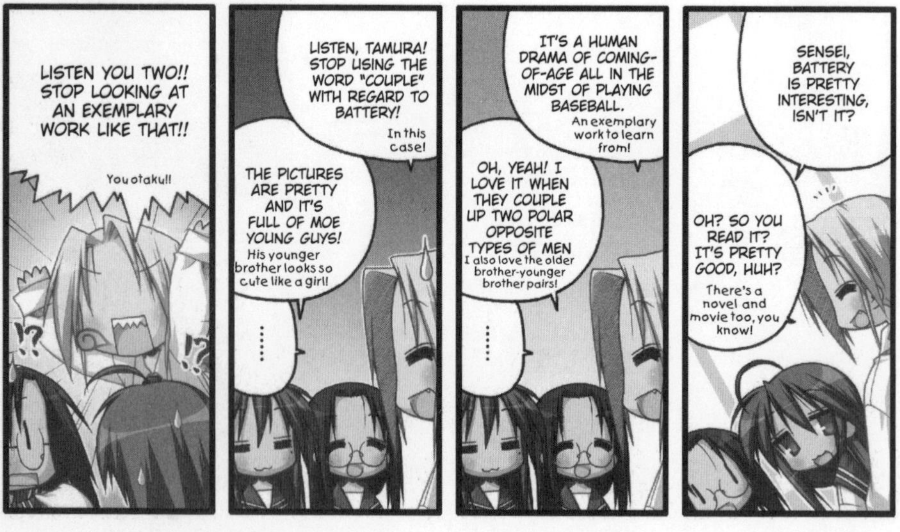
SENSEI, BATTERY IS PRETTY INTERESTING, ISN'T IT?
OH? SO YOU READ IT? IT'S PRETTY GOOD, HUH?
There's a novel and movie too, you know!
IT'S A HUMAN DRAMA OF COMING-OF-AGE ALL IN THE MIDST OF PLAYING BASEBALL.
An exemplary work to learn from!
OH, YEAH! I LOVE IT WHEN THEY COUPLE UP TWO POLAR OPPOSITE TYPES OF MEN
I also love the older brother-younger brother pairs!
......
LISTEN, TAMURA! STOP USING THE WORD "COUPLE" WITH REGARD TO BATTERY!
In this case!
THE PICTURES ARE PRETTY AND IT'S FULL OF MOE YOUNG GUYS!
His younger brother looks so cute like a girl!
......
LISTEN YOU TWO!! STOP LOOKING AT AN EXEMPLARY WORK LIKE THAT!!
You otaku!!
!?
!?

NO. 22 GETTING WORKED UP
An introduction to the TV anime adaptation of Shounen Onmyouji.
(2006, October issue)

NO. 23 DREAM
Introduction to the decision to make Lucky ☆ Star an anime and the Shounen Ace 12-year anniversary campaign.
(2006, November issue)

NO. 24 MISSION
An introduction to The Melancholy of Haruhi Suzumiya Vol. 3 manga and the Lucky ☆ Star anime.
(2006, December issue)

No. 22 getting worked up

SEMPAI, DID YOU LISTEN TO THE DRAMA CD I LENT YOU EARLIER?
YOU MEAN SHOUNEN ONMYOUJI? YEAH, I SURE DID! IT WAS GREAT!
THE STORY WAS SO PURE AND RIGHTEOUS! I FELT CLEANSED AFTER!
AndI was really moved!
DIDN'T YOU THINK THE CHARAC-TERS WERE CHARMING AND MULTI-FACETED?
ABSO-LUTELY! I'M EVEN THINKING OF PICKING UP THE NOVELS!
THAT'S A GOOD IDEA! AND IT'S GOING TO BE AN ANIME STARTING IN OCTOBER!
Let's soak it all in!
REALLY? THEY'RE ANIMAT-ING IT?!
WAIT! SEMPAI, YOU CAN'T JUST WATCH THE ANIME! A TRUE FAN WOULD ALSO READ THE ORIGINAL WORK!
And enjoy them both for what they are!
HA HA HA! YOU'RE A BET-TER INFLUENCE THAN KAGAMI IS, HIYORIN!
In fact, if you sug-gested the books on Kagami, she'd probably be happy!

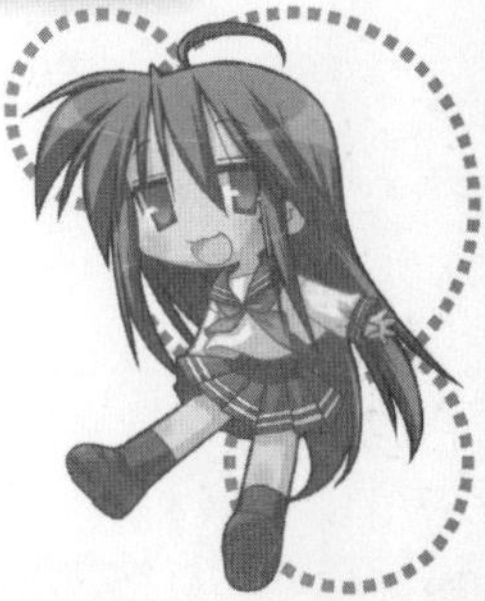

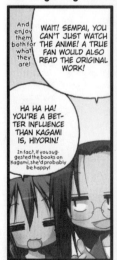

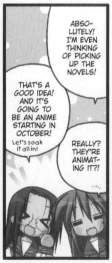

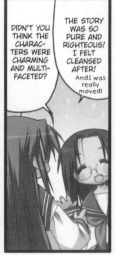

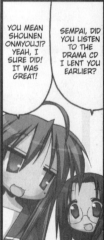

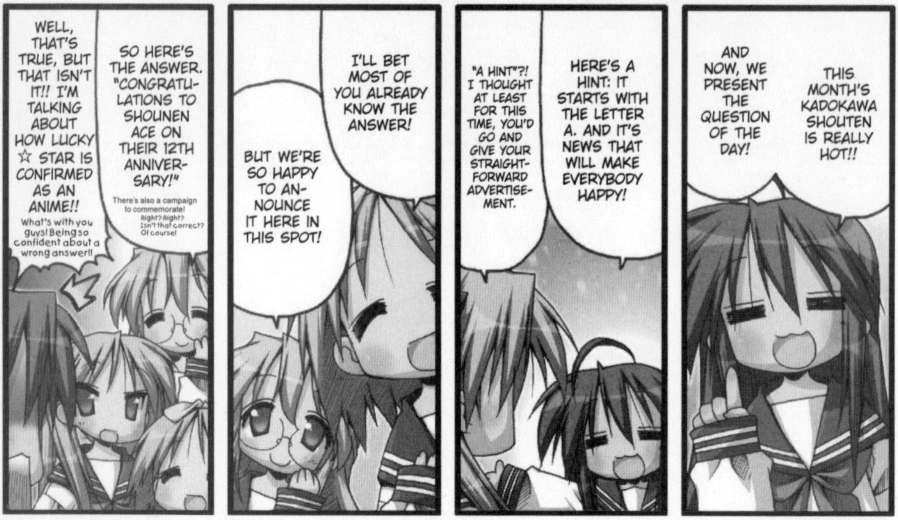
AND NOW, WE PRESENT THE QUESTION OF THE DAY!
THIS MONTH'S KADOKAWA SHOUTEN IS REALLY HOT!!
HERE'S A HINT: IT STARTS WITH THE LETTER A. AND IT'S NEWS THAT WILL MAKE EVERYBODY HAPPY!
"A HINT"?! I THOUGHT AT LEAST FOR THIS TIME, YOU'D GO AND GIVE YOUR STRAIGHT-FORWARD ADVERTISE-MENT.
I'LL BET MOST OF YOU ALREADY KNOW THE ANSWER!
BUT WE'RE SO HAPPY TO AN-NOUNCE IT HERE IN THIS SPOT!
SO HERE'S THE ANSWER. "CONGRATU-LATIONS TO SHOUNEN ACE ON THEIR 12TH ANNIVER-SARY!"
There's also a campaign to commemorate! Right? Right? Isn't that correct? Of course!
WELL, THAT'S TRUE, BUT THAT ISN'T IT!! I'M TALKING ABOUT HOW LUCKY ☆ STAR IS CONFIRMED AS AN ANIME!!
What's with you guys! Being so confident about a wrong answer!!

No. 23 dream

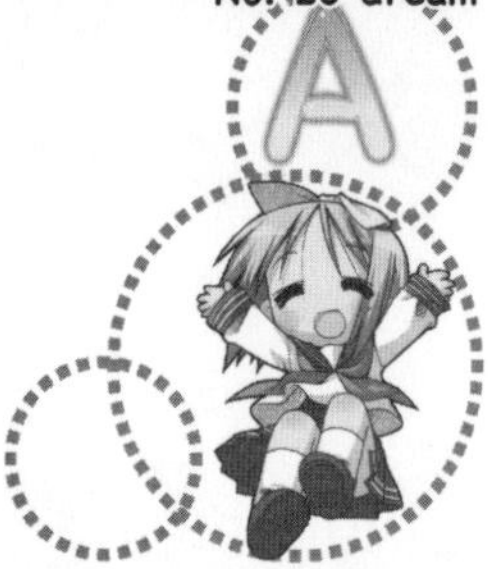
A

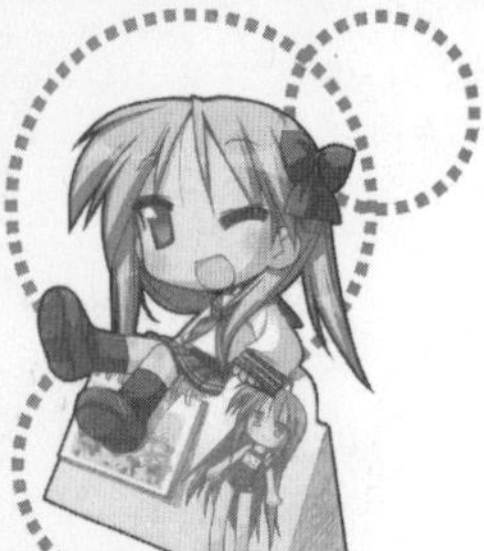

No. 24 mission

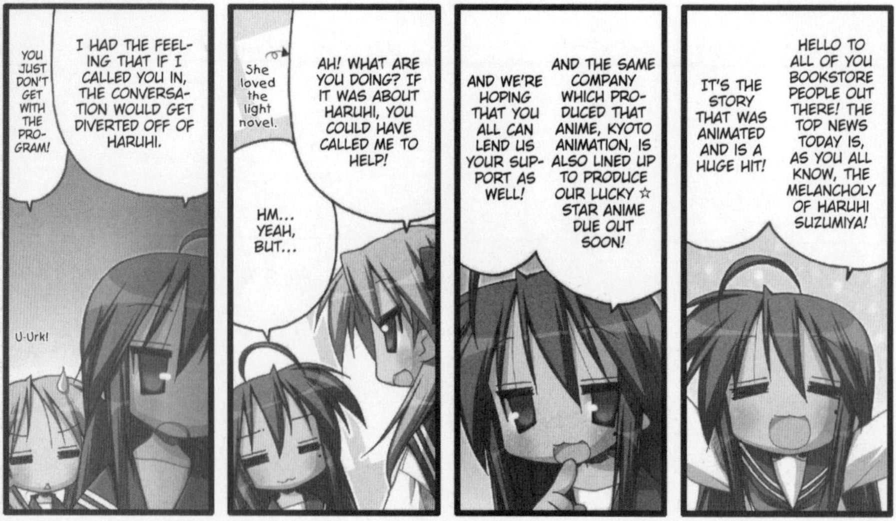
HELLO TO ALL OF YOU BOOKSTORE PEOPLE OUT THERE! THE TOP NEWS TODAY IS, AS YOU ALL KNOW, THE MELANCHOLY OF HARUHI SUZUMIYA!
IT'S THE STORY THAT WAS ANIMATED AND IS A HUGE HIT!
AND THE SAME COMPANY WHICH PRO-DUCED THAT ANIME, KYOTO ANIMATION, IS ALSO LINED UP TO PRODUCE OUR LUCKY ☆ STAR ANIME DUE OUT SOON!
AND WE'RE HOPING THAT YOU ALL CAN LEND US YOUR SUP-PORT AS WELL!
AH! WHAT ARE YOU DOING? IF IT WAS ABOUT HARUHI, YOU COULD HAVE CALLED ME TO HELP!
She loved the light novel.
HM... YEAH, BUT...
I HAD THE FEEL-ING THAT IF I CALLED YOU IN, THE CONVERSA-TION WOULD GET DIVERTED OFF OF HARUHI.
YOU JUST DON'T GET WITH THE PRO-GRAM!
U-Urk!

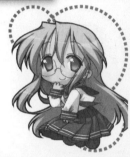

NO. 25 PINCH THIS
The Lucky ☆ Star cast gives their New Year's greetings and hopes.
(2007, January issue)

NO. 26 CHARM
An introduction to Sgt. Frog 2 and Battery movies.
(2007, February issue)

NO. 27 THE GOES-ALL-OUT GANG
An introduction to Sgt. Frog 2 and Battery movies plus the Lucky ☆ Star TV anime.
(2007, March issue)

No. 25 pinch this

A HAPPY NEW YEAR TO ALL OF YOU!
THIS YEAR, THE TALKS TO PRODUCE A SECOND LUCKY ☆ STAR GAME AND THE ANIME ARE ALL PROCEEDING NICELY, SO IT LOOKS TO BE A GREAT YEAR FOR US!
AND THE THANKS GO ENTIRELY TO YOU!
WE SEND OUT OUR WISHES THAT THIS YEAR IS AN EXCEPTIONAL YEAR FOR ALL OF YOU.
AND I'D LIKE TO SAY AGAIN, PLEASE KEEP UP YOUR FAITHFUL SUPPORT OF LUCKY ☆ STAR THIS YEAR TOO.
BOW
HUH? BUT THIS MAKES IT NOT SO MUCH A 4-PANEL STRIP, BUT JUST A REGULAR GREETINGS ADVERTISEMENT.
IT CAN'T BE...
RELAX! WE HAVEN'T HAD MUCH IN THE WAY OF A STORY-LINE, SET-UPS, OR PUNCH LINES SO FAR, SO WHY START NOW?
We're just taking care of business this time.

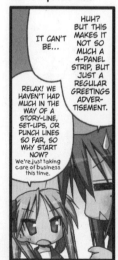

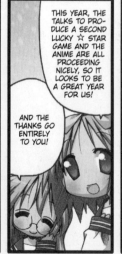

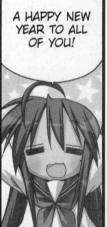

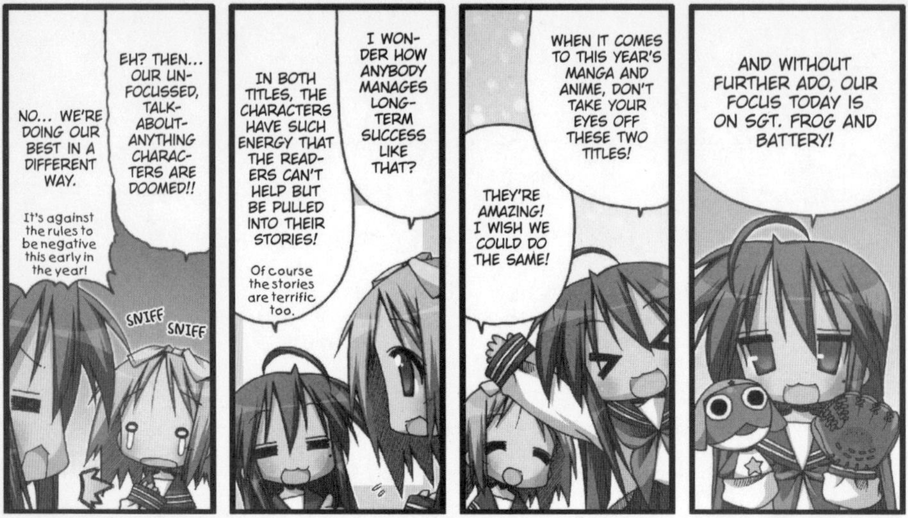
AND WITHOUT FURTHER ADO, OUR FOCUS TODAY IS ON SGT. FROG AND BATTERY!
WHEN IT COMES TO THIS YEAR'S MANGA AND ANIME, DON'T TAKE YOUR EYES OFF THESE TWO TITLES!
THEY'RE AMAZING! I WISH WE COULD DO THE SAME!
I WONDER HOW ANYBODY MANAGES LONG-TERM SUCCESS LIKE THAT?
IN BOTH TITLES, THE CHARACTERS HAVE SUCH ENERGY THAT THE READERS CAN'T HELP BUT BE PULLED INTO THEIR STORIES!
Of course the stories are terrific too.
EH? THEN... OUR UNFOCUSSED, TALK-ABOUT-ANYTHING CHARACTERS ARE DOOMED!!
NO... WE'RE DOING OUR BEST IN A DIFFERENT WAY.
It's against the rules to be negative this early in the year!
SNIFF SNIFF

No. 26 charm

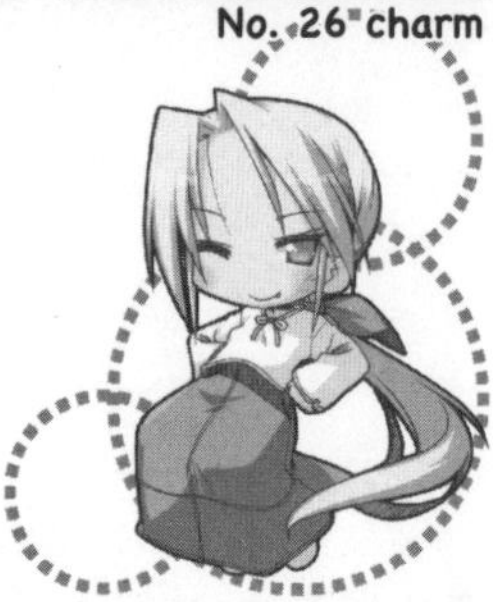

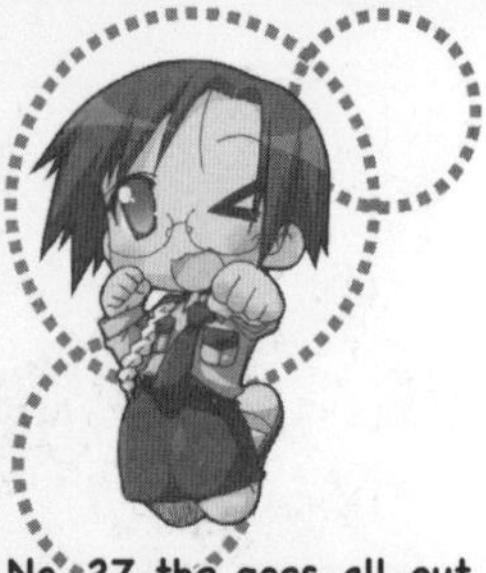

No. 27 the goes-all-out gang

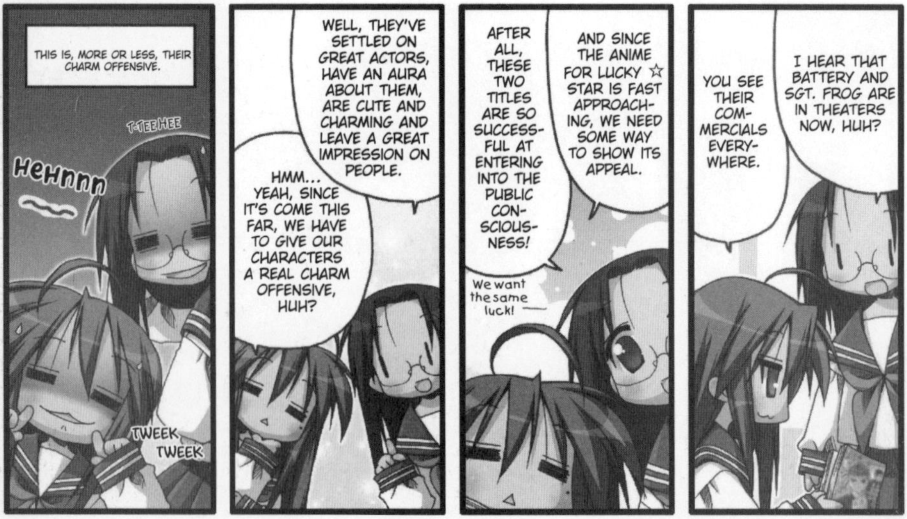
I HEAR THAT BATTERY AND SGT. FROG ARE IN THEATERS NOW, HUH?
YOU SEE THEIR COMMERCIALS EVERYWHERE.
AND SINCE THE ANIME FOR LUCKY ☆ STAR IS FAST APPROACHING, WE NEED SOME WAY TO SHOW ITS APPEAL.
AFTER ALL, THESE TWO TITLES ARE SO SUCCESSFUL AT ENTERING INTO THE PUBLIC CONSCIOUSNESS!
We want the same luck! —
WELL, THEY'VE SETTLED ON GREAT ACTORS, HAVE AN AURA ABOUT THEM, ARE CUTE AND CHARMING AND LEAVE A GREAT IMPRESSION ON PEOPLE.
HMM... YEAH, SINCE IT'S COME THIS FAR, WE HAVE TO GIVE OUR CHARACTERS A REAL CHARM OFFENSIVE, HUH?
THIS IS, MORE OR LESS, THEIR CHARM OFFENSIVE.
T-TEE HEE
HEHNNN ~~
TWEEK TWEEK

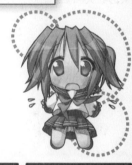

NO. 28 FOUR PANEL
An introduction to Lucky ☆ Star Vol. 4, and the Spring Lucky Fair 2007.
(2007, April issue)

NO. 29 ALREADY OUT OF TIME
An introduction to The Melancholy of Haruhi Suzumiya, Sgt. Frog and Battery.
(2007, May issue)

NO. 30 ILLUSION
An introduction to Evangelion Vol. 11 and The Melancholy of Haruhi Suzumiya Vol. 4.
(2007, June issue)

No. 28 four panel

THE ANIME HAS FINALLY STARTED!!
WE MOVE! WE TALK! SO SUPPORT US!!
We're animated by the famous Kyo-ani!!
YAAAY!
AND ALONG WITH IT, THIS MONTH OUR MANGA VOLUME 4 IS ARRIVING ON THE STANDS. PLEASE SUPPORT THAT TOO!
EH HEH
HEH
ALSO, WE WILL BE COMMENCING THIS YEAR'S SPRING LUCKY FAIR 2007. WE HOPE YOU'RE ALL AS EXCITED AS WE ARE.
W-WAIT A SECOND HERE!
WHAT IS THIS? IT'S JUST A COMMERCIAL!
DON'T WORRY ABOUT IT. THIS IS JUST A 4-PANEL STRIP! NOBODY ACTUALLY READS IT!
DOESN'T THAT COMPLETELY NEGATE OUR ENTIRE PURPOSE FOR EXISTING?!
Are you sure you want that?

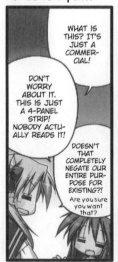

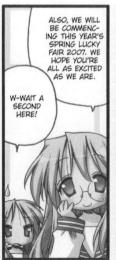

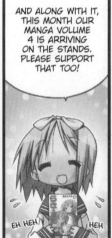

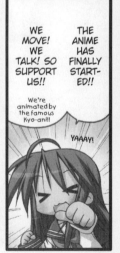

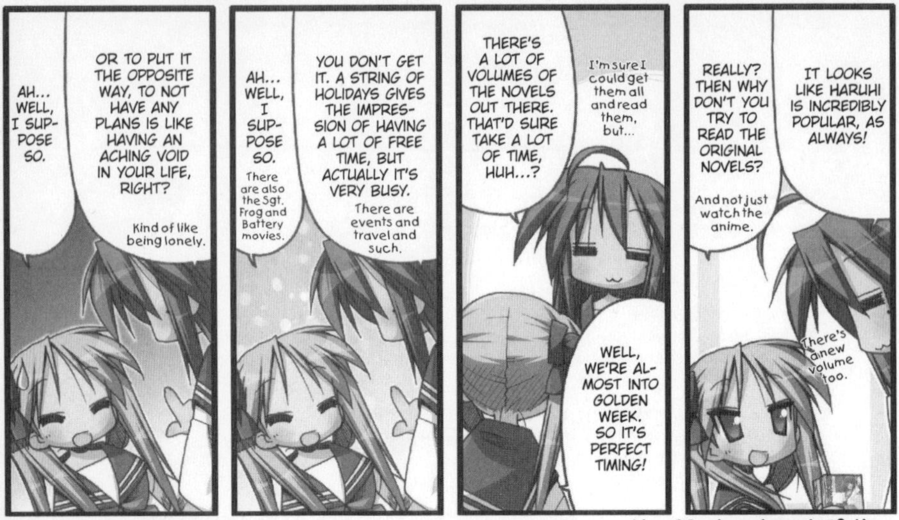
IT LOOKS LIKE HARUHI IS INCREDIBLY POPULAR, AS ALWAYS!
REALLY? THEN WHY DON'T YOU TRY TO READ THE ORIGINAL NOVELS?
And not just watch the anime.
There's a new volume too.
THERE'S A LOT OF VOLUMES OF THE NOVELS OUT THERE. THAT'D SURE TAKE A LOT OF TIME, HUH...?
I'm sure I could get them all and read them, but...
WELL, WE'RE AL-MOST INTO GOLDEN WEEK. SO IT'S PERFECT TIMING!
YOU DON'T GET IT. A STRING OF HOLIDAYS GIVES THE IMPRES-SION OF HAVING A LOT OF FREE TIME, BUT ACTUALLY IT'S VERY BUSY.
There are events and travel and such.
AH... WELL, I SUP-POSE SO.
There are also the Sgt. Frog and Battery movies.
OR TO PUT IT THE OPPOSITE WAY, TO NOT HAVE ANY PLANS IS LIKE HAVING AN ACHING VOID IN YOUR LIFE, RIGHT?
Kind of like being lonely.
AH... WELL, I SUP-POSE SO.

No. 29 already out of time

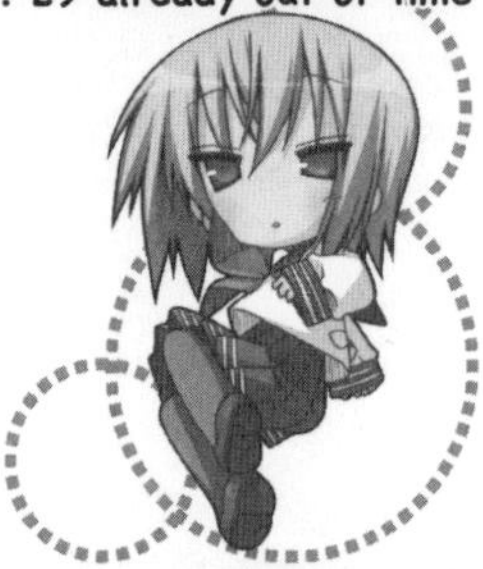

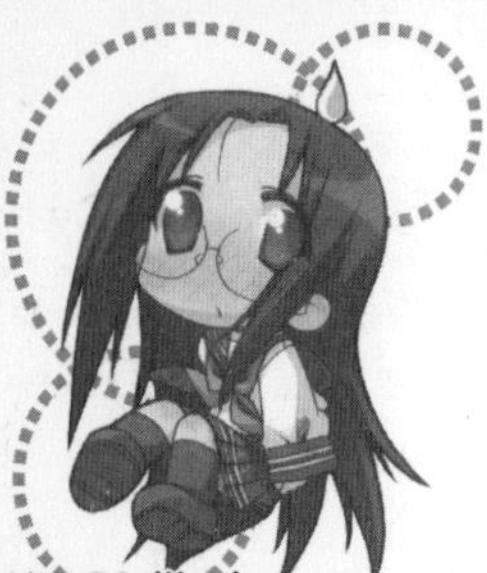

No. 30 illusion

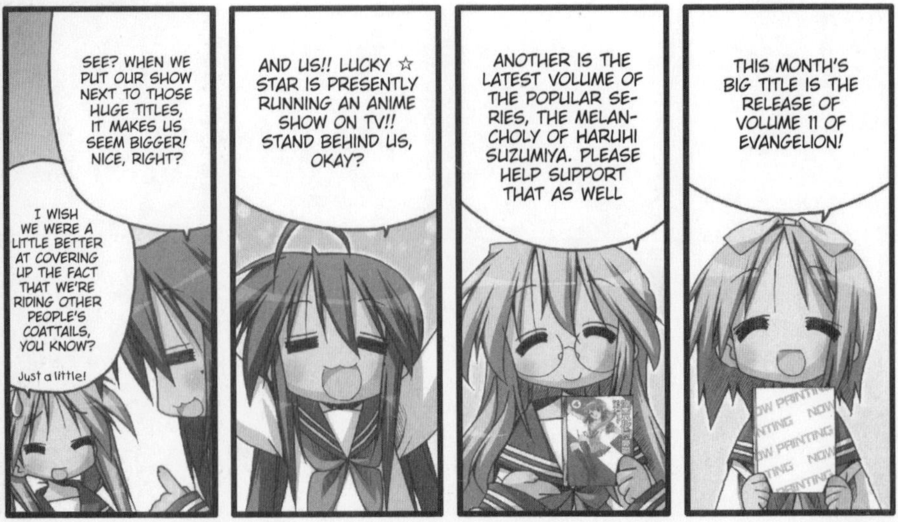
THIS MONTH'S BIG TITLE IS THE RELEASE OF VOLUME 11 OF EVANGELION!
NOW PAINTING
ANOTHER IS THE LATEST VOLUME OF THE POPULAR SE-RIES, THE MELAN-CHOLY OF HARUHI SUZUMIYA. PLEASE HELP SUPPORT THAT AS WELL
AND US!! LUCKY ☆ STAR IS PRESENTLY RUNNING AN ANIME SHOW ON TV!! STAND BEHIND US, OKAY?
SEE? WHEN WE PUT OUR SHOW NEXT TO THOSE HUGE TITLES, IT MAKES US SEEM BIGGER! NICE, RIGHT?
I WISH WE WERE A LITTLE BETTER AT COVERING UP THE FACT THAT WE'RE RIDING OTHER PEOPLE'S COATTAILS, YOU KNOW?
Just a little!

NO. 31 EMPHASIS
An introduction to Sgt. Frog Vol. 15, Welcome to the NHK Vol. 8, and the Lucky ☆ Star series in the supplemental magazine.
(2007, July issue)

NO. 32 FRIENDLY AND FUN
An introduction to the Lucky ☆ Star Official Guide, the special collection, and Nichijou Vol. 1.
(2007, August issue)

NO. 33 HONESTLY MOTIVATED PEOPLE
An introduction to Lucky ☆ Star Vol. 5 and Fate/Stay Night Vol. 4.
(2007, September issue)

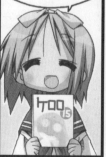

No. 31 emphasis

THIS MONTH, THE EXTREMELY POPULAR SGT. FROG'S MUCH AWAITED VOLUME 15 COMES OUT!
ALSO, THE HIT AND TALKED-ABOUT WELCOME TO THE NHK'S FINALE, VOLUME 8 FINDS ITS WAY TO THE SHELVES. PLEASE LEND YOUR SUPPORT!
NHKにようこそ! 8
AND US TOO! WE KNOW YOU ALL LOVE OUR ANIME, AND NOW LUCKY ☆ STAR GETS A SPECIAL-EDITION MAGAZINE TO RUN THE STRIPS! WE'RE GIVING IT OUR BEST, SO PLEASE STAY WITH US!
THIS TIME, HAVING OUR STORY SURROUNDED BY HUGE TITLES MAKES US LOOK BIG! MAYBE IT REALLY DOES LOOK LIKE RIDING COAT-TAILS, HUH?
LISTEN YOU! YOU'RE DOING THIS ON PURPOSE, AREN'T YOU?
You did exactly the same thing last month!

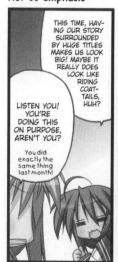

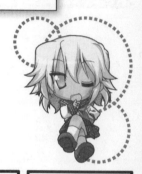

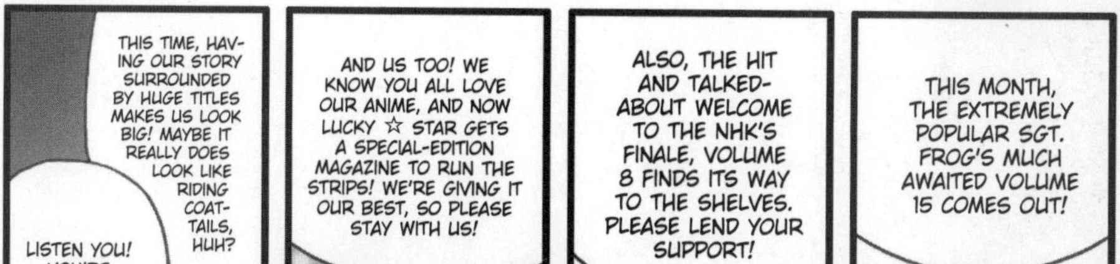

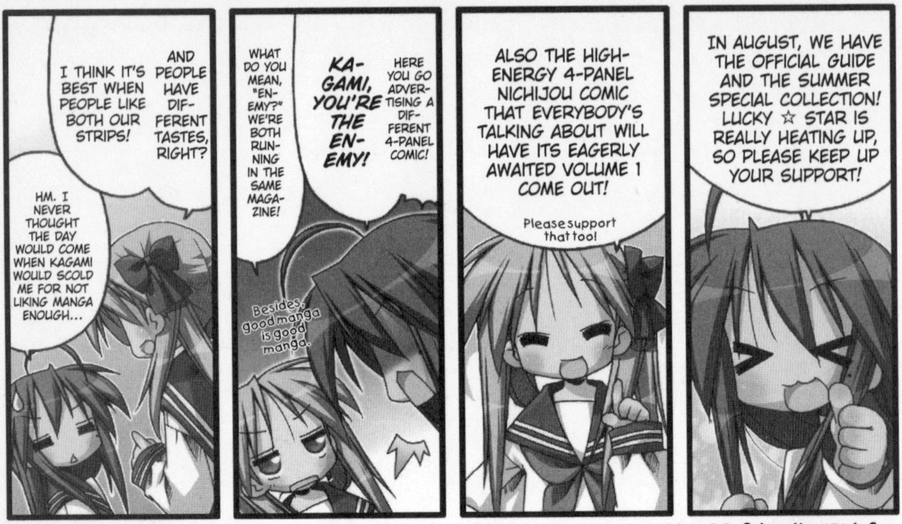
IN AUGUST, WE HAVE THE OFFICIAL GUIDE AND THE SUMMER SPECIAL COLLECTION! LUCKY ☆ STAR IS REALLY HEATING UP, SO PLEASE KEEP UP YOUR SUPPORT!
ALSO THE HIGH-ENERGY 4-PANEL NICHIJOU COMIC THAT EVERYBODY'S TALKING ABOUT WILL HAVE ITS EAGERLY AWAITED VOLUME 1 COME OUT!
Please support that too!
HERE YOU GO ADVERTISING A DIFFERENT 4-PANEL COMIC!
KAGAMI, YOU'RE THE ENEMY!
WHAT DO YOU MEAN, "ENEMY?" WE'RE BOTH RUNNING IN THE SAME MAGAZINE!
Besides, good manga is good manga.
AND PEOPLE HAVE DIFFERENT TASTES, RIGHT?
I THINK IT'S BEST WHEN PEOPLE LIKE BOTH OUR STRIPS!
HM. I NEVER THOUGHT THE DAY WOULD COME WHEN KAGAMI WOULD SCOLD ME FOR NOT LIKING MANGA ENOUGH...

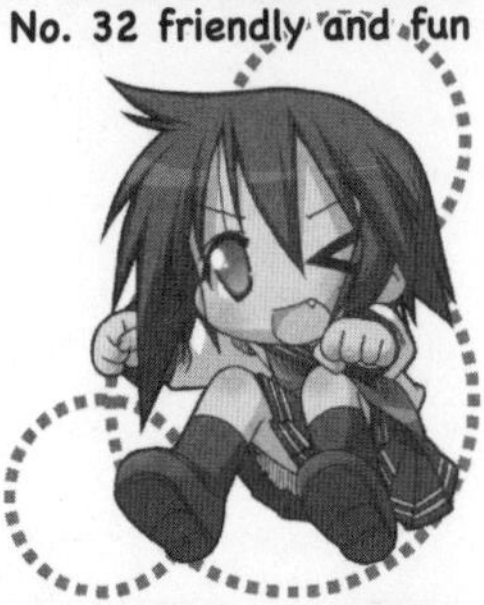

No. 32 friendly and fun

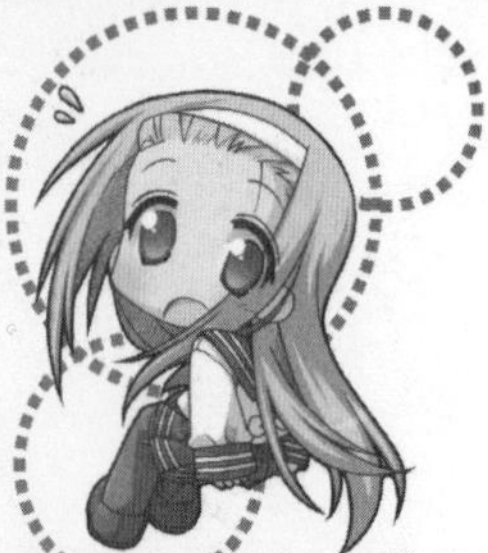

No. 33 honestly motivated people

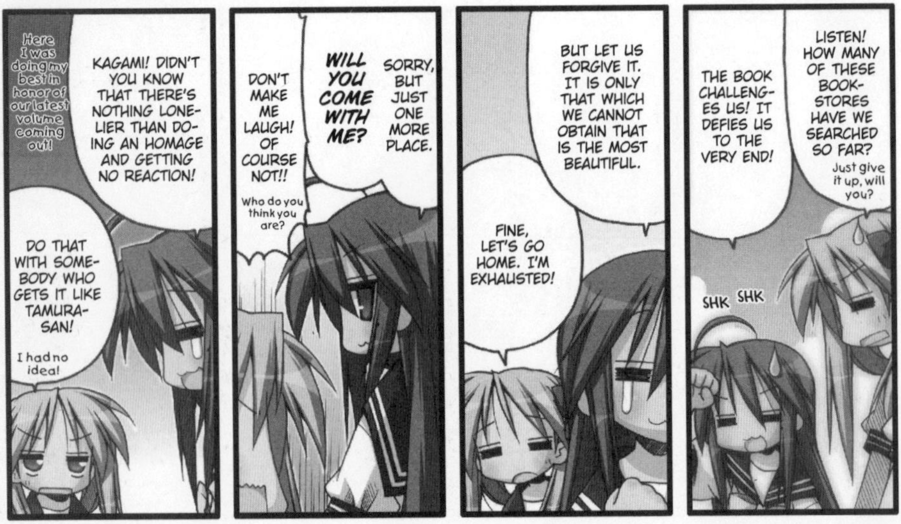
LISTEN! HOW MANY OF THESE BOOKSTORES HAVE WE SEARCHED SO FAR?
THE BOOK CHALLENGES US! IT DEFIES US TO THE VERY END!
Just give it up, will you?
SHK SHK
BUT LET US FORGIVE IT. IT IS ONLY THAT WHICH WE CANNOT OBTAIN THAT IS THE MOST BEAUTIFUL.
FINE, LET'S GO HOME. I'M EXHAUSTED!
SORRY, BUT JUST ONE MORE PLACE.
WILL YOU COME WITH ME?
DON'T MAKE ME LAUGH! OF COURSE NOT!!
Who do you think you are?
KAGAMI! DIDN'T YOU KNOW THAT THERE'S NOTHING LONELIER THAN DOING AN HOMAGE AND GETTING NO REACTION!
Here I was doing my best in honor of our latest volume coming out!
DO THAT WITH SOMEBODY WHO GETS IT LIKE TAMURA-SAN!
I had no idea!

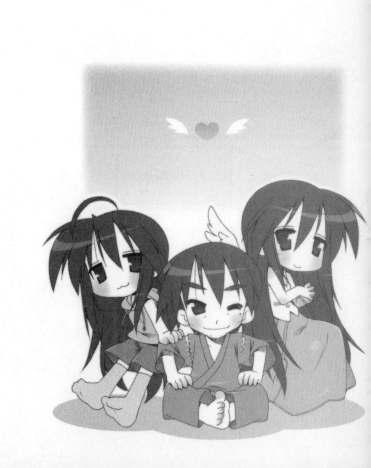

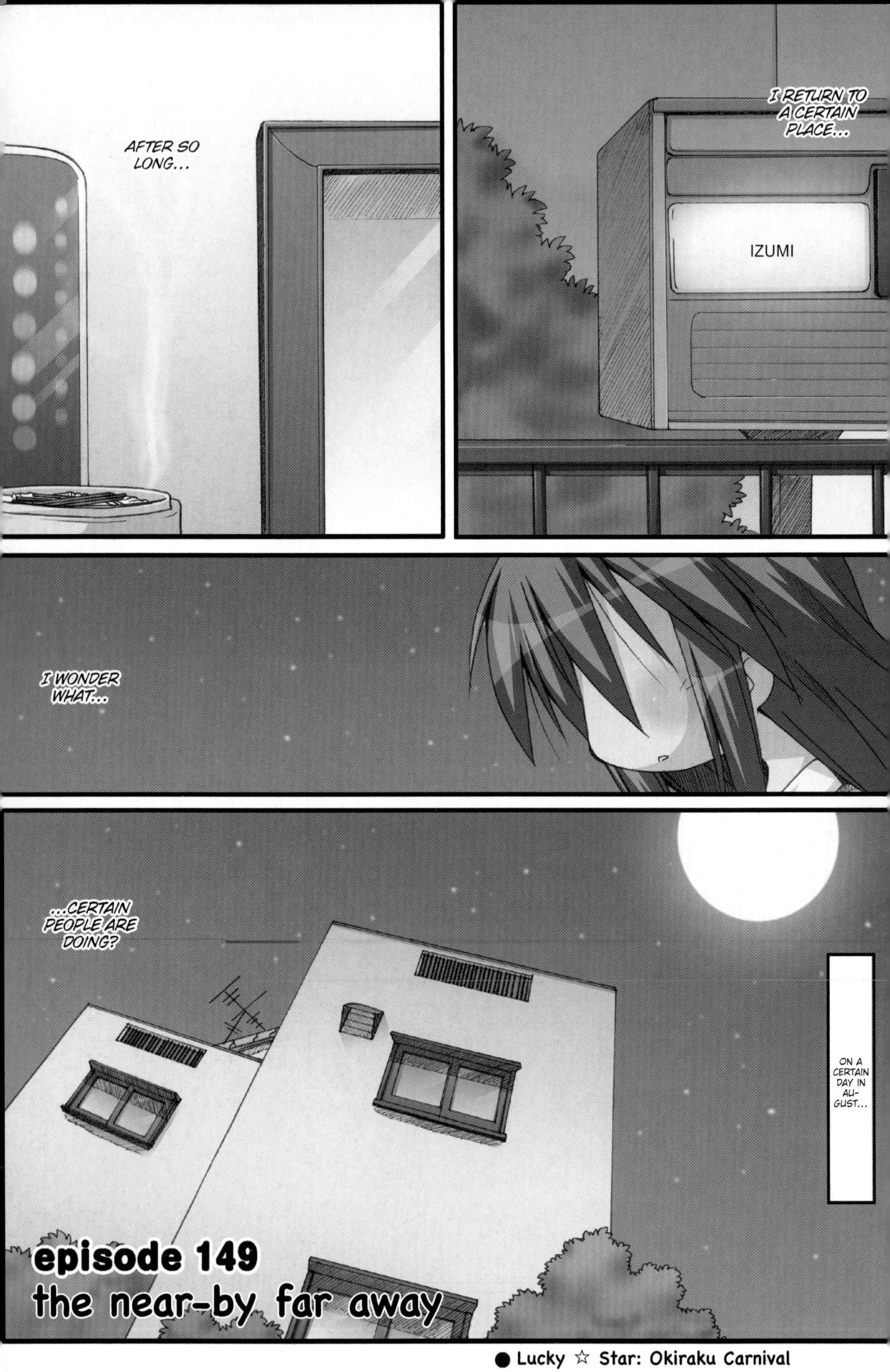
I RETURN TO A CERTAIN PLACE...
IZUMI
AFTER SO LONG...
I WONDER WHAT...
...CERTAIN PEOPLE ARE DOING?
ON A CERTAIN DAY IN AU-GUST...
episode 149
the near-by far away

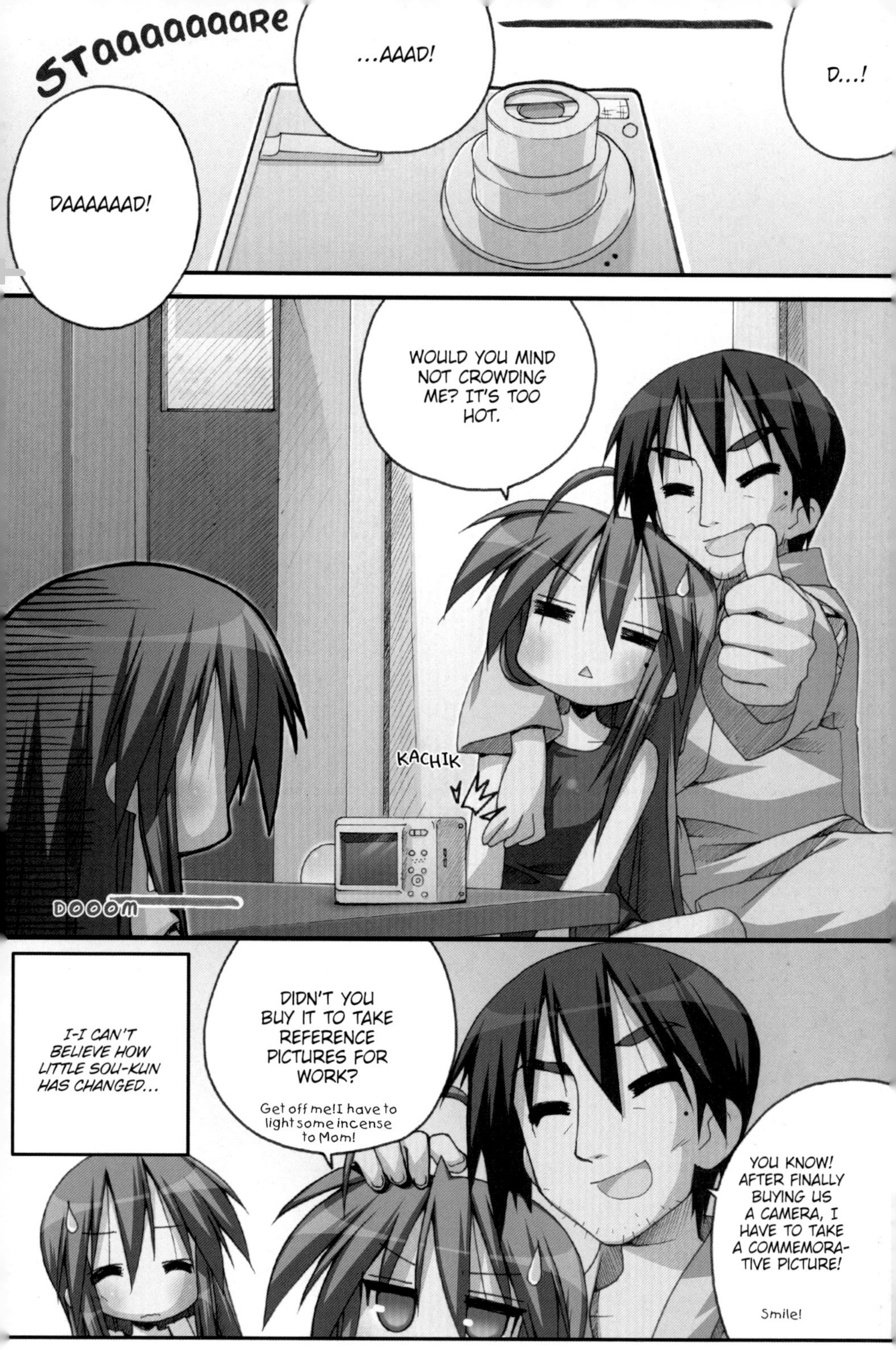
D...!
...AAAD!
Staaaaaaare
DAAAAAAD!
WOULD YOU MIND NOT CROWDING ME? IT'S TOO HOT.
KACHIK
DOOOM
YOU KNOW! AFTER FINALLY BUYING US A CAMERA, I HAVE TO TAKE A COMMEMORA-TIVE PICTURE!
Smile!
DIDN'T YOU BUY IT TO TAKE REFERENCE PICTURES FOR WORK?
Get off me! I have to light some incense to Mom!
I-I CAN'T BELIEVE HOW LITTLE SOU-KUN HAS CHANGED...

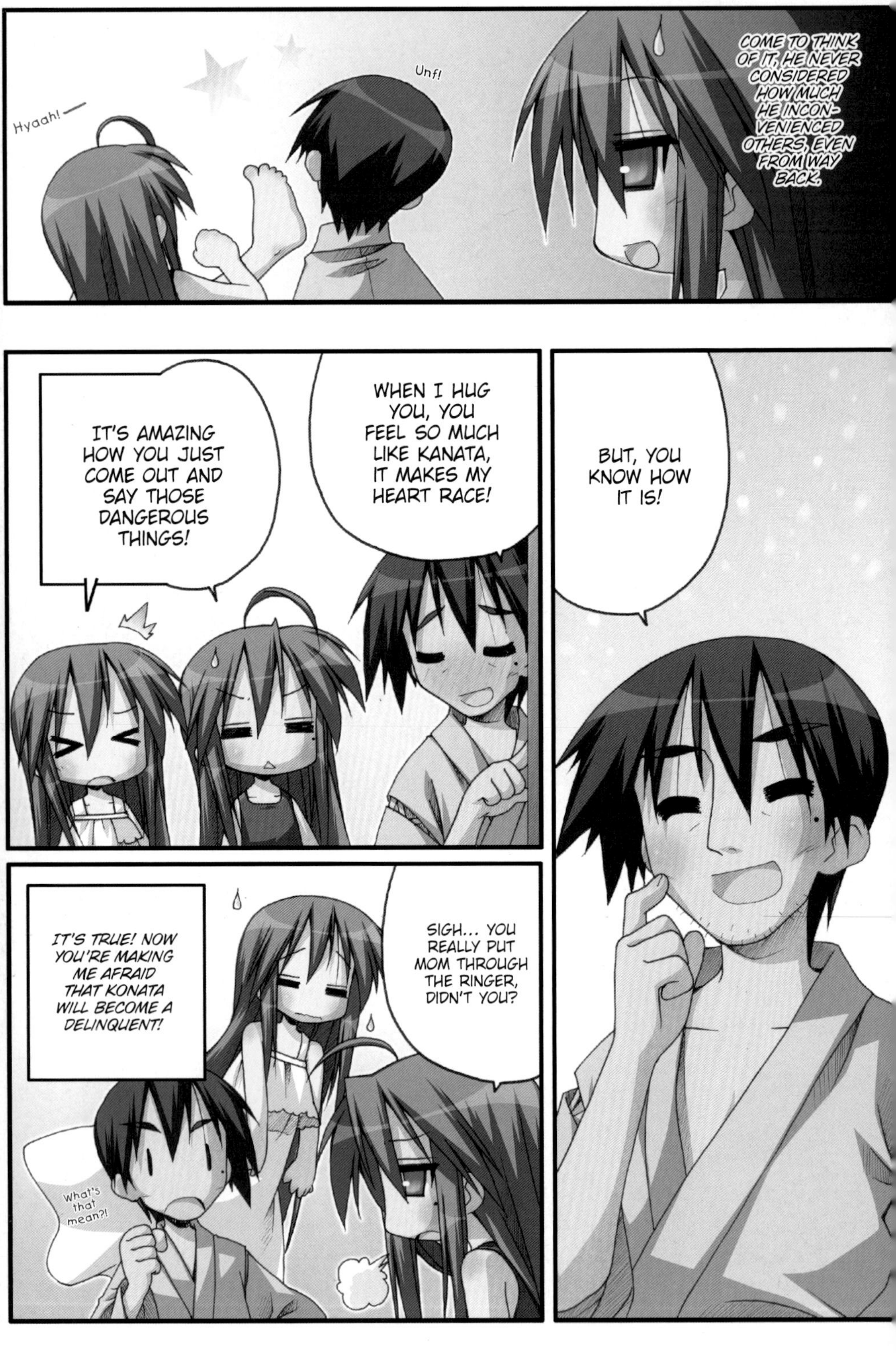
COME TO THINK OF IT, HE NEVER CONSIDERED HOW MUCH HE INCON-VENIENCED OTHERS, EVEN FROM WAY BACK.
Unf!
Hyaah!
BUT, YOU KNOW HOW IT IS!
WHEN I HUG YOU, YOU FEEL SO MUCH LIKE KANATA, IT MAKES MY HEART RACE!
IT'S AMAZING HOW YOU JUST COME OUT AND SAY THOSE DANGEROUS THINGS!
SIGH... YOU REALLY PUT MOM THROUGH THE RINGER, DIDN'T YOU?
IT'S TRUE! NOW YOU'RE MAKING ME AFRAID THAT KONATA WILL BECOME A DELINQUENT!
What's that mean?!

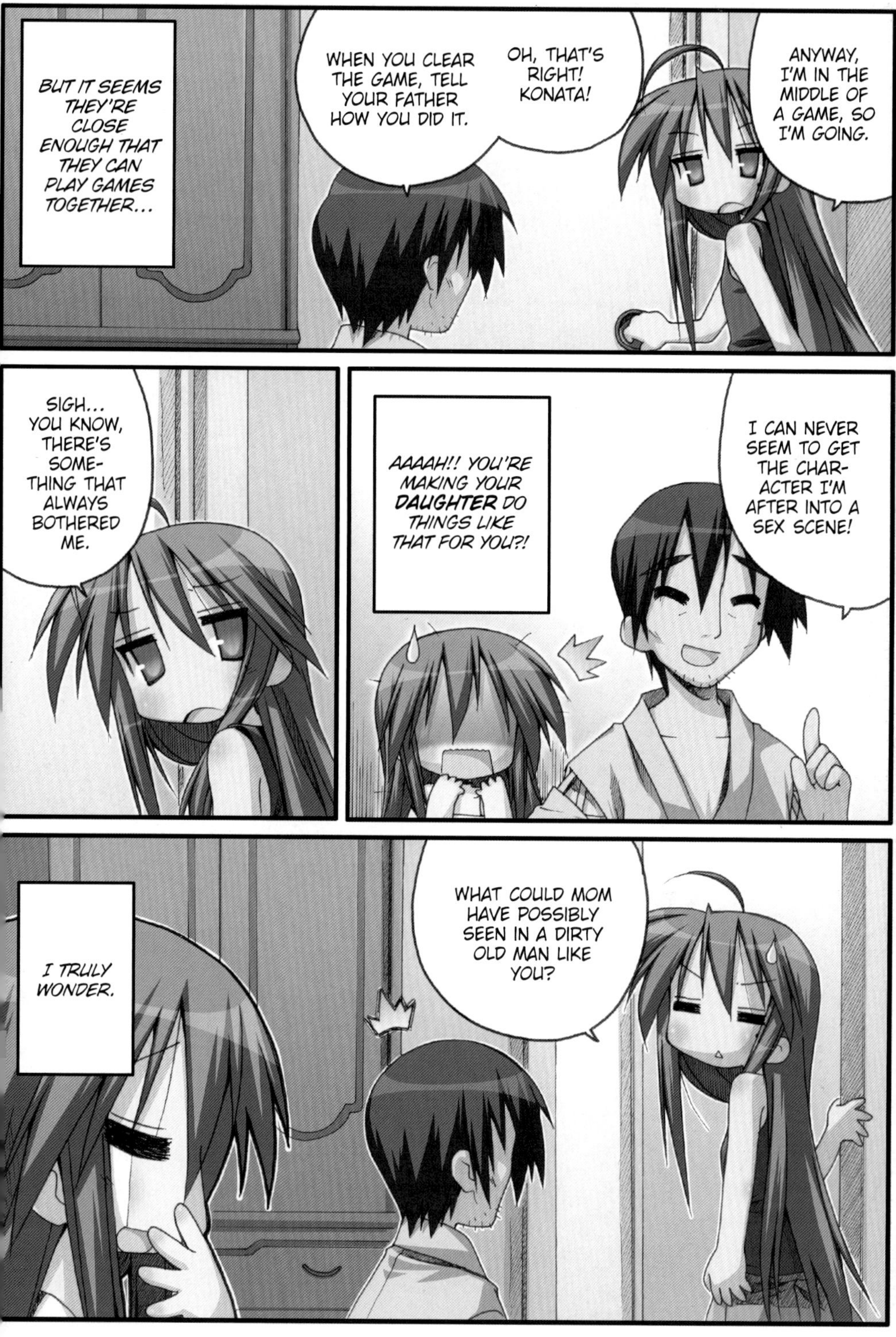
ANYWAY, I'M IN THE MIDDLE OF A GAME, SO I'M GOING.
OH, THAT'S RIGHT! KONATA!
WHEN YOU CLEAR THE GAME, TELL YOUR FATHER HOW YOU DID IT.
BUT IT SEEMS THEY'RE CLOSE ENOUGH THAT THEY CAN PLAY GAMES TOGETHER...
I CAN NEVER SEEM TO GET THE CHAR-ACTER I'M AFTER INTO A SEX SCENE!
AAAAH!! YOU'RE MAKING YOUR DAUGHTER DO THINGS LIKE THAT FOR YOU?!
SIGH... YOU KNOW, THERE'S SOME-THING THAT ALWAYS BOTHERED ME.
WHAT COULD MOM HAVE POSSIBLY SEEN IN A DIRTY OLD MAN LIKE YOU?
I TRULY WONDER.

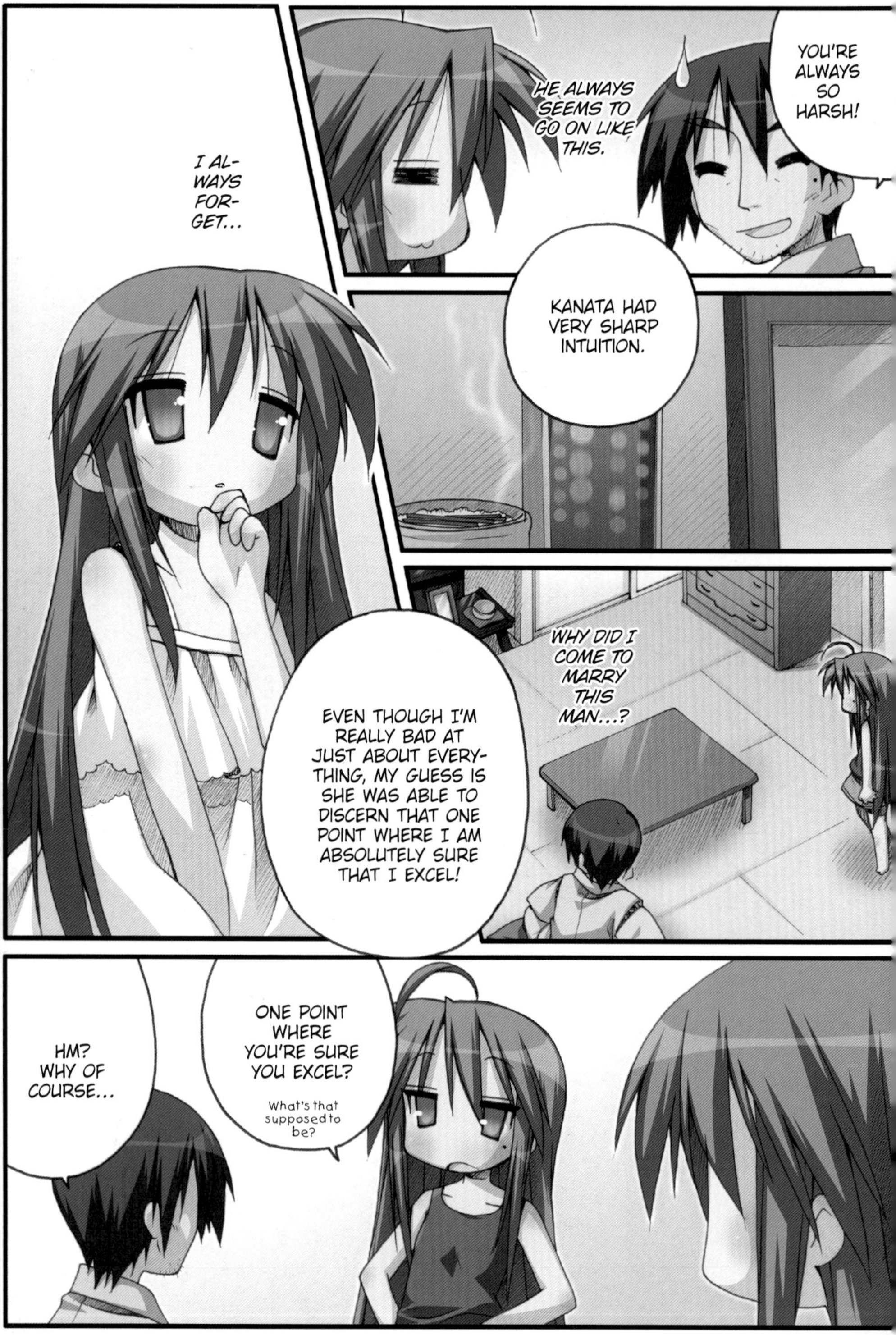
YOU'RE ALWAYS SO HARSH!
HE ALWAYS SEEMS TO GO ON LIKE THIS.
I AL-WAYS FOR-GET...
KANATA HAD VERY SHARP INTUITION.
WHY DID I COME TO MARRY THIS MAN...?
EVEN THOUGH I'M REALLY BAD AT JUST ABOUT EVERY-THING, MY GUESS IS SHE WAS ABLE TO DISCERN THAT ONE POINT WHERE I AM ABSOLUTELY SURE THAT I EXCEL!
ONE POINT WHERE YOU'RE SURE YOU EXCEL?
What's that supposed to be?
HM? WHY OF COURSE...

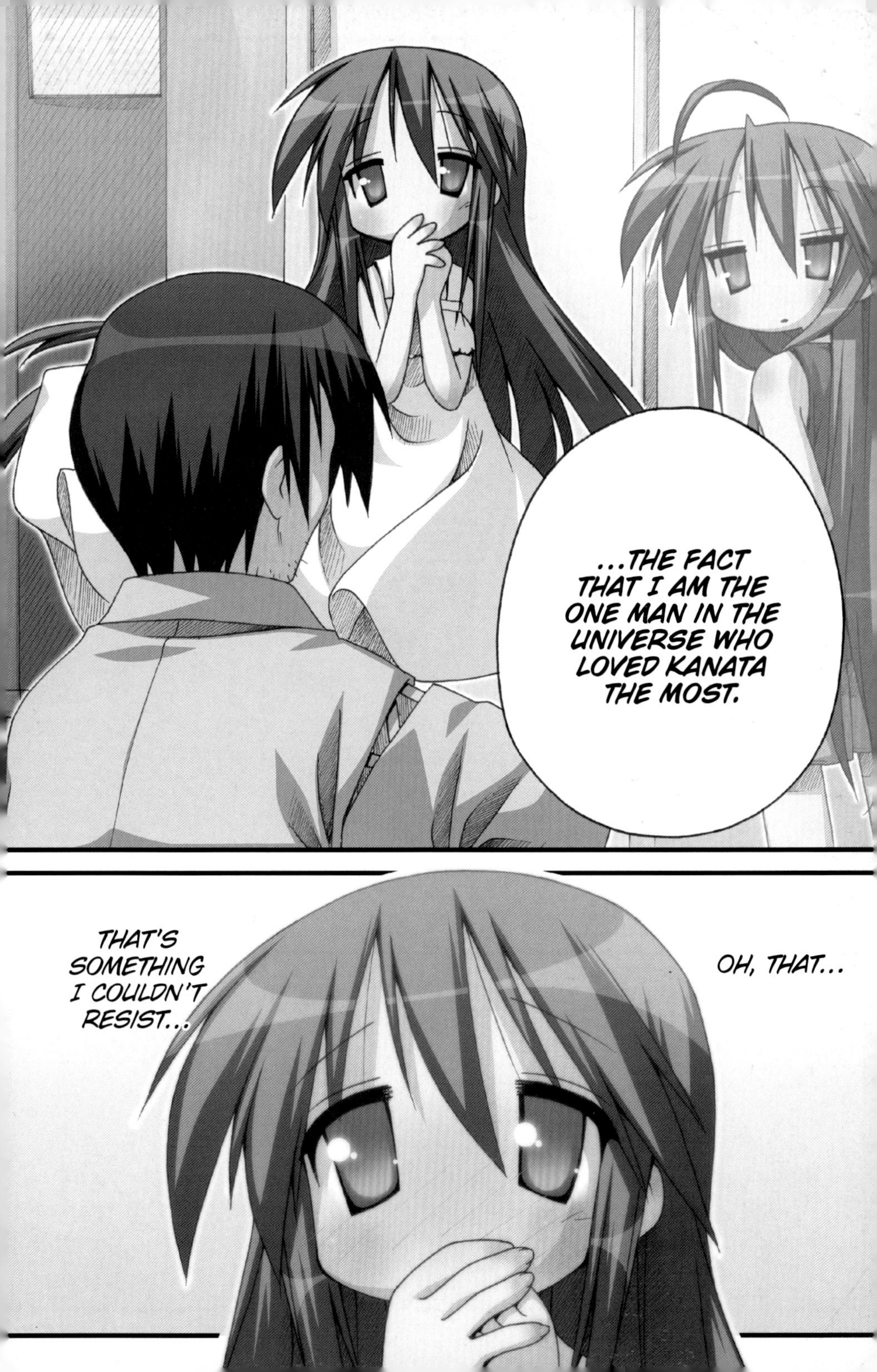
...THE FACT THAT I AM THE ONE MAN IN THE UNIVERSE WHO LOVED KANATA THE MOST.
OH, THAT...
THAT'S SOMETHING I COULDN'T RESIST...

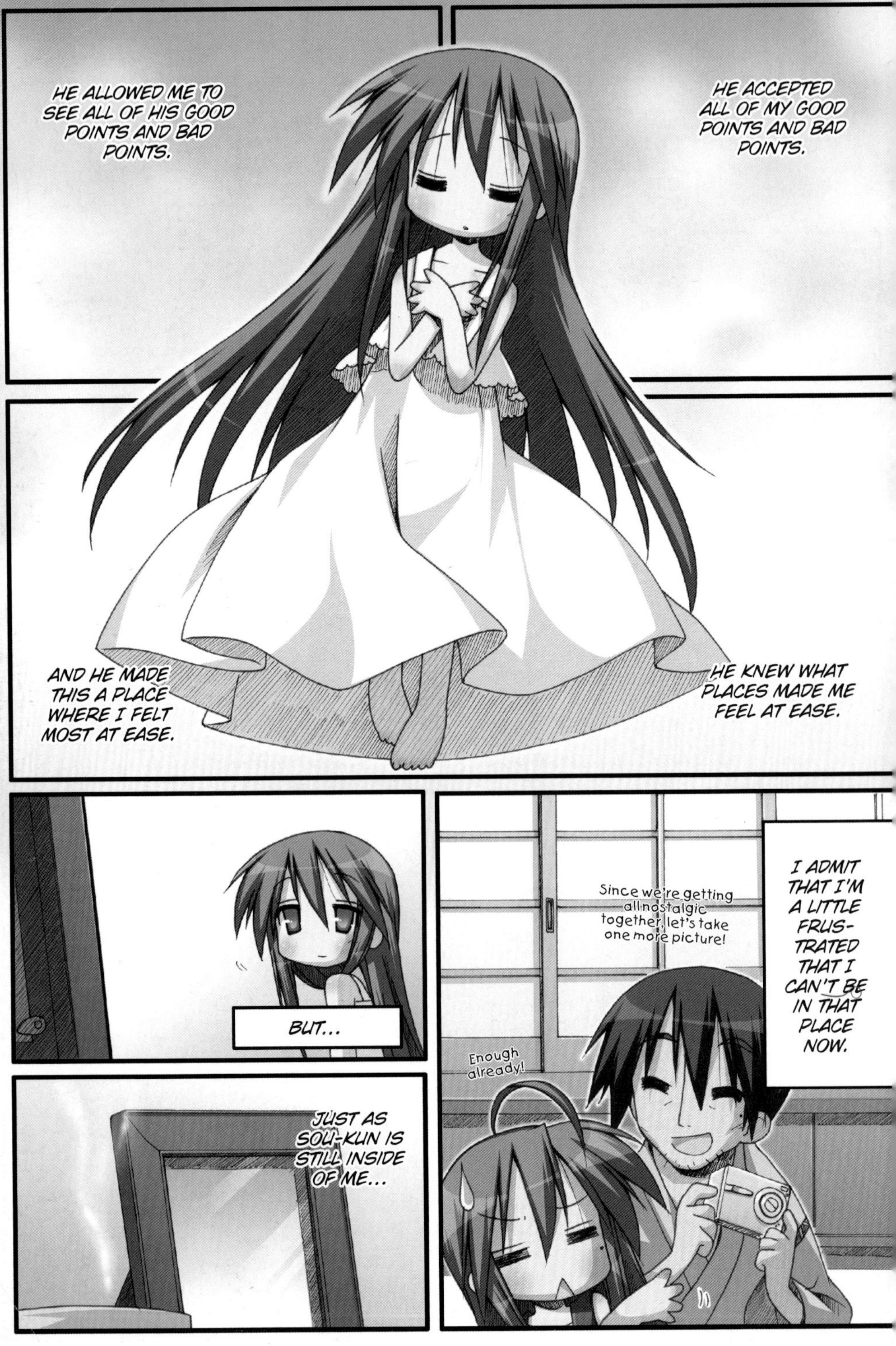
HE ACCEPTED ALL OF MY GOOD POINTS AND BAD POINTS.
HE ALLOWED ME TO SEE ALL OF HIS GOOD POINTS AND BAD POINTS.
HE KNEW WHAT PLACES MADE ME FEEL AT EASE.
AND HE MADE THIS A PLACE WHERE I FELT MOST AT EASE.
I ADMIT THAT I'M A LITTLE FRUS-TRATED THAT I CAN'T BE IN THAT PLACE NOW.
Since we're getting all nostalgic together, let's take one more picture!
Enough already!
BUT...
JUST AS SOU-KUN IS STILL INSIDE OF ME...

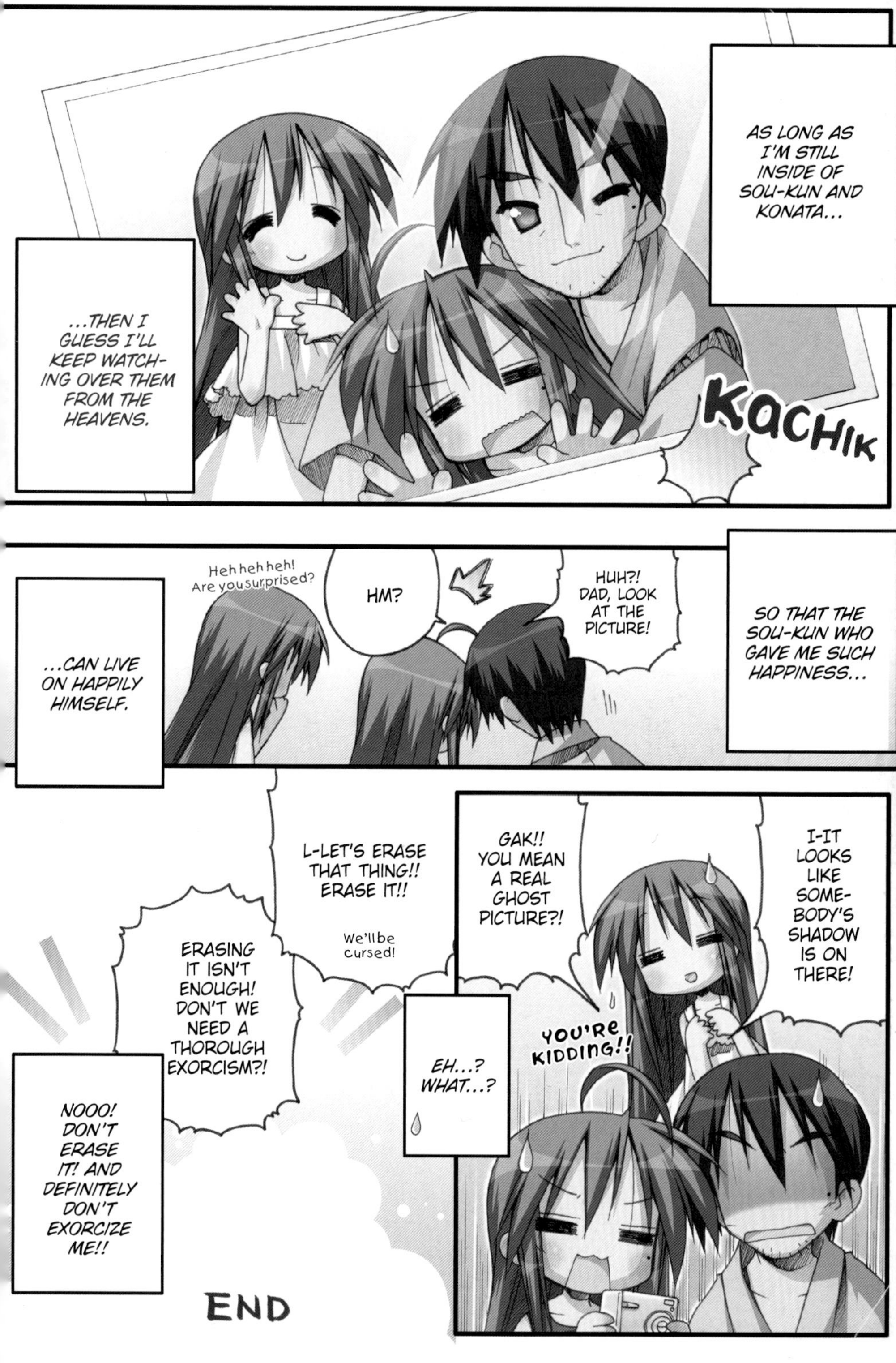
AS LONG AS I'M STILL INSIDE OF SOU-KUN AND KONATA...
KACHIK
...THEN I GUESS I'LL KEEP WATCHING OVER THEM FROM THE HEAVENS.
SO THAT THE SOU-KUN WHO GAVE ME SUCH HAPPINESS...
HUH?! DAD, LOOK AT THE PICTURE!
HM?
Heh heh heh! Are you surprised?
...CAN LIVE ON HAPPILY HIMSELF.
I-IT LOOKS LIKE SOMEBODY'S SHADOW IS ON THERE!
GAK!! YOU MEAN A REAL GHOST PICTURE?!
YOU'RE KIDDING!!
EH...? WHAT...?
L-LET'S ERASE THAT THING!! ERASE IT!!
We'll be cursed!
ERASING IT ISN'T ENOUGH! DON'T WE NEED A THOROUGH EXORCISM?!
NOOO! DON'T ERASE IT! AND DEFINITELY DON'T EXORCIZE ME!!
END

special
bonus 3

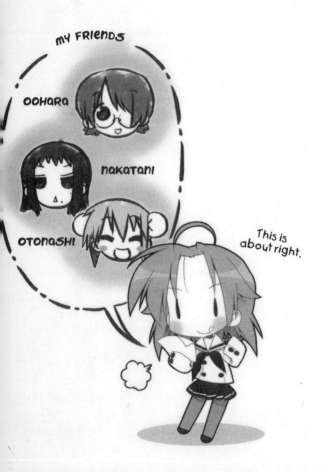

MY FRIENDS

OOHARA

NAKATANI

OTONASHI

This is about right.

the true face behind the smiling face

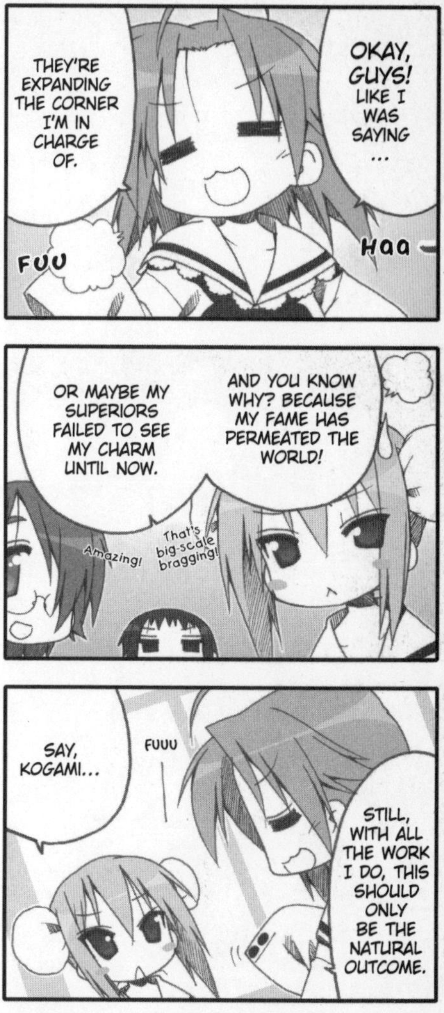
OKAY, GUYS! LIKE I WAS SAYING ...
THEY'RE EXPANDING THE CORNER I'M IN CHARGE OF.
Haa–
FUU
AND YOU KNOW WHY? BECAUSE MY FAME HAS PERMEATED THE WORLD!
OR MAYBE MY SUPERIORS FAILED TO SEE MY CHARM UNTIL NOW.
That's big-scale bragging!
Amazing!
FUUU
STILL, WITH ALL THE WORK I DO, THIS SHOULD ONLY BE THE NATURAL OUTCOME.
SAY, KOGAMI...
...THE CAMERA ON YOUR "NEW EXPANDED CORNER" IS ALREADY RUNNING. ARE YOU OKAY WITH THAT?
GAK!
HI, EVERYBODY! HI-LUCKY! ☆
THANKS TO ALL YOUR SUPPORT, LUCKY ☆ CHANNEL IS GOING ON THE ROAD! SO ROOT FOR US, PLEEZ!! ♥
TWIRL

an idol's privilege

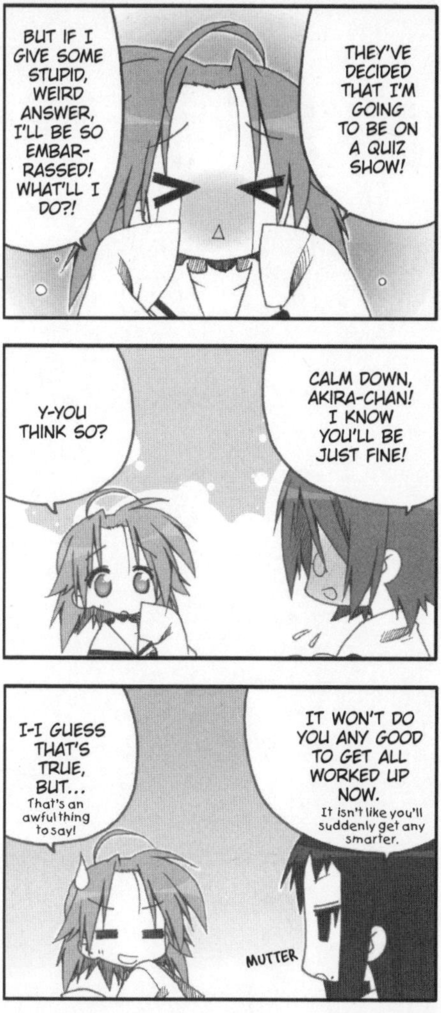
THEY'VE DECIDED THAT I'M GOING TO BE ON A QUIZ SHOW!
BUT IF I GIVE SOME STUPID, WEIRD ANSWER, I'LL BE SO EMBARRASSED! WHAT'LL I DO?!
CALM DOWN, AKIRA-CHAN! I KNOW YOU'LL BE JUST FINE!
Y-YOU THINK SO?
IT WON'T DO YOU ANY GOOD TO GET ALL WORKED UP NOW.
It isn't like you'll suddenly get any smarter.
I-I GUESS THAT'S TRUE, BUT...
That's an awful thing to say!
MUTTER
AND DON'T PEOPLE LIKE IDOLS MORE WHEN THEY SEEM A BIT DUMB?
I get that feeling.
......
THAT MIGHT BE RIGHT, HUH?
I'll do that!
THAT'S PERFECT FOR YOU!!
HeHn

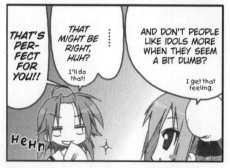

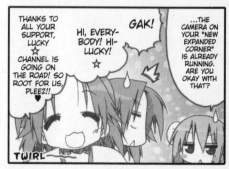

akira really is famous

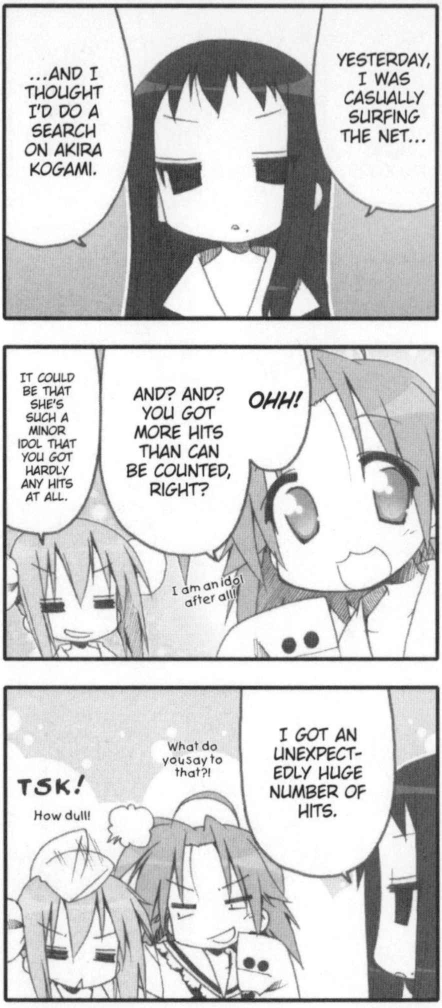
YESTERDAY, I WAS CASUALLY SURFING THE NET...
...AND I THOUGHT I'D DO A SEARCH ON AKIRA KOGAMI.
OHH!
AND? AND? YOU GOT MORE HITS THAN CAN BE COUNTED, RIGHT?
IT COULD BE THAT SHE'S SUCH A MINOR IDOL THAT YOU GOT HARDLY ANY HITS AT ALL.
I am an idol after all!
I GOT AN UNEXPECTEDLY HUGE NUMBER OF HITS.
What do you say to that?!
TSK!
How dull!
BUT THE VAST MAJORITY WERE LINKS TO IDOL SITES THAT HAVE NOTHING TO DO WITH HER.
WHAT WAS THAT?!
But even so, the fact they link to her name means that she's pretty famous, I'm sure!
HEH HEH

so busy with work

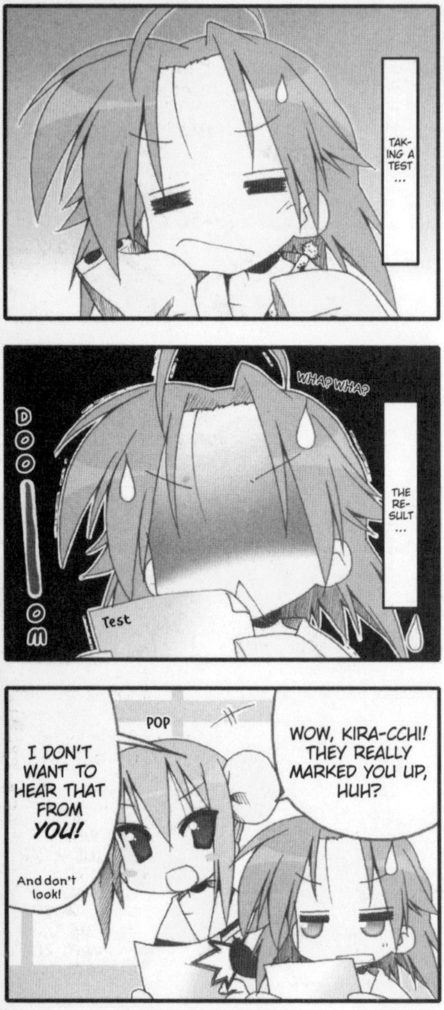
TAKING A TEST...
THE RESULT...
WHA? WHA?
DOOOOM
Test
WOW, KIRA-CCHI! THEY REALLY MARKED YOU UP, HUH?
POP
I DON'T WANT TO HEAR THAT FROM YOU!
And don't look!
IDOLS ARE CONSTANTLY BEING "CALCULATING," SO I THOUGHT YOU'D GET A BETTER SCORE.
Right?
LISTEN YOU! WHY DO YOU ALWAYS GIVE ME AN OVERLY BIASED VIEWPOINT?!
And don't give me, "Right"!

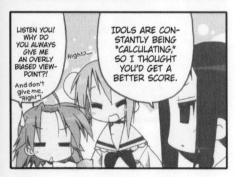

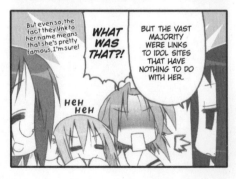

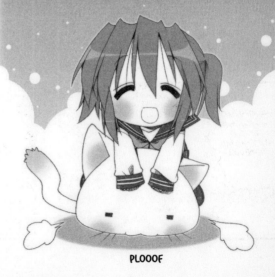

WELL DONE, EVERYBODY!

PLOOOF

nothing works

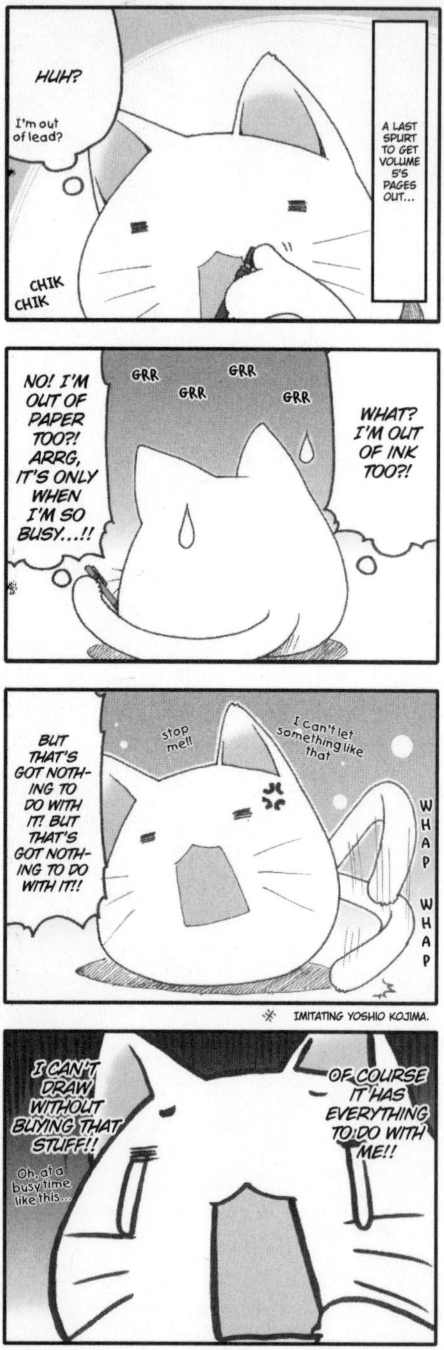
A LAST SPURT TO GET VOLUME 5'S PAGES OUT...
HUH?
I'm out of lead?
CHIK CHIK
WHAT? I'M OUT OF INK TOO?!
GRR GRR GRR GRR
NO! I'M OUT OF PAPER TOO?! ARRG, IT'S ONLY WHEN I'M SO BUSY...!!
WHAP WHAP
I can't let something like that
stop me!!
BUT THAT'S GOT NOTHING TO DO WITH IT! BUT THAT'S GOT NOTHING TO DO WITH IT!!
OF COURSE IT HAS EVERYTHING TO DO WITH ME!!
I CAN'T DRAW WITHOUT BUYING THAT STUFF!!
Oh, at a busy time like this...

※ IMITATING YOSHIO KOJIMA.

influences at work

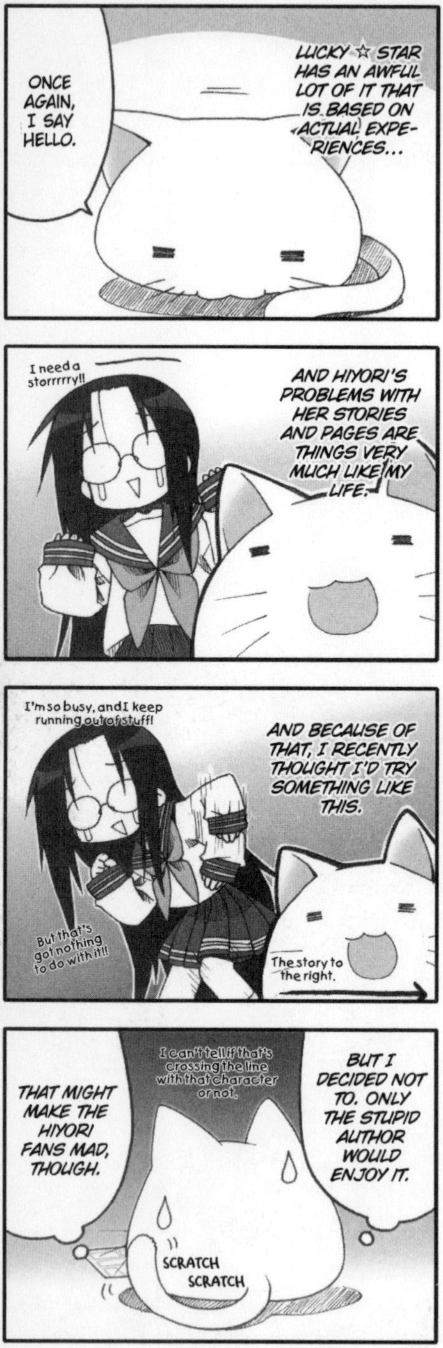
LUCKY ☆ STAR HAS AN AWFUL LOT OF IT THAT IS BASED ON ACTUAL EXPE-RIENCES...
ONCE AGAIN, I SAY HELLO.
AND HIYORI'S PROBLEMS WITH HER STORIES AND PAGES ARE THINGS VERY MUCH LIKE MY LIFE.
I need a storrrrry!!
AND BECAUSE OF THAT, I RECENTLY THOUGHT I'D TRY SOMETHING LIKE THIS.
I'm so busy, and I keep running out of stuff!
But that's got nothing to do with it!!
The story to the right.
BUT I DECIDED NOT TO. ONLY THE STUPID AUTHOR WOULD ENJOY IT.
I can't tell if that's crossing the line with that character or not.
THAT MIGHT MAKE THE HIYORI FANS MAD, THOUGH.
SCRATCH SCRATCH

self destruction

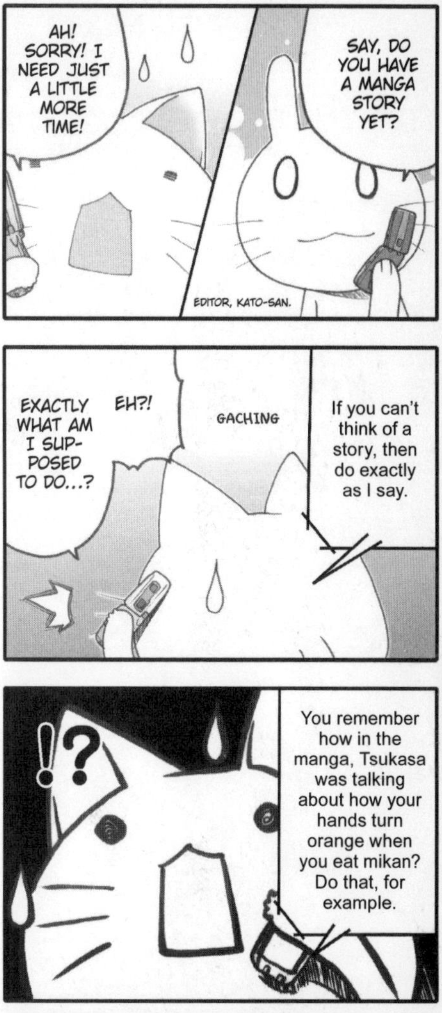
SAY, DO YOU HAVE A MANGA STORY YET?
AH! SORRY! I NEED JUST A LITTLE MORE TIME!
EDITOR, KATO-SAN.
If you can't think of a story, then do exactly as I say.
GACHING
EH?!
EXACTLY WHAT AM I SUP-POSED TO DO...?
You remember how in the manga, Tsukasa was talking about how your hands turn orange when you eat mikan? Do that, for example.
I NEED A STORY! A STORY!!
IF I DON'T COME UP WITH SOME-THING, I'LL DIE! I'LL KILL MYSELF!!
umm
umm
umm
umm

what it's like to be an author

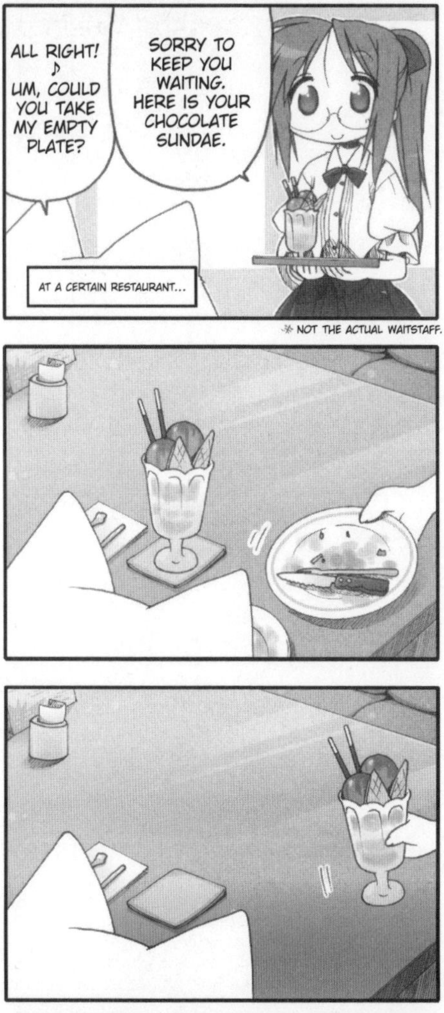
SORRY TO KEEP YOU WAITING. HERE IS YOUR CHOCOLATE SUNDAE.
ALL RIGHT! ♪ UM, COULD YOU TAKE MY EMPTY PLATE?
AT A CERTAIN RESTAURANT...
※ NOT THE ACTUAL WAITSTAFF.
HUH...? HUH...?
EVERY ONE OF THE CHARACTERS IN LUCKY ☆ STAR IS A PART OF ME, BUT CONSIDERING MY TRUE SELF, I THINK I'M PROB-ABLY MOST LIKE TSUKASA.
Where's my chocolate sundae?

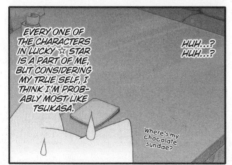

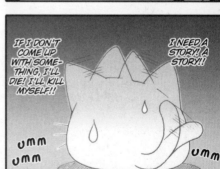

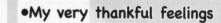

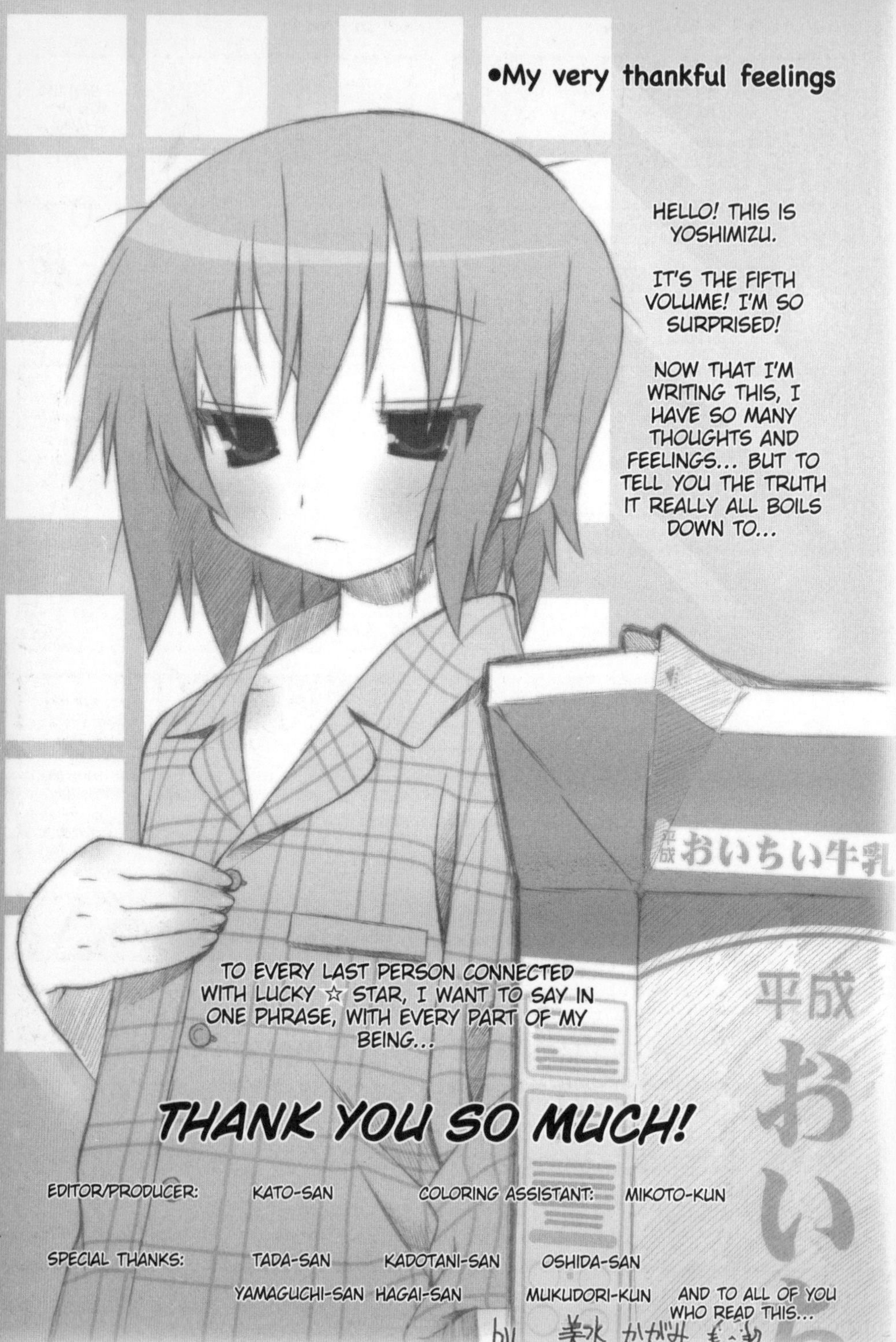

●My very thankful feelings

HELLO! THIS IS
YOSHIMIZU.

IT'S THE FIFTH
VOLUME! I'M SO
SURPRISED!

NOW THAT I'M
WRITING THIS, I
HAVE SO MANY
THOUGHTS AND
FEELINGS... BUT TO
TELL YOU THE TRUTH
IT REALLY ALL BOILS
DOWN TO...

TO EVERY LAST PERSON CONNECTED
WITH LUCKY ☆ STAR, I WANT TO SAY IN
ONE PHRASE, WITH EVERY PART OF MY
BEING...!

THANK YOU SO MUCH!

EDITOR/PRODUCER: KATO-SAN   COLORING ASSISTANT: MIKOTO-KUN

SPECIAL THANKS: TADA-SAN   KADOTANI-SAN   OSHIDA-SAN

YAMAGUCHI-SAN HAGAI-SAN   MUKUDORI-KUN   AND TO ALL OF YOU
WHO READ THIS...

by 美水 かがみ
YOSHIMIZU KAGAMI

TRANSLATOR NOTES

P.6   *AYA HIRANO:*   THE LEAD VOICE ACTRESS IN THE MELANCHOLY OF HARUHI SUZUMIYA, WHO ALSO HAPPENS TO PLAY THE PART OF KONATA IZUMI IN THE ANIME VERSION OF A MANGA CALLED LUCKY STAR.

P.15   *JUKU*   THESE ARE AFTER-SCHOOL SCHOOLS THAT SUPPLEMENT THE EDUCATION OF NORMAL SCHOOLS USUALLY FOR THE PURPOSE OF PASSING ENTRANCE EXAMS. JUKU IS OFTEN TRANSLATED AS "CRAM SCHOOL."

P.20   *TSUKKOMI*   THE "STRAIGHT MAN" OF THE TRADITIONAL 2-MAN COMEDY ACT CALLED MANZAI. THIS PART USUALLY POINTS OUT IN AN ANGRY-SOUNDING VOICE WHAT IS WRONG WITH DUMB THINGS SAID BY THE BOKE OR DUMB GUY IN THE ACT.

P.23   *MELON BREAD*   A ROUND SWEET-BREAD SNACK. ITS HALF-SPHERICAL SHAPE AND CROSS-CUT MARKINGS MAKES IT LOOK LIKE A CUT MELON, AND THAT IS WHERE IT GOT ITS NAME. IT TYPICALLY DOES NOT HAVE A MELON TASTE (ALTHOUGH SOME VARIATIONS ARE MADE WITH MELON-CREAM FILLING OR MELON FLAVORING BAKED INTO THE BREAD).

    CAFETERIA SOLD OUT   TYPICALLY, CAFETERIA FOOD IN JAPANESE HIGH SCHOOLS IS FARMED OUT TO LOCAL BAKERIES AND CATERING COMPANIES. THESE COMPANIES ARE NOTORIOUS FOR BRINGING ONLY ENOUGH FOOD SO THAT THEY WILL SELL OUT EVERY DAY, AND SO THERE IS A COMPETITION AMONG THE STUDENTS FOR THE TASTIEST FOOD, AND TOWARDS THE END OF THE FOOD LINE, FOR ANY FOOD AT ALL.

P.25   *COFFEE JELLY*   COFFEE-FLAVORED JELLY IS A PACKAGED SNACK, AND IT COMES WITH SWEETENED CREAM SYRUP THAT IS POURED ON THE JELLY GIVING THE CONCOCTION A FLAVOR SIMILAR TO CAFÉ LATTE.

P.26   *CUP YAKI-SOBA*   YAKI-SOBA IS NOODLES PAN OR GRIDDLE FRIED ALONG WITH MEATS, VEGGIES AND SAUCE. CUP YAKI-SOBA IS MADE BY ADDING BOILING WATER, THEN POURING OFF THE EXCESS WATER AFTERWARDS. SINCE IT ISN'T FRIED, IT CAN'T REALLY BE CALLED YAKI-SOBA, BUT THAT DOESN'T STOP IT FROM BEING A HUGE SELLER.

P. 27   *DORA-CHAN*   "DORA-CHAN" IS THE THEME SONG FOR THE CHILD-ORIENTED ANIME DORAEMON. "CHRARAMERA" DESCRIBES THE TUNE PLAYED BY VENDORS WHO SELL FROM THEIR VEHICLES (ALA ICE-CREAM TRUCKS IN THE STATES).

    INSURANCE DUCK AFLAC INSURANCE HAS A BIG PRESENCE ON JAPANESE TELEVISION USING THE SAME DUCK AS ON THE AMERICAN COMMERCIALS. HOWEVER THE APPROACH IS A LITTLE DIFFERENT, AND ONE SET OF JAPANESE AFLAC COMMERCIALS FEATURES A FEMALE VOCALIST (AND THE DUCK) SINGING A JINGLE THAT IS POPULAR WITH CHILDREN.

P.30   *NII-SAN*   AS DESCRIBED IN THE NOTES FOR PREVIOUS VOLUMES, ONEE-SAN MEANS "OLDER SISTER," AND CAN BE USED WITH ONE'S BLOOD RELATION OLDER SISTER OR WITH ANYONE WHO IS AN OLDER-SISTER FIGURE. IT HAS VARIANTS SUCH AS LEAVING OFF THE "O" AT THE BEGINNING (NEE-SAN) OR COMBINING IT WITH A NAME SUCH AS IN YUI-NEESAN. THE "OLDER BROTHER" TITLE IS ONII-SAN AND HAS THE SAME VARIATIONS.

P.32   *THIGH GAL*   THERE IS AN OTAKU TERM CALLED ZETTAI RYOUIKI WHICH LITERALLY TRANSLATED MEANS "ABSOLUTE TERRITORY," BUT THAT IT REFERS TO ARE THOSE GIRLS WHO WEAR THIGH-HIGH BOOTS OR STOCKINGS ALONG WITH HOT-PANTS OR SHORT SKIRTS AND WIND UP EXPOSING THEIR THIGHS.

P.39   *ORICON CHART*   LIKE THE BILLBOARD CHARTS IN THE U.S., THE ORICON COMPANY SURVEYS SOME TWENTY-FIVE HUNDRED SHOPS IN JAPAN TO LIST THE NATIONAL BEST-SELLERS IN MUSIC AND OTHER VARIETIES OF ENTERTAINMENT.

P.46   *ULTRAMAN*   ULTRAMAN IS JAPAN'S MOST POPULAR SUPER HERO. STARTED IN THE 60'S, RIGHTEOUS YOUNG MEN (USUALLY) CAN TRANSFORM INTO THE SOLAR-POWERED GIANT WHO SHOOTS RAYS FROM HIS ARM. HIS SIGNATURE SOUND EFFECT IS "SHUWA."

    MISAKICHI   MANY, IF NOT MOST, JAPANESE NAMES ARE MADE UP OF TWO KANJI, AND IN MANY CASES, THE SECOND KANJI CAN DETERMINE THE GENDER. MALE-SOUNDING SECOND KANJI HAVE SOUNDS LIKE KICHI, HIKO, ROU, AND TAKA (AMONG MANY OTHERS). SO FOR KONATA TO CALL MISAO, "MISAKICHI" MAKES HER NAME SOUND MANLY.

P.49   *DEVIATION VALUE*   DEVIATION VALUE IS A STATISTICAL REPORT INDICATING THAT LIKELIHOOD OF STUDENTS PASSING THEIR ENTRANCE EXAMS TO GET INTO A HIGH-RANKED UNIVERSITY. A DEVIATION VALUE OF 70 IS CONSIDERED EXCELLENT.

P.54   *PERVERT*   TRAINS ARE CROWDED PLACES, ESPECIALLY DURING COMMUTE TIMES, AND CERTAIN SEXUAL PREDATORS USE THE ANONYMITY OF THIS SITUATION TO "COP A FEEL." FORTUNATELY, IN THE PAST DECADE OR SO, JAPANESE GIRLS ARE LEARNING THAT GRABBING THE OFFENDER'S HAND AND SCREAMING (OR OTHERWISE DRAWING ATTENTION TO THEMSELVES AND THE CRIMINAL) IS AN EFFECTIVE WAY TO GET THESE PREDATORS ARRESTED.

P.58   *RIRATTANU*   THERE IS A KIND OF TEDDYBEAR IN JAPAN CALLED A RIRAKKUMA (RIRA BEAR). THE RIRATANU WOULD BE THE LUCKY STAR'S VERSION OF THIS. THE "TANU" WOULD BE SHORT FOR TAKUKI OR "RACCOON DOG."

P.59   *FIRE A GUN*   THE DECISION CHANT WHICH TSUKASA IS SAYING WOULD BE SOMETHING LIKE EENY-MEENY-MINY-MO METHOD OF DECIDING THINGS FOR WESTERN KIDS. THE "FIRE A GUN" PART IS A LITTLE-KNOWN BUT TRADITIONAL CONTINUATION OF IT.

P.62   *HEADACHES*   THE JAPANESE CONSIDER ONE OF THE COMMON CAUSES FOR HEADACHES IS TENSE MUSCLES IN THE BACK AND SHOULDERS. FOR EXAMPLE, WHEN ONE'S SHOULDERS ARE STIFF, THE JAPANESE FEEL ONE IS PRONE TO HEADACHES FROM THE TENSION. ALSO, LARGE BREASTS ARE CONSIDERED A CAUSE FOR STIFF SHOULDERS.

P.66   *THE OPPOSITE*   MY GUESS IS THAT IN THIS STRIP, KONATA IS REFERRING TO HOW MUCH OTAKU PIRATE VIDEOS.

    POSTCARDS   JAPANESE BANKS AND UTILITIES SEND THEIR CUSTOMERS SENSITIVE ACCOUNT INFORMATION ON A SPECIAL KIND OF POSTCARD THAT PEELS OPEN INTO THREE SECTIONS. SINCE THE PEEL-ABLE ADHESIVE TENDS TO BE STRONG, IT TAKES A BIT OF FORCE TO OPEN THESE KINDS OF POSTCARDS.

P.67   *BISHOUJO*   BISHOUJO IS JAPANESE FOR "BEAUTIFUL YOUNG GIRL," AND BISHOUJO GAMES ARE USUALLY EROTIC OR EVEN PORNOGRAPHIC GAMES WHERE ONE'S CHARACTER SEDUCES SUCH YOUNG WOMEN.

P.71 **KOTATSU** THERE IS A LOW TABLE, ABOUT COFFEE-TABLE HEIGHT, THAT IS EQUIPPED WITH A HEATER ON THE BOTTOM SIDE AND CAN BE DRAPED WITH A QUILT-LIKE FUTON THAT FITS BETWEEN THE FRAME AND THE TABLETOP. IN THE SUMMER IT CAN BE USED AS A REGULAR TABLE (WITH THE FUTON REMOVED), BUT IT'S REAL CALL TO SERVICE IS IN THE WINTER WHEN IT KEEPS PEOPLE'S LEGS AND FEET WARM IN THE COLD WEATHER. IT CAN BECOME RATHER HOT BENEATH THE TABLE.

P.79 **JUGS OF...** THIS IS A LOCALIZATION OF AN UNTRANSLATABLE JAPANESE PUN. THE ORIGINAL HAD A WORD WRITTEN IN KANJI WHICH, WHEN READ ONE WAY COMES OUT TO "SEINYUU" WHICH MEANS MILK FRESH FROM THE COW (UNPASTEURIZED). BUT IT CAN BE READ A DIFFERENT WAY AS "NAMA CHICHI," WHICH WOULD MEAN "REAL-LIFE BREASTS."

P.94 **DS SOFTWARE** IT ISN'T AS PREVALENT NOW AS IT WAS A FEW YEARS AGO WHEN THIS STRIP WAS PUBLISHED, BUT AT THE TIME THERE WERE MANY POPULAR GAMES FOR THE NINTENDO DOUBLE SCREEN (DS) AIMED AT ADULTS IN JAPAN. GAMES TO IMPROVE HANDWRITING, STUDY HISTORY, IMPROVE BRAIN FUNCTION, ETC.

P.99 **CHAKUSHIN ARI** THIS IS THE JAPANESE NAME OF A SERIES OF NOVELS BY YASUSHI AKIMOTO AND THE POPULAR MOVIE STARRING KOU SHIBASAKI AND DIRECTED BY TAKASHI MIIKE. IT'S TRANSLATED VARIOUSLY AS ONE MISSED CALL, YOU'VE GOT A CALL, AMONG OTHERS DEPENDING ON THE COUNTRIES IN WHICH IT WAS RELEASED.

SGT. FROG A MANGA WITH THE JAPANESE TITLE OF KERORO GUNSOU ABOUT A SMALL GROUP OF ALIENS WHO ARRIVE ON EARTH INTENDING TO CONQUER IT, BUT GETTING SIDETRACKED BY SUCH DISTRACTIONS AS PLASTIC GUNDAM MODELS AND THE INTERNET.

P.104 **CHIBI VAMPIRE** A MANGA BY YUNA KAGESAKI CALLED KARIN IN JAPANESE. IT WAS THE STORY OF A DAUGHTER IN A VAMPIRE FAMILY TRYING TO LIVE AS A NORMAL PERSON.

P.105 **NHK** ALTHOUGH FOR MOST JAPANESE, THE NHK MEANS NIPPON HOUSOU KOUKAI AND IS THE JAPANESE VERSION OF PUBLIC TELEVISION, THIS REFERENCE IS TO THE POPULAR MANGA WELCOME TO THE NHK. THE PLOT IS PRETTY MUCH AS KONATA DESCRIBES IT.

P.109 **BUNKO VERSION** BUNKO IS THE NAME FOR THE TRIM SIZE OF JAPANESE MASS-MARKET PAPERBACK BOOKS. AT A LITTLE OVER 4 INCHES BY JUST SHORT OF 6 INCHES, IT IS MUCH SMALLER THAN AND LESS EXPENSIVE THAN OTHER JAPANESE BOOKS.

TRUNKS THERE WAS A CONTEST AS A PART OF KADOKAWA'S NEGATIVE CAMPAIGN WHERE ONE CAN BE ENTERED INTO A DRAWING FOR SPECIAL PROMOTIONAL UNDERWEAR.

P.110 **BATTERY** BATTERY IS A BASEBALL MANGA BY ATSUKO ASANO. THE WORD "BATTERY": IN BASEBALL REFERS TO THE TEAMING OF A PITCHER AND CATCHER.

P.112 **SHOUNEN ONMYOUJI** SHOUNEN ONMYOUJI (BOY MEDIUM) IS A SERIES OF LIGHT NOVELS BY MITSURU YUUKI ABOUT A GRANDSON OF THE HISTORICAL MEDIUM ABE NO SEIMEI SET DURING THE HEIAN PERIOD OF JAPANESE HISTORY (794-1185). AS OF EARLY 2010, IT HAS 29 NOVELS IN THE SERIES.

P.117 **GOLDEN WEEK** GOLDEN WEEK IS A SERIES OF CONSECUTIVE HOLIDAYS IN MAY THAT ADDED UP TO ABOUT A WEEK'S WORTH OF VACATION TIME FOR MOST OF JAPAN'S WORKERS AND STUDENTS. MOST OF THE JAPANESE PLAN SOME SORT OF VACATION OR DAY TRIPS FOR GOLDEN WEEK.

EVANGELION THE SEMINAL GIANT-ROBOT ANIME SERIES OF THE '90S FEATURING SEVERAL DYSFUNCTIONAL MAIN CHARACTERS TRYING TO STOP A MYSTERIOUS ALIEN INVASION. THE MANGA IS DRAWN BY THE CHARACTER DESIGNER OF THE ANIME AND HAS BEEN SLOWLY RELEASED OVER MORE THAN A DECADE SINCE THE RELEASE OF THE ANIME.

COATTAILS THE ORIGINAL PROVERB THAT KONATA QUOTED, TORA NO I WO KARIRU KITSUNE, IS ABOUT A FOX THAT BORROWS THE SKIN OF A TIGER TO BLUFF HIS WAY THROUGH.

P.121 **AUGUST** AUGUST IS THE TIME OF OBON, A FESTIVAL TO HONOR ONES ANCESTORS AND DEPARTED LOVED ONES. IT'S HIGHLIGHTED BY BIG FAIRS AND FESTIVALS AT TEMPLES, INCLUDING FIREWORKS, BUT IT IS ALSO NOTED BY ANNUAL VISITS TO THE GRAVE SITES OF DEPARTED LOVED ONES. AUGUST IS ALSO A TIME TO TELL GHOST STORIES.

NEAR-BY FAR AWAY KONATA'S MOTHER'S NAME IS KANATA, WHICH IS A JAPANESE WORD FOR "FAR AWAY." IN THIS CASE, THE TITLE COULD MEAN EITHER SOMETHING THAT IS "BOTH CLOSE AND FAR AWAY," OR THAT "KANATA IS CLOSE BY."

P.130 **QUIZ SHOW** UNLIKE AMERICAN QUIZ SHOWS THAT FEATURE NORMAL PEOPLE COMPETING FOR PRIZES, JAPANESE QUIZ SHOWS FEATURE CELEBRITIES WHO DO THEIR BEST TO ENTERTAIN THE TV AUDIENCE DURING THE SHOW REGARDLESS OF WHO IS WINNING OR LOSING. IN ONE QUIZ SHOW, CERTAIN CELEBRITIES PLAY ESPECIALLY DUMB CHARACTERS GIVING FUNNY, INACCURATE ANSWERS TO THE TRIVIA QUESTIONS. THESE DUMB CHARACTERS CAN BECOME VERY POPULAR WITH THE AUDIENCE.

P.131 **KIRA-CCHI** THIS IS ANOTHER VARIATION ON THE -CHAN HONORIFIC.

P.133 **THAT'S GOT NOTHING** YOSHIO KOJIMA BROKE ONTO THE STAND-UP COMEDY ARENA WITH A NEARLY NUDE (WEARING ONLY SPEEDO-STYLE SWIM TRUNKS) OFF-THE-WALL RAP AND DANCE ROUTINE WHERE HE DESCRIBES HIS FAILURES IN LIFE, AND ENDS EACH FUNNY STORY WITH A FIST-PUMPING ACTION AND THE CHANT, "SONNA HA KANKEI GA NEE," WHICH TRANSLATES OUT TO, "THAT'S GOT NOTHING TO DO WITH IT!" THIS CATCH PHRASE WAS EXTREMELY POPULAR IN JAPAN DURING 2007 WHERE KOJIMA APPEARED ON NEARLY EVERY VARIETY PROGRAM AND HIS CATCH PHRASE WAS IMITATED BY CELEBRITIES AND COMMON PEOPLE FAR AND WIDE. BUT LIKE MOST FADS, THIS ONE DIED WITHIN A YEAR, AND NOW KOJIMA IS RELEGATED TO ONLY A FEW VARIETY PROGRAMS WHILE HE SEARCHES FOR HIS NEXT HIT CATCHPHRASE.

Lucky☆Star

Yoshimizu★Kagami

5

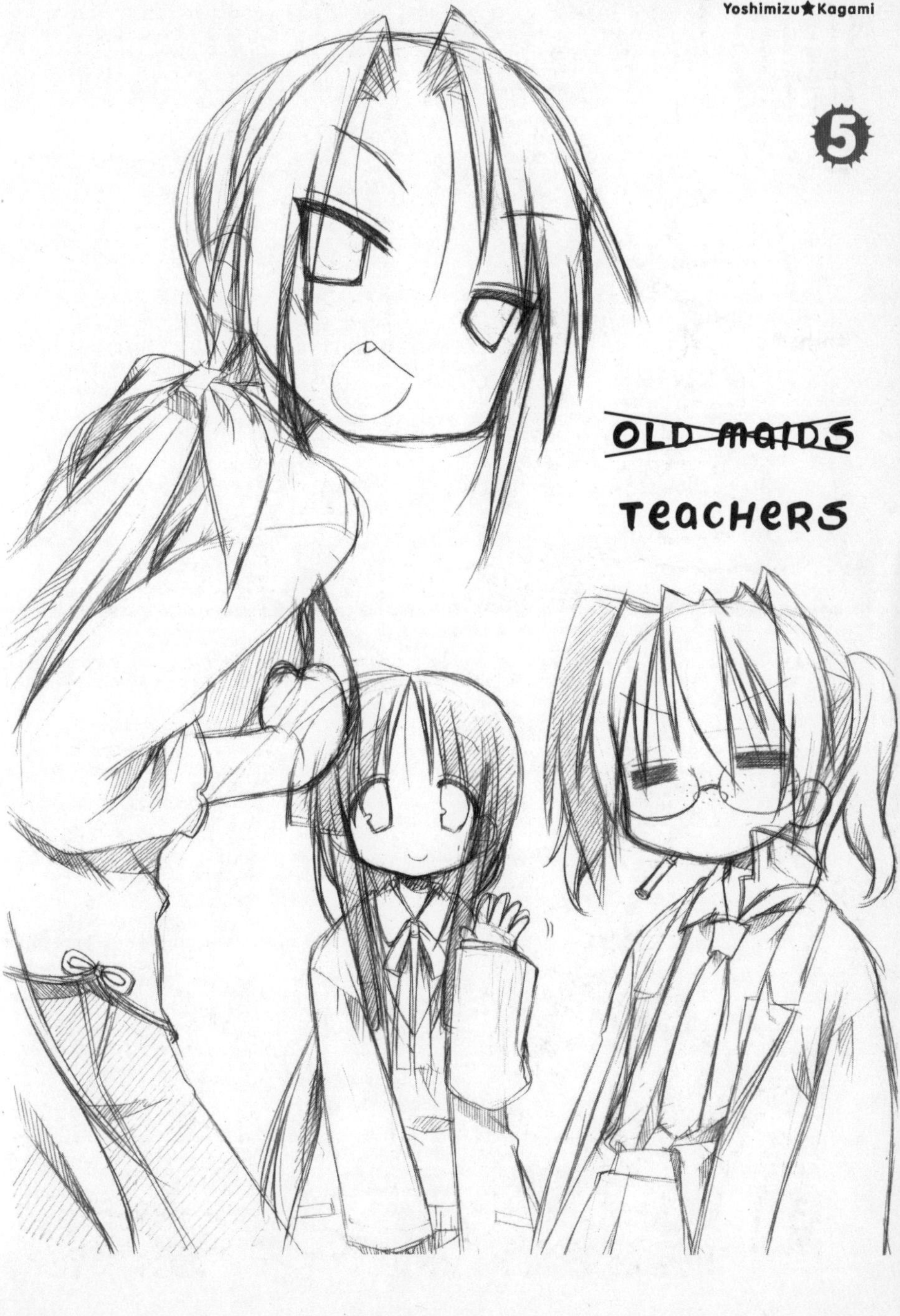

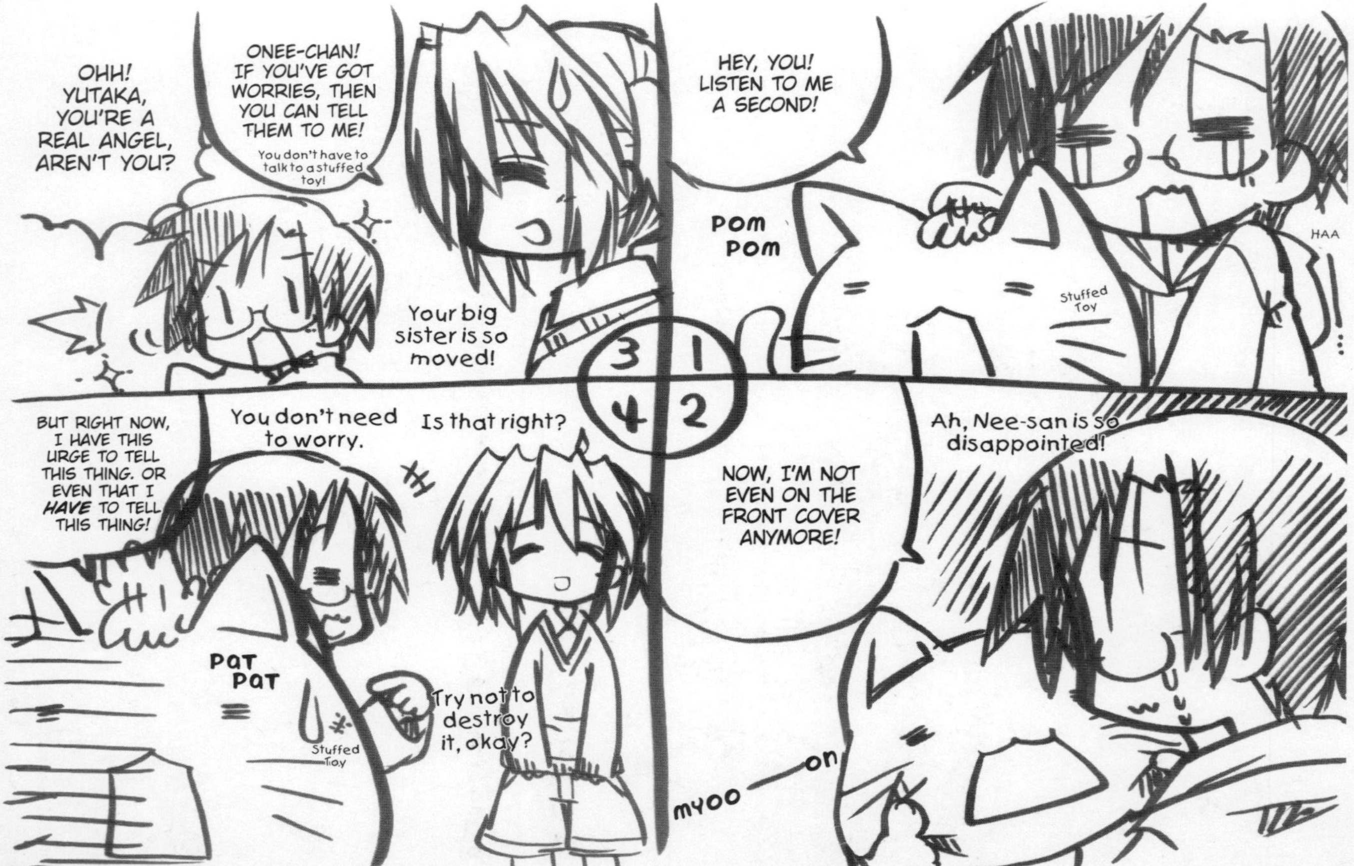
HEY, YOU! LISTEN TO ME A SECOND!
POM POM
Stuffed Toy
HAA
...!
NOW, I'M NOT EVEN ON THE FRONT COVER ANYMORE!
Ah, Nee-san is so disappointed!
myoo—on
ONEE-CHAN! IF YOU'VE GOT WORRIES, THEN YOU CAN TELL THEM TO ME!
You don't have to talk to a stuffed toy!
Your big sister is so moved!
OHH! YUTAKA, YOU'RE A REAL ANGEL, AREN'T YOU?
Is that right?
You don't need to worry.
BUT RIGHT NOW, I HAVE THIS URGE TO TELL THIS THING. OR EVEN THAT I HAVE TO TELL THIS THING!
PAT PAT
Stuffed Toy
Try not to destroy it, okay?

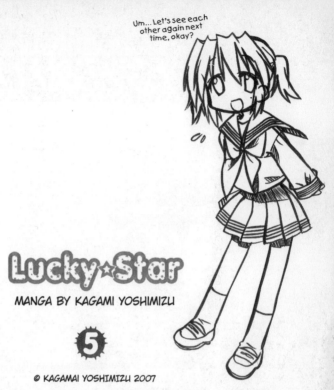

Um... Let's see each other again next time, okay?

Lucky ★ Star

MANGA BY KAGAMI YOSHIMIZU

5

© KAGAMAI YOSHIMIZU 2007

FIRST PUBLISHED IN JAPAN IN 2007 BY KADOKAWA SHOTEN PUBLISHING CO., LTD., TOKYO.

ENGLISH TRANSLATION RIGHTS ARRANGED WITH KADOKAWA SHOTEN PUBLISHING CO., LTD., TOKYO.

ENGLISH CREDITS

TRANSLATION BY	WILLIAM FLANAGAN
LETTERING BY	ERIKA TERRIQUEZ
COVER PRODUCTION BY	KIT LOOSE
COPY EDITED BY	TAKU OTSUKA
EDITED BY	ROBERT PLACE NAPTON
PUBLISHED BY	KEN IYADOMI

FIRST BANDAI ENTERTAINMENT INC EDITION PUBLISHED IN JUNE 2010

PRINTED IN CANADA

ISBN 1-978-1-60496-115-7

10, 9, 8, 7, 6, 5, 4, 3, 2, 1

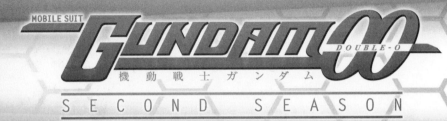

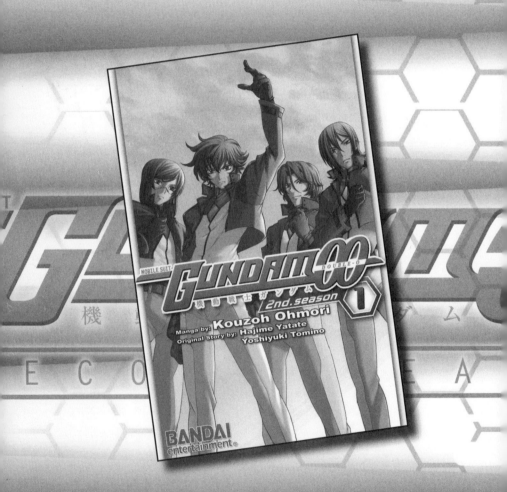

CELESTIAL BEING RISES AGAIN!
ON SALE NOW!

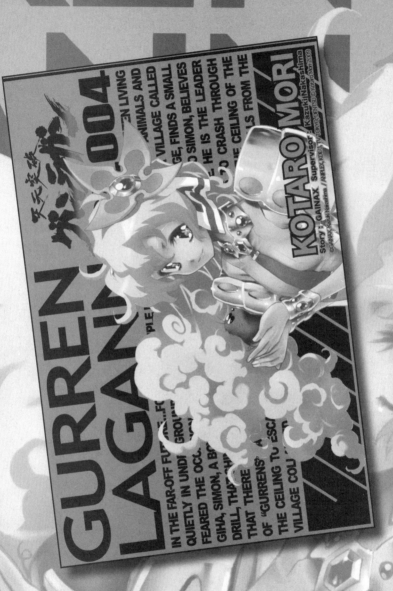

GURREN LAGANN

004

KOTARO MORI

Story : Kazuki Nakashima
Supervisor : GAINAX

IN THE FAR-OFF FUTURE...

THE MANGA ADAPTATION OF THE HIT
ANIME CONTINUES!
ON SALE NOW!

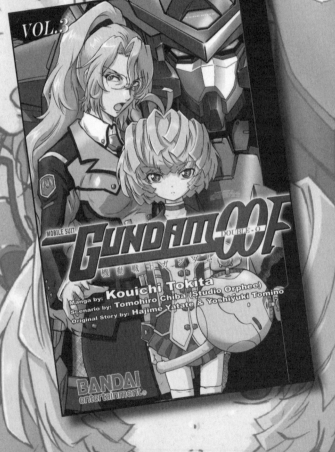

THE BATTLE BETWEEN THE GUNDAM MEISTERS IS
ABOUT TO BEGIN! AVAILABLE IN MAY!

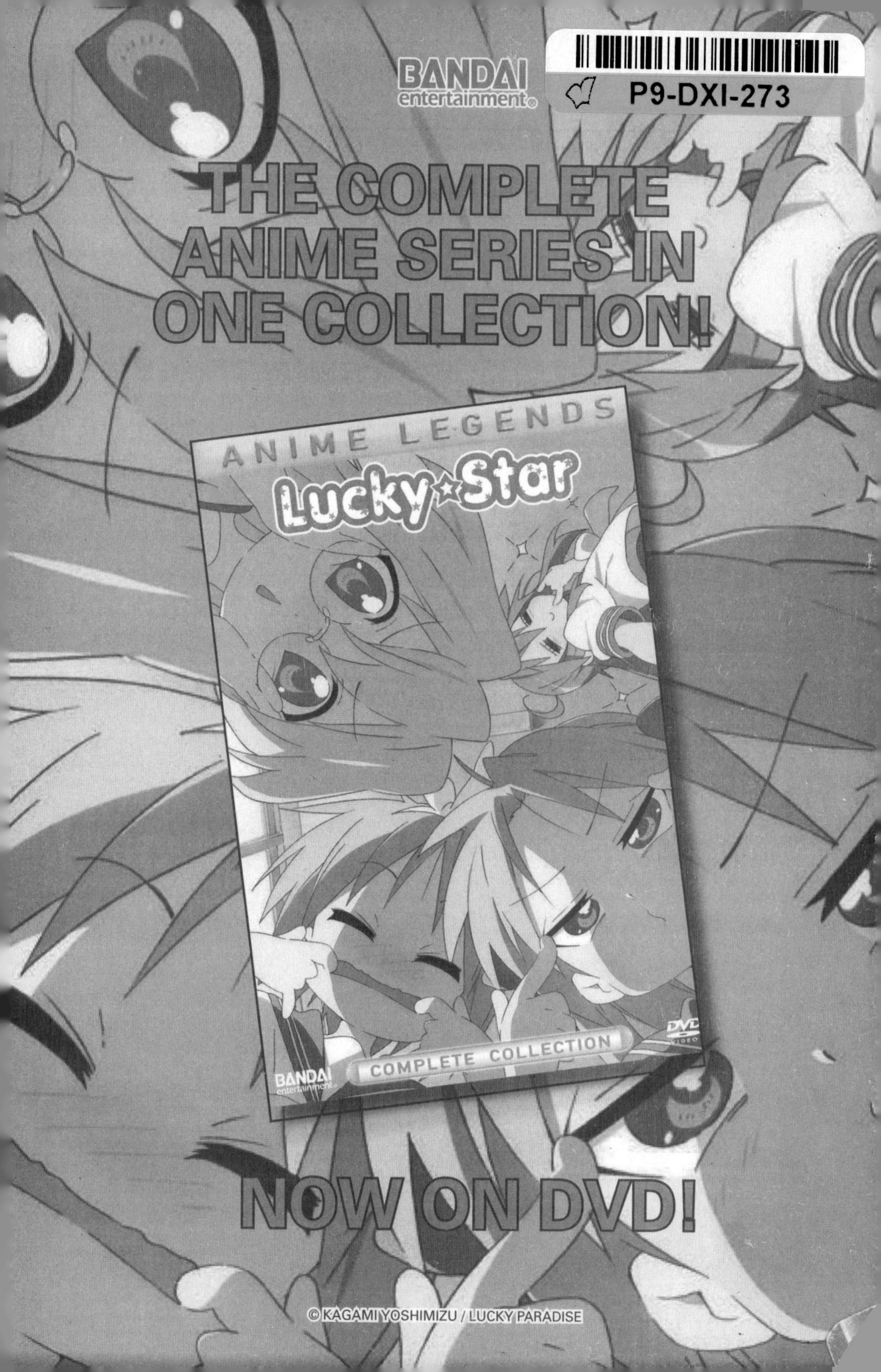
P9-DXI-273
BANDAI entertainment
THE COMPLETE ANIME SERIES IN ONE COLLECTION!
ANIME LEGENDS
Lucky☆Star
COMPLETE COLLECTION
BANDAI entertainment
DVD VIDEO
NOW ON DVD!
© KAGAMI YOSHIMIZU / LUCKY PARADISE